Volume Four of
THE PLANNING OF INVESTMENT PROGRAMS
Alexander Meeraus and Ardy J. Stoutjesdijk, Editors

A World Bank Research Publication

The Planning of Investment Programs
Alexander Meeraus and Ardy J. Stoutjesdijk, Editors

Loet B. M. Mennes

Ardy J. Stoutjesdijk

Multicountry Investment Analysis

Published for The World Bank
THE JOHNS HOPKINS UNIVERSITY PRESS
Baltimore and London

The Johns Hopkins University Press
Baltimore, Maryland 21218, U.S.A.

Library of Congress Cataloging in Publication Data

Mennes, L. B. M.
    Multicountry investment analysis.

  (The Planning of investment programs; v. 4)
(A World Bank research publication)
    "Published for the World Bank."
    Includes index.
    1. Public investments—Evaluation—Mathematical
models—Case studies. 2. Fertilizer industry—
Latin America—Evaluation—Mathematical models.
I. Stoutjesdijk, Ardy J., 1938-   . II. International
Bank for Reconstruction and Development. III. Series.
IV. Series: World Bank research publication.
HC79.P83M46 1985   332.6′73′0724   85-45104

ISBN 0-8018-3138-5
ISBN 0-8018-3141-5 (pbk.)

Contents

Tables

Figures

Maps

Editors' Note to the Series

THIS IS THE FOURTH VOLUME in a series that deals with the use of mathematical programming methods in investment analysis. This volume treats the use of such methods for the analysis of investment programs in a multicountry framework. The exposition of the methodology follows closely that adopted in the other volumes in this series.

It should be emphasized that the series relies essentially on one among a number of possible approaches to investment planning and specifically employs mixed-integer programming to analyze investment problems in the presence of economies of scale. Alternative approaches, such as dynamic programming, are successfully used to address selected aspects of the investment planning problem by other investigators. For multicountry investment analysis, however, we considered that mathematical programming offered the best prospects for operational use, as demonstrated by the case study in this volume relating to the Andean Common Market.

ALEXANDER MEERAUS
ARDY J. STOUTJESDIJK

Preface

ECONOMIC INTEGRATION among developed and developing countries alike is a process fraught with difficulties of implementation. This book does not pretend to provide a panacea for such difficulties. It is principally addressed to one, and only one, of the many problems that multicountry cooperation schemes have encountered; that is, the absence of a practicable approach to investment analysis that not only can take into account economies of scale—an important justification for the establishment of such schemes—but also can address issues of equity among the countries involved. With that objective in mind, we have adapted to a multicountry context the investment methodology developed in companion volumes in this series for subsector analysis on a national basis.

The case study included in this volume covers the Andean Common Market. It was financed by the World Bank, the Inter-American Development Bank (IDB), and the Andean Common Market Secretariat, and it involved staff from all three organizations.

From the side of the Andean secretariat, Rodrigo Donoso, Norberto Galdo, and Gustavo Flórez participated; Donoso directed the work locally, which involved the supervision of country consultants as well as local computing activities. In connection with the latter, Alfredo Dammert should be mentioned for his advice. The country consultants were Alfonso Avilés (Ecuador), Alberto Gómez (Colombia), Henry Harman (Peru), Oscar Lovera (Venezuela), and Hugo Ossío (Bolivia). Efraín Guevara was in charge of the coordination of local data collection. From the World Bank, William Sheldrick and Harald Stier, then of the Industrial Projects Department's Fertilizer Unit, should be mentioned for their contributions throughout the study. José Nuñez del Arco and

xi

Frank Meisner took an active interest on behalf of the IDB in the progress of the study. Havelock Brewster of the United Nations Conference on Trade and Development provided useful comments on an earlier partial draft of the study.

The final formulation of the models presented in this volume and the implementation of the various versions of the Andean model in Washington would not have been possible without the continued assistance of Alexander Meeraus, the coeditor of this series, and his staff in the Analytic Support Unit of the World Bank's Development Research Department. In particular, Piet Bleyendaal and Sethu Palaniappan deserve mention for their excellent support.

Thus, many persons contributed to this study, and in particular the case study benefited greatly from the collaboration with the Andean secretariat. Nonetheless, it should be emphasized that the opinions expressed are those of the authors, and that they do not reflect views held by others who participated in the study.

PART ONE

General Methodology

1
Introduction

A GROWING NUMBER of developing countries have begun to realize that the opportunities for efficient industrial growth on the basis of the domestic market alone are severely limited and that sooner or later high-cost production units will begin to emerge that require increasingly protective barriers against competitive imports from abroad. At the same time, there is now ample evidence available that export-oriented development strategies—particularly if supported by a pervasive, well-publicized, and stable government commitment to exports—can result in superior economic performance.[1]

The outstanding examples of success of export-promotion policies are the so-called newly industrializing economies: Brazil, Hong Kong, Mexico, the Republic of Korea, Portugal, Singapore, Spain, Taiwan, and

---

1. Ian Little, Tibor Scitovsky, and Maurice Scott, *Industry and Trade in Some Developing Countries* (London: Oxford University Press, 1970); Bela Balassa and associates, *The Structure of Protection in Developing Countries* (Baltimore, Md.: Johns Hopkins University Press, 1971); Anne O. Krueger, *Foreign Trade Regimes and Economic Development: Liberalization Attempts and Consequences* (New York: Ballinger for the National Bureau of Economic Research, 1978); Juergen B. Donges and Lotte Müller-Ohlsen, *Auszenwirtschaftsstrategien und Industrialisierung in Entwicklungsländern* (Tübingen: Institut für Weltwirtschaft an der Universität Kiel, J. C. B. Mohr [Paul Siebeck], 1978); Bela Balassa and associates, *Development Strategies in Semi-Industrial Countries* (Baltimore, Md.: Johns Hopkins University Press, 1982); Anne O. Krueger, *Trade and Employment in Developing Countries,* vol. 3: *Synthesis and Conclusions* (Chicago: University of Chicago Press for the National Bureau of Economic Research, 1983); and Anne O. Krueger, "Trade Policies in Developing Countries," in Ronald W. Jones and Peter B. Kenen, eds., *Handbook of International Economics*, vol. 1, (Amsterdam: North-Holland, 1984).

Yugoslavia. Recently, this group has been joined by a group of sixteen "second tier" developing countries that succeeded in achieving a breakthrough with respect to two significant measures: scale and rate of growth of manufactured exports. These countries are Chile, Cyprus, Haiti, Indonesia, Jordan, Macao, Malaysia, Malta, Mauritius, Morocco, Peru, the Philippines, Sri Lanka, Thailand, Tunisia, and Uruguay.[2] Turkey may in the meantime be added to this ever-growing list. Not only is export performance clearly and positively correlated with economic growth; evidence is also accumulating that such export-oriented policies are consistent with the objectives of better income distribution[3] and more productive employment opportunities.[4]

In aggregate terms, developing countries have been able to expand their exports of manufactures to a considerable extent during the last fifteen to twenty years. Between 1965 and 1973, total exports of manufactures from developing countries increased at constant (1980) prices by over 15 percent annually. From 1973 to 1980 such exports increased somewhat less rapidly at 12.4 percent a year in constant prices. Because of the world economic recession this annual rate of increase amounted to no more than between 4 and 5 percent for the period 1980–83.[5] At present, however, cautious optimism is being expressed with respect to the prospects for resumed rapid growth of developing countries' exports of manufactures.[6]

In spite of this formidable achievement in aggregate terms, it should be noted that the majority of developing countries have not yet been able to build up a competitive, export-oriented industrial sector. The reasons for this failure vary from country to country and may include such diverse factors as:

- lack of clear comparative advantage
- absence of a skilled and disciplined labor force
- insufficient entrepreneurship

2. See "A New Wave of Industrial Exporters," *OECD Observer*, no. 119 (November 1982).

3. Krueger, *Foreign Trade Regimes*, p. 268.

4. Anne O. Krueger, "Alternative Trade Strategies and Employment in LDCs," *American Economic Review*, vol. 68, no. 2 (May 1978); and Krueger, *Trade and Employment*, vol. 3, ch. 9.

5. See, for example, *World Development Report 1983* (Oxford: Oxford University Press, 1983), p. 10, table 2.2.

6. See, for example, *World Development Report 1983*, pp. 29–31, and International Monetary Fund, *World Economic Outlook*, Occasional Paper No. 27 (Washington, D.C.: International Monetary Fund, 1984), pp. 70–71.

- distance from markets
- lack of adequate government incentives
- government-induced distortions in factor and product markets
- inefficiencies arising from past mistakes in industrial strategy
- unavailability of risk capital for export-oriented projects
- competition from more experienced suppliers
- poor market prospects in potential product lines.

A number of countries have attempted to improve their export prospects by embarking on a process of regional economic integration. Normally, this process involves the gradual abolition of barriers to trade among adjacent countries, with or without the harmonization of a number of social and economic policies, and sometimes the joint operation of a number of common services.[7] Regional economic integration can be considered as one of four possible options that may be adopted, singly or in combination, by developing countries as a part of their overall strategy for economic development: development in a national framework, regional economic integration, increased trade with developing countries in other regions, and participation in the international division of labor.[8] Although regional economic integration is defined in this way as an alternative to a policy that aims at exporting to world markets, this need not necessarily be the case: it could be seen as a variant to the latter, with the risk somewhat reduced as a result of a collaborative agreement. Moreover, to the extent the regional market leads to increased efficiency, it may provide an improved basis for capturing world markets.

In theory, regional economic integration offers many advantages. A substantial body of literature on the subject exists, spelling out under what conditions this policy is likely to lead to improvements in efficiency.[9]

---

7. See Fritz Machlup, *History of Thought on Economic Integration* (New York: Columbia University Press, 1977) for an extensive description of history and terminology.

8. See Bela Balassa and Ardy Stoutjesdijk, "Economic Integration among Developing Countries," *Journal of Common Market Studies*, vol. 14, no. 1 (September 1975), pp. 37-55.

9. Bela Balassa, *The Theory of Economic Integration* (London: Allen and Unwin, 1961); F. Kahnert and others, *Economic Integration among Developing Countries* (Paris: Organization for Economic Cooperation and Development, 1969); Peter Robson, ed., *International Economic Integration* (New York: Penguin Books, 1971); L. B. M. Mennes, *Planning Economic Integration among Developing Countries* (Rotterdam: Rotterdam University Press, 1973); Jean Waelbroeck, "Measuring the Degree or Progress of Economic Integration," in Fritz Machlup, ed., *Economic Integration: Worldwide, Regional, Sectoral* (London: Macmillan, 1976); Constantine V. Vaitsos, "Crisis in Regional Economic Cooperation (Integration) among Developing Countries: A Survey," *World Devel-*

In practice, regional economic integration among developing countries has made very little progress. This is due to various factors.[10] First, the power of special interests makes item-by-item negotiations on tariff reductions difficult. Second, agreements on trade liberalization are hard to reach because of differences in the level of industrial development among the prospective partners. Third, it has been difficult to determine the benefits to be derived from integration. Moreover, to the extent that benefits did materialize, they often led to disputes among partner countries relating to their distribution. Finally, most governments are reluctant to proceed with integration because they are anxious to safeguard their sovereignty.

The growing evidence of the difficulties of integration has led to pressure for reexamining the traditional prointegration arguments.[11] Nonetheless, there is empirical evidence that substantial benefits can be obtained through intraindustry specialization among developing countries.[12] The opportunities that such intraindustry specialization offers for successful regional cooperation among developing countries were already suggested by Grubel and Lloyd in their well-known study on intraindustry trade.[13]

As an alternative to across-the-board tariff reductions, countries increasingly favor a project or sector approach. With this approach, a specific sector, usually characterized by significant economies of scale, is singled out for analysis on the basis of the joint market, and projects within the sector are allocated among the countries through negotiations in which economic and political arguments play a role.

---

opment, vol. 6, no. 6 (June 1978), pp. 719–69; Peter Robson, "Regional Economic Cooperation among Developing Countries: Some Further Considerations," World Development, vol. 6, no. 6 (June 1978), pp. 771–77; Peter Robson, The Economics of International Integration (London: Allen and Unwin, 1980); and Ali M. El-Agraa, ed., International Economic Integration (London: Macmillan, 1982).

10. See, for example, Bela Balassa, "Types of Economic Integration," in Machlup, Economic Integration.

11. See, for instance, Helen Hughes, "Opening Statement for Group Discussions," in Machlup, Economic Integration.

12. Bela Balassa, "Intra-Industry Trade and the Integration of Developing Countries in the World Economy," in Herbert Giersch, ed., On the Economics of Intra-Industry Trade (Tübingen: Institut für Weltwirtschaft an der Universität Kiel, J. C. B. Mohr [Paul Siebeck], 1979).

13. Herbert G. Grubel and P. J. Lloyd, Intra-Industry Trade: The Theory and Measurement of International Trade in Differentiated Products (London: Macmillan, 1975), pp. 145–48.

While this project or sector approach has several appealing features, its implementation is not without difficulties. First, the main economic rationale for sectoral collaboration will almost always be related to the presence of economies of scale in production, which gives rise to complicated problems of investment analysis. Second, the allocation of projects among countries, in particular when equity considerations are added to efficiency criteria, is usually far from straightforward and may often lead to lengthy political negotiations. It may be impossible to reach agreement, unless more than one sector is involved and the so-called package approach is adopted, further complicating the scope and nature of investment planning and implementation problems.

In this book, we shall describe in some detail an approach to the analysis of investment programs in a multicountry context. To avoid confusion, we shall generally use the terms "cooperation" and "cooperation projects" in recognition of the fact that collaboration is possible among countries that have no intention of embarking upon a generalized scheme of removal of trade barriers. The techniques to be described enable the explicit incorporation of economies of scale and result in project-specific recommendations about location, scale, timing, technology, and product mix. Moreover, as the analysis makes use of high-speed computers, it is possible to assist the project negotiation phase with rapid and fully quantified alternatives to the initially proposed allocation of projects among the countries, which may be of importance during the negotiations.

The Project Approach in General Terms

In the next chapter we will give a fairly detailed description of the project approach to economic cooperation and indicate the type of problems that may occur in its analysis and subsequent implementation. Here we shall give a brief synopsis of that description.[14]

Many activities exhibit economies of scale, necessitating a minimum accessible market for efficient operation. If such a minimum accessible market can only be obtained by combining the markets of a number of countries, recourse may be had to the project approach to cooperation,

---

14. The countries involved in cooperation efforts do not need to be adjacent, although they usually are; unless otherwise stated, in what follows we shall assume they are part of the same region.

which involves agreement on the establishment and the operation of specific projects or specific sectors. The project approach can be used in conjunction with the application of a general trade liberalization scheme. In case the conditions for implementing a trade liberalization scheme are not fulfilled, the project approach may be adopted with provisions made for intercountry trade in the products involved. Tinbergen has described the latter scheme as a partial customs union *cum* investment plan.[15]

In this context a project is a scheme to invest resources which is strictly defined in terms of scale, location, product mix, timing, and technology. A sector is defined as a set of interdependent projects. The project approach may refer to one single project, a single sector, or more sectors. The approach may involve a large number of projects, facilitating the distribution of projects over the prospective partner countries, and thus may be more aptly termed a package approach.

We shall draw a distinction between regional and international goods and services, following Mennes, Tinbergen, and Waardenburg,[16] although not using exactly the same definitions. In the present volume, regional goods and services are defined as those that are not normally traded over long distances, and their availability within the multicountry market depends on intraregional supply. Examples of such goods and services are electricity, railways, roads, irrigation, universities, and telecommunications. In contrast, international goods and services are traded internationally and do not have to be produced inside the cooperation area in order to be available to consumers. This category of goods and services includes most agricultural and industrial products.

The distinction between regional and international goods and services is important in this context. For regional goods and services, the choice of desired production structure is between national production and regional production: imports from countries other than the cooperation partners are by definition excluded from the possibilities. Given this fairly clear-cut choice, it is necessary to evaluate the relative costs and benefits of national and regional production and to determine whether a good case can be made for regionally integrated production facilities. In the case of international goods and services, imports from outside the cooperation area are possible in addition to national and regional production. As a consequence, more possible supply patterns have to be eval-

15. Jan Tinbergen, *International Economic Integration* (Amsterdam: Elsevier, 1965).

16. L. B. M. Mennes, Jan Tinbergen, and J. George Waardenburg, *The Element of Space in Development Planning* (Amsterdam: North-Holland, 1969).

uated, and it is generally much more difficult to demonstrate the relative merits of each.

Although regional goods and services usually involve fewer analytical possibilities than international goods and services, both types of products are likely to pose difficult planning problems: the main rationale for considering different production structures for them in a multicountry framework is that their production is likely to exhibit economies of scale. The next section will briefly address the complications arising in such cases (chapter 3 deals with this topic in much more detail).

Economies of Scale and the Need for Systematic Analysis

Economies of scale have always complicated economic analysis. In many instances, the complications are so significant that analysts have been forced to assume that increasing returns can legitimately be ignored. At best they have fallen back on rules of thumb and partial equilibrium models.[17] This is not the place to take issue with such assumptions. However, it appears evident that economies of scale cannot be ignored in the analysis of a set of economic policies that are to a large extent designed to capture the advantages associated with scale in a number of economic activities.

In this context, what are the complications that can be expected to arise from the explicit incorporation of economies of scale in the framework of analysis? Economic activities exhibit economies of scale if total costs per unit fall as scale of production increases. This phenomenon gives rise to several complications in investment analysis. Larger units will have lower costs per unit than smaller units, so there will be a tendency toward centralized production facilities in given market areas. However, before deciding on such a production structure, it is important to assess carefully its implications for transport and other distribution costs, as these can be expected to be higher than in the case of a decentralized production pattern. Similarly, if demand for the relevant products is increasing over time, it may pay to postpone investments until the market has reached a certain size, so that a larger plant can be built; even then, a certain amount of overcapacity in the early years may be efficient.

17. Lance Taylor, *Macro Models for Developing Countries* (New York: McGraw-Hill, 1979), sec. 13.5.

Moreover, in the presence of economies of scale, it is often necessary to consider several interdependent projects simultaneously, as interindustry demand may give rise to larger production units. These complications render investment planning in the presence of economies of scale on a national basis difficult enough. In a multicountry context, in addition to increasing the size of the planning problem, issues associated with the distribution of costs and benefits among partner countries complicate matters even further.

In the orthodox theory of economic integration economies of scale do not find a place, but they have been introduced in partial equilibrium terms by Corden.[18] It is striking, however, how little attention is given to this important motive for economic cooperation in a recent survey by the same author.[19]

The approach we advocate in this book is essentially an extension of the sectorwide investment planning technique that is described in the other volumes in this series.[20] We shall rely on the technique of mathematical programming to determine an optimal pattern of production, investment, and trade for a set of interdependent activities, taking economies of scale explicitly into account. The approach involves the specification of relevant products in the sector concerned, their production possibilities and technologies, and investment, distribution, and production costs, as well as import prices. On the basis of projected final demand, including export demand, and, if desired, specified by marketing region, the approach permits the identification of the supply pattern that meets demand at lowest resource costs. For national investment analysis, the usefulness of this approach was demonstrated by case studies.[21] For multicountry investment planning, the proposed method has additional advantages. To increase the attraction of a regional investment plan to prospective partner countries and to enhance the stability of an agreement, it is vital that the regional plan is economically sound, which

---

18. W. M. Corden, "Economies of Scale and Customs Union Theory," *Journal of Political Economy*, vol. 80, no. 3 (1972, pt. 1), pp. 465–75.

19. W. M. Corden, "The Normative Theory of International Trade," in Jones and Kenen, *Handbook of International Economics*, vol. 1, p. 123.

20. See David Kendrick and Ardy J. Stoutjesdijk, *The Planning of Industrial Investment Programs: A Methodology*, The Planning of Investment Programs, vol. 1 (Baltimore, Md.: Johns Hopkins University Press, 1978).

21. The fertilizer industry in volume 2 and the steel sector in volume 3 of the series.

at the minimum means that the emerging supply pattern is competitive with imports.[22]

As noted before, increased efficiency is rarely the sole objective of countries negotiating a joint investment program: perceived equity is equally important. This means that frequently initially proposed investment allocations are modified during the negotiation phase and thus require additional analysis. The proposed computer-based method permits this additional analysis to be carried out extremely rapidly. In fact, as it is often possible to anticipate which different supply patterns may be of interest to policymakers, the initial set of proposals could already include reference to the existence and relative merits of schemes different from the one proposed. This is in sharp contrast to more conventional approaches to investment planning, which in the end result in a single proposal for cooperative action.

The Organization of the Volume

Following this chapter, the scope for cooperation projects will be described in general terms, making a distinction among goods and services that is based upon international mobility. That chapter will also pay attention to the problems of evaluation and implementation of integration projects and will give an overall assessment of the approach.

Chapter 3 gives a brief but comprehensive introduction to investment analysis in the presence of economies of scale, summarizing the method discussed in more detail in the first volume in this series.[23] In chapter 4, the planning method is adapted to a multicountry framework. This implies in the first place a rather trivial expansion of the geographic coverage of the models to more than one country. However, because an investment analysis involving more than one country will have to focus on efficiency as well as equity, it also requires expansion of the model's restrictions and objectives. Chapter 4 provides a systematic description of

---

22. We neglect now the case of regional protectionism, where integration is the alternative not to free trade but to national protectionism of each participating country. See Eduardo Lizano, "Integration of Less Developed Areas and of Areas on Different Levels of Development," in Machlup, *Economic Integration*, p. 277.

23. Kendrick and Stoutjesdijk, *Planning of Industrial Investment Programs*.

how this expansion may be achieved. Chapters 3 and 4 are designed to provide the reader with the methodological background necessary to formulate a multicountry investment planning model that is appropriate to specific situations.

In chapter 5, we offer a candid assessment of the uses and limitations of the planning method. Not surprisingly, we conclude that the models represent a potentially powerful tool in the formulation of investment scenarios in a multicountry context and may be of considerable use in the negotiation phase. We emphasize, however, that there is a variety of important issues that they are not particularly suited to deal with. This chapter concludes the general part of the volume.

Part two consists of a case study of the fertilizer sector of the Andean Common Market in South America. Following a brief introduction to the Andean group of countries in chapter 6, chapter 7 presents the empirical background needed for the case study in the form of a conventional narrative. In chapter 8, this information is reorganized in a more systematic manner to fit directly into the structure of a planning model that can be used to analyze alternative investment strategies. The treatment of the material in that chapter is done with the potential user of the planning method in mind and is as explicit as possible about how to handle certain classes of data problems and modeling situations. The same applies to the discussion of results in chapter 9, which follows the sequence of scenarios that the Andean secretariat chose to evaluate before drawing up proposals. Chapter 10 focuses on a number of extensions of the Andean model that were carried out in Washington and that included an evaluation of several so-called equity conditions. Chapter 11 presents some general conclusions.

2

The Project Approach to Economic Cooperation

ONE OF THE PRINCIPAL AIMS of multicountry investment agreements is the establishment of projects that serve a wider than national market. Such projects may emerge either through the free operation of market forces in a region where trade barriers have been removed or as a result of an explicit agreement between two or more countries which may or may not be part of a trade liberalization scheme. Projects of this nature will be referred to as cooperation projects.

In discussing economic cooperation, it is useful to realize that goods and services are not as mobile as they are usually assumed to be in international trade theory. Imperfect mobility is the basis for the well-known distinction suggested by Little and Mirrlees between tradables and non-tradables.[1] Similarly, and somewhat more usefully for our purpose, Mennes, Tinbergen, and Waardenburg suggest terminology that distinguishes between local, regional, national, continental, and international or world goods and services.[2] In both cases, the distinction is drawn on the basis of a variety of economic and technical considerations; however, transport costs are the single most important factor in the determination of each category. It is useful to make a distinction between national, regional (which, unlike the terminology used by Mennes and others,

1. I. M. D. Little and J. A. Mirrlees, *Project Appraisal and Planning for Developing Countries* (London: Heinemann Educational Books, 1974).
2. L. B. M. Mennes, Jan Tinbergen, and J. George Waardenburg, *The Element of Space in Development Planning* (Amsterdam: North-Holland, 1969).

13

means here multicountry), and international goods and services. National goods and services, including perishables, construction, housing, retail trade, most services, government, and primary and secondary education, can by definition be excluded from the discussion of cooperation projects, as they are normally not traded among countries. Regional and international goods and services both qualify as candidates for cooperation projects, where regional goods and services may be provided on a national basis as well as jointly for a group of neighboring countries (for example, electricity, railways, roads, and irrigation). International goods and services may be procured on a national and regional basis as well as from world markets (for example, agricultural, mining, and manufactured products).

At this point, it is useful to discuss briefly the sources of economies of scale that we consider in this context; in the next two sections, we shall elaborate upon the sources of gains as they relate to specific types of cooperation project. Our approach to the analysis of scale effects meets the conditions set out in a recent survey on economies of scale, that is, it is focused on products similar enough to be regarded as competitive in relevant markets, on comparable stages of production, and on essentially common technologies where similar inputs are used to produce similar products.[3]

Many activities exhibit economies of scale in investment, in the sense that investment costs are independent of capacity over a certain range or that they increase less than proportionately with capacity. Examples of the former are laboratories and electronic control units in chemical plants; examples of the latter are tanks, pressure vessels, and pipes. Both lead to nonlinearities in the investment cost function such that, for example, a doubling of capacity leads to less than a doubling of investment costs, up to a certain point which will vary from activity to activity. Stylized facts relating to this source of economies of scale are relatively well known, particularly for the process industries such as fertilizers, steel, or cement, and are determined on technical grounds. They can, therefore, be taken into account without much difficulty in investment analysis.

The other main source of economies of scale relates to indivisibilities in operating cost elements. These may be due to indivisibilities such as expenditures for senior management or development and design cost for

3. See Bela Gold, "Changing Perspectives on Size, Scale and Returns: An Interpretive Survey," *Journal of Economic Literature*, vol. 19, no. 1 (March 1981).

new products. In those cases, their inclusion in the investment analysis resembles that of investment cost. However, they may also be attributable to factors relating to the organization of production within a plant, such as the length of the production run. The direct benefit of lengthening production runs is that set-up costs can be distributed over a larger volume of output. Moreover, it is likely that cost savings due to learning by doing can be achieved more rapidly with relatively long production runs. The continuous production of a good can lead not only to cost reductions but also to quality improvements due to increased technical competence in handling components or processes.

The latter source of economies of scale may be very important, particularly in the developing countries. In fact, there is evidence that even in many sectors of developed countries the potential advantages of economies of scale on this score have not yet been fully exploited and represent a resource for further economic growth in the long run.[4] The main problems we face in the realization of this type of economies of scale are that such economies are much more plant specific than those associated with investment cost elements or management and design cost and that they are dependent upon factors that are difficult to quantify in the framework of a planning model, such as managerial skill and the level of training or degree of trainability of the labor force. In many cases, fairly crude assumptions will have to be made with regard to the cost savings that will be possible on account of these sources of economies of scale over time. It should be noted, however, that this may be less important for investment analysis in the process industries—the main subject of this series of volumes—than in the nonprocess industrial sectors.

The Gains from Cooperation Projects: Regional Goods and Services

Cooperation projects in this category may be found in transportation and communications, public utilities, education and research, and a few other fields. They bring economic benefits if production on a regional scale leads to cost savings compared with their production on a national scale, taking into account production as well as distribution costs. Cost savings may be achieved directly through large-scale operations, fuller

---

4. See C. T. Saunders, "Industrial Specialization and Trends in Industrial Policies," in United Nations, *Factors and Conditions of Long-Term Growth* (New York, 1974).

utilization of existing capacity, greater specialization in production, joint management, and the coordinated use of jointly owned resources, such as a river basin. Savings may also be achieved indirectly, for example, by investments in infrastructure that are principally designed to promote trade within the region.

Transport provides examples of direct and indirect benefits from cooperation projects. First, cost savings may be achieved through the coordinated planning and operation of transport facilities (for example, a joint airline or a regionally integrated railway network with identical railway gauges). Second, coordinated investments in transport may have beneficial effects of an indirect nature in promoting trade among the partner countries. Opportunities for such projects include the development of regional shipping companies and the construction of international transport links, such as occurred in the Central American Highway System. Cost savings and quality improvements may also be achieved by the coordinated planning and operation of regional communications networks, which require tariff agreements, the rationalization of signaling systems, and similar measures.

Among public utilities, electric power production and the development and management of water resources offer scope for cooperation projects. Both types of project supply output that is normally not internationally tradable unless distances are short. In such cases, cooperation projects may offer benefits by exploiting economies of scale and, in some instances, by using the resources from within the region that lead to lower production costs. For example, in hydropower, the investment cost in 1980 U.S. dollars per kilowatt installed may vary from $1,100 for a large hydropower plant to $3,500 for a minihydro plant, and the resulting delivered power cost can range from 2.4 cents per kilowatt-hour to 12.7 cents per kilowatt-hour. Moreover, cooperation in power supply among neighboring countries may permit the exploitation of differences in fuel endowment. This may be even more important than the exploitation of economies of scale, given that power generation costs vary widely depending on fuel used.[5]

In the category of water supply projects, the principal case for coordinated action is with respect to the development of international river basins. A number of schemes of this nature exist (for example, the lower Mekong Basin) with the major benefits, apart from power, to be derived

---

5. See World Bank, *Energy in the Developing Countries* (Washington, D.C., 1980), pp. 42–44. All dollar figures are U.S. dollars.

from improved flood control and more intensive use of the water resources for irrigation. Moreover, projects located on international waters may cause problems of environmental pollution in other countries, necessitating coordination of action.

Joint projects in the field of education and research can lead to cost savings due to the better utilization of indivisible factors, such as teaching and research staff and equipment, and may result in qualitative improvements in education and research as well. The encouragement of regional universities and technical colleges and the investigation of area-specific problems, jointly financed and managed by the participating countries, come into this category. Examples are organizations for research in agriculture, veterinary medicine, pesticides, forestry, and fishing in the East African Economic Community, the International Laboratory for Research on Animal Diseases, and the International Livestock Center for Africa. In Central America, the Central American Higher University Council has developed a coordinated system of regional specialized education in agriculture, and there is also a regional organization for agricultural health. An example of Asian integrated training and research activities is the Asian Statistical Institute. Other areas where integrated research and training may be advantageous are intermediate technology, small-scale industry, computer programming, and health and disease prevention. Cooperation projects in the category of research are not necessarily restricted to regional arrangements, and successful global undertakings exist, such as the International Rice Research Institute.

The list of categories of cooperation projects among regional goods and services given so far is by no means exhaustive, and a variety of other fields should be mentioned where scope for such projects exists. These include projects aiming at regional computer facilities, the promotion of tourism, the expansion of regional exports through regional trade promotion centers, the development of mineral resources, and the provision of meteorological services.

The Gains from Cooperation Projects: International Goods and Services

This category of projects consists chiefly of agricultural and industrial activities; their principal characteristic is that they can be internationally traded so that their availability in the region is not contingent upon production within the region. In agriculture, there are examples of countries' agreeing to limit the expansion of production in order to improve their terms of trade (as in the case of coffee). Such agreements are usually of a global nature; they are considered to be outside the scope of this study. There are also possibilities for agreements on specialization in agricultural production between countries with different resource endowments. However, to the extent that economies of scale can be obtained in the national framework, cooperation projects in agriculture are usually linked with processing.

If regional planning permits the identification and establishment of efficient facilities to process, for example, cocoa, cotton, rubber, forest resources, or livestock, such projects are properly classified as cooperation projects. To the extent that such facilities are dependent on the supply of inputs from the region as a whole, agreements among the participating countries may be required to guarantee compatible agricultural produce. Often a transit country can exploit its geographic location by processing the exports of a landlocked country, which are allowed duty free into the transit country. If the landlocked country were to process its agricultural produce for exports, the transit country could impose import duties on the processed product. This issue has arisen a few times in practice, for example, in West Africa with respect to livestock produced in the inland states of Mali and Niger. Agreements on such projects can be reached either by establishing cooperation projects in the landlocked country or by including processing facilities in a package deal consisting of a variety of projects to be distributed among partner countries.

Many cooperative efforts among developing countries have as their main objective the promotion of industrial growth, and most existing cooperation agreements devote special attention to industrial investments. This is primarily due to the belief that the widening of the domestic market through regional cooperation enables the capturing of economies of scale that characterize most economic activities, leading to lower average costs of production.

Lower average costs of production can be the result of higher rates of capacity utilization in the case of existing plants. In such cases, partner countries may be induced to forgo investments in such activities. Second, cost savings may be achieved by the establishment of production units at a larger scale than would have been possible for the domestic market alone.

Third, cost savings may result from the exploitation of the advantages associated with specialization, either at the product or the process level. Petrochemicals, fertilizer, and machinery provide possibilities for product specialization, with countries producing different varieties within a product category. Process specialization occurs if a group of countries agrees to specialize in different components for the manufacture of machinery or transport equipment. In both cases, the main source of cost savings is the economies of scale associated with indivisibilities in plant, equipment, and management and with cost elements dependent on the length of the production run.

A considerable amount of evidence has been assembled on the importance of economies of scale in industrial processes. A well-known source for data is Pratten, but others exist.[6] Information on economies of scale may serve as a first indication of industrial activities that may be attractive candidates for cooperation projects, in the sense that the more important the economies of scale, the more substantial the potential cost savings attributable to a widening of the accessible market. However, it should be remembered that the larger market involves higher transport and distribution costs; their incidence on total delivered cost to marketing centers constitutes a detrimental effect on total cost savings. Moreover, energy requirements increasingly become a negative factor in the assessment of industrial opportunities, particularly in the developing countries.

The Problems Associated with Cooperation Projects

In the preceding sections, we have described the scope for cooperation projects and the potential gains that can be derived from them. In spite of the apparent advantages that such projects may have in comparison to alternative production structures, however, relatively few have been established. In this section, we shall briefly discuss some of the reasons that may explain the limited success of this approach.

A first set of problems is associated with the selection and appraisal of cooperation projects. One of the main arguments in favor of cooperation projects is the exploitation of economies of scale that many economic activities exhibit. Unfortunately, project selection in the presence of econo-

---

6. C. F. Pratten, *Economies of Scale in Manufacturing Industry* (Cambridge: Cambridge University Press, 1971). See also John Haldi and Donald Whitcomb, "Economies of Scale in Industrial Plants," *Journal of Political Economy*, vol. 75 (1967), pp. 373–85; Frederick T. Moore, "Economies of Scale: Some Statistical Evidence," *Quarterly Journal of Economics*, vol. 73 (1959), pp. 232–45; and Aubrey Silberston, "Economies of Scale in Theory and Practice," *Economic Journal*, vol. 82 (1972), pp. 369–91.

mies of scale poses a number of complex planning problems with respect to the determination of optimal scale, timing, and location of projects, for which no easy-to-apply planning techniques have as yet been developed. The best available methodology for the selection and optimal design of projects in the presence of economies of scale is mixed-integer programming, but the few attempts that have been made to apply this technique to practical problems have indicated that there are some difficulties with its use.[7]

Transport costs need to be taken into account in the selection of cooperation projects to avoid an overestimate of the efficiency gains that can be attained through the exploitation of economies of scale and the benefits of specialization. This is perhaps best explained by considering an example. Two countries may decide that it is more advantageous to establish one steel mill to meet their joint demand for steel than to construct separate steel mills designed to meet domestic demand in each country; naturally, the argument is based on the economies of scale under which steel is produced. However, total transport costs of steel to all regional users will usually be higher from one regional steel mill than from two national steel mills, and those costs may conceivably wipe out the advantages in production costs. Clearly, the case for cooperation projects cannot be made on the basis of production cost arguments alone; transport costs and other distributional costs have to be taken into account. As these costs vary with the degree of dispersion of the market, it is impossible to come up with general recommendations regarding cooperation projects, even for a specific activity such as steel production.

Another complication in cooperation project selection is related to the effect of the introduction of risk and uncertainty into the project analysis exercise. The explicit recognition of risk and uncertainty tends to weaken the case for large production units, even under economies of scale. As a plant designed to meet requirements for a regional market faces greater uncertainty than one that caters to a national market only, in the sense that regional cooperation may be discontinued, the *expected* benefits of a cooperation project are correspondingly lower.

Although many industrial processes exhibit economies of scale over a range of plant sizes, at some point such economies of scale will usually be

---

7. Much progress has, however, been made during the last decade both in the efficiency of computers and their ability to use and process large, complex data sets and in the availability of software for data organization, model representation, and solution algorithms. What were difficult problems to solve only ten years ago are now routinely handled by experienced analysts.

exhausted, and the average costs of production will then rise. The reasons for this trend may vary from case to case but are mostly associated with plant management problems. In developed countries, diseconomies of scale may not occur except in the case of very large plants; in developing countries, however, with a less well-trained labor force, greater problems of raw material supply, and, sometimes, less skilled management, such diseconomies of scale may occur at smaller plant scales than in developed countries.

To the extent that the cooperation project has as its output an internationally tradable commodity, the project may divert trade and promote the inefficient use of regional resources. There is no inherent reason for cooperation projects to be import substitution projects. In practice, however, many such projects are designed to produce for the regional market alone without due regard to the scope for exports to outside the region. To the extent that cooperation projects divert attention away from the overseas export market, an inefficient allocation of resources in the region may result.

In many cases, the approach to economic cooperation based on projects leads to the establishment of monopolies. If, moreover, restrictions are placed on competing imports, privately managed cooperation projects will follow pricing and output policies that may not be consistent with economic policy objectives in partner countries. There is therefore clearly a tradeoff between the exploitation of economies of scale that might arise from establishing relatively few productive units and the achievement of given policy objectives that might arise from a different organization of supply.

A second set of problems, usually paramount in discussions pertaining to cooperation projects, relates to the distribution of gains and benefits.[8] Unless the location of a project is dictated by natural resource constraints, it is extremely difficult to get countries to agree on the location of a cooperation project. The more "visible" a project, the more difficult such negotiations may be, and it may be impossible to achieve agreement or, if an agreement can be reached, the allocation of projects may be so inefficient that the net gain of cooperation is eliminated. Judging by the experience of the last decade, problems of this nature are most severe in the case of cooperation projects in international goods and services,

8. For a good survey of this set and a third set of problems see Arthur Hazlewood, "The End of the East African Community: What Are the Lessons for Regional Integration Schemes?" *Journal of Common Market Studies*, vol. 43, no. 1 (September 1979), pp. 40–58.

many of which are "footloose," in the sense that they may be placed in any of a number of locations.

Apart from the problem of which country provides the location for which set of cooperation projects, problems may arise with regard to the distribution of perceived costs and benefits. Clearly, one project may generate more domestic value added and employment, and require less foreign exchange and domestic capital, than another. The distributional formula, therefore, contains many elements, and it may be difficult to agree on the weights to be attached to each element. Disputes may also arise over regional transfer prices of the output of such projects following unilateral attempts to rectify imbalances in the distribution of gains and losses; it should be noted here that optimal pricing policies under economies of scale are very difficult to implement. Even more important, the ex ante allocation of cooperation projects agreeable to all partners may not materialize because some countries may be unable to mobilize domestic and foreign resources required for their establishment (investment capital) and operation (managerial talent).

It is clearly impossible to list all possible problems that may arise, but one final point should be mentioned, as it is often heard in developing countries. Project identification, selection, appraisal, and implementation are more complex—and the uncertainties are much greater—for cooperation projects than for domestic projects. Given the scarcity of human resources available to carry out the economic planning function, it appears unattractive to national governments to assign resources to cooperation project planning. Therefore, the identification and planning of such projects are often performed by planners from outside the region, unaware of the political sensitivities and desires in the countries concerned. This may further complicate the negotiation process.

A third set of problems can be grouped together under the heading of political economy. A nation's greatest political rivals are frequently its nearest neighbors. Thus the countries most quickly thought of as candidates for cooperation in regional investment schemes are precisely those that are most suspicious of one another. For this reason it may be appropriate at times to study cooperation schemes among noncontiguous countries.

When neighboring countries rival one another they do not want to be dependent on each other for vital material needs for any substantial period of time. For this reason it may be important to study various time-phasing patterns of locations of projects among countries so as to reduce interdependence to acceptable levels.

Potential political changes also add to the risk and uncertainty associated with cooperation projects. For example, an agreement reached between two countries at one time may be abrogated following a change of administration in one of the countries.

Mathematical programming models of joint investment schemes cannot fully incorporate these kinds of problems in political economy. However, they can provide a highly automated aid to negotiations among countries on cooperation projects. The models provide an efficient means of making rough estimates of the relative costs of serving markets for regional and international goods and services from national facilities, as opposed to serving those markets from cooperation projects. Only in cases where these economic gains are substantial will it be worthwhile to engage in political negotiations. At this time the model may serve the valuable role of permitting very efficient and rapid calculations of the cost and benefits of alternative sets of cooperation projects proposed by the negotiating countries.

The Relative Importance of Cooperation Projects

It should be apparent from the foregoing discussion that it makes about as little economic sense to state categorically that cooperation projects are or are not justified on economic grounds as to state that the minimum economic size of cement plants is 600,000 tons a year. Both statements are oversimplifications, designed to guide decisionmaking under conditions that do not permit adequate appraisal of the planning problem. In an attempt to go beyond this simplistic approach, we shall give a qualitative assessment of cooperation projects in this section, making use of the previously mentioned distinction between international, regional, and national goods and services.

It is perhaps not surprising that most existing cooperation projects are to be found in the category of regional projects. The production of national goods is by definition not eligible for cooperation. The production of international goods and services is eligible for production within the region (either on a regional or national scale) but poses more complex problems of planning. If regional goods and services are to be made available, two alternative modes of production exist, namely, in national projects and in regional projects; imports from outside the region are by definition excluded. Under such conditions, project planning takes place in an environment that is fully controlled by the region itself, as a result of which fairly firm estimates can be made of the net gains or losses associated with any specific production structure. In contrast, in the case of international goods and services, an alternative to national or regional projects is presented in the form of imports from world markets. The uncertainty related to future import prices greatly complicates the assessment of potential costs and benefits of cooperation projects and usually weakens the case for projects in this category. A further reason can be noted for the more frequent occurrence of regional cooperation projects than international ones—the greater stability associated with the former.

In the case of a cooperation project producing a regional good or service, the alternative of national production exists but cannot be realized instantly. Lengthy gestation periods are usually required to attain full operation of a new project. However, in the case of projects dealing with international goods and services, project cooperation can be terminated at once by activating the import alternative. These factors have in particular hampered the establishment of cooperation projects in the industrial sector.

Import prices for industrial goods often vary by source and over time, while wide fluctuations in ocean shipping rates further complicate projections of c.i.f. import prices (those including cost, insurance, and freight). Under such conditions, it is difficult to make plausible quantitative estimates of the potential net gains to be derived from cooperation projects in this sector, and countries have understandably been reluctant to agree to a production structure that may prove to be inefficient in the medium and long term. If the structure does prove to be inefficient, one of two situations may arise. First, the producing country may lose its regional market and end up with an underutilized plant. Second, if the regional market is maintained, all participating countries may suffer net losses because of relatively high-cost regional production. The former alternative is more likely, and this likelihood distinguishes cooperation projects sharply from national projects. For, if a national project turns out to be based on an erroneous projection of c.i.f. import prices and is relatively high cost, domestic pressures to prevent the shutdown of the project will be severe, usually resulting in higher protection from imports than originally envisaged. In the case of a cooperation project, such pressures from the project's host country can be assumed to be less effective in the partner countries.

The Package Approach

Cooperation projects may be established as part of an arrangement that makes pressures on maintaining the regional market in adverse circumstances more effective. The so-called package approach is frequently advocated with this purpose in mind. The package approach specifically and explicitly aims at enhancing the durability of the multicountry market structure by ensuring that each participating country obtains at least one cooperation project. For this purpose the number of cooperation projects should not be too small. Although both the identification and planning and the implementation of the package approach to cooperation projects pose severe problems, it appears in principle at least that, because unilateral withdrawal from the regional scheme inflicts losses on the withdrawing country itself, the approach has a built-in device for promoting stability.

The effectiveness of this device, however, may vary considerably from case to case. Some projects in the package will usually be more efficient than others because of the region's comparative advantage. Countries with efficient projects in the category of international goods and services may be better off than countries with projects in the category of regional goods and services, as the latter cannot, by definition, be exported outside the region. In general, the package approach is more likely to achieve its goal of stability in the regional market if the projects included are relatively efficient compared with national projects, in the case of regional goods and services, and compared with imports, for international goods and services. If high protective barriers are necessary for some or all of the projects included in the category of international goods and services, it is conceivable that the cost of trade diversion to a partner country is so high as to offset the loss associated with underutilization of the capacity of its cooperation projects following withdrawal from the scheme.

It should be clear that the identification and appraisal of cooperation projects presents a complex problem and that the success of the package approach depends to a large extent on the manner in which this task is carried out. Unfortunately, as was indicated earlier, cooperation projects belong to a category of projects for which planning techniques are not yet well developed. Therefore it is possible that, because of the lack of appropriate planning methodologies, optimal projects and optimal packages of projects are not considered for inclusion in the final investment program, so that even at the outset the gains of economic cooperation on this score may seem small.

The package approach usually presents problems related to the distribution of cooperation projects among participating countries, except if very pronounced resource advantages dictate the location of projects. If an allocation is eventually decided upon, it may not be the most efficient one from the point of view of the region as a whole. Moreover, if an allocation is agreed upon by participating countries, special arrangements may need to be made to ensure that each project is implemented. Some of the projects may be located in a relatively unattractive part of the regional market, and it may be difficult to find capital and managerial talent to establish the project.

A number of dynamic problems related to the package approach should be explicitly mentioned. First, even if the original allocation of projects was agreeable to all partner countries, some projects may appear so inefficient while in operation that problems arise relating to the distribution of costs and benefits. Similarly, an incorrect projection of import prices, or demand, may render some projects less efficient than predicted. Finally, as demand for different products is likely to increase at different rates, some of the projects in the package may become independent of the regional market for efficient operation at an earlier stage than others, leading to instability over time.

In combination with the package approach, some regional financing scheme may be attractive to promote stability in the conditions underlying cooperation projects. It would seem that the joint financing of cooperation projects tends to spread the financial risk among partner countries, which may result in greater solidarity among partner countries in the face of adverse conditions affecting one or more cooperation projects. At the same time, however, it should be noted that the joint financing of projects may be extremely difficult to accomplish, and substantial leverage by lending agencies may need to be exercised to bring it about. The international company approach, as proposed by Little,[9] focuses on the distribution of direct financial costs and benefits of economic cooperation. It is unlikely to be successful on its own, as it does not provide a solution for disputes on other issues, such as industrial development, employment, or foreign exchange earnings.

In conclusion, it can be stated that multicountry investment planning is an approach to economic cooperation among developing countries. For production activities with economies of scale, market-sharing ar-

9. I. M. D. Little, "Regional International Companies as an Approach to Economic Integration," *Journal of Common Market Studies*, vol. 5, no. 2 (1966–67), pp. 181–86.

rangements may be the only way in which efficient development can occur. This is true particularly for regional goods and services, because they cannot be imported from overseas and have to be produced within the region. For international goods and services, the planning problem is much more complex, and very careful analysis of projects in this category is required to ensure the selection and implementation of efficient ones. Provided such careful analysis takes place, it would appear that, for activities with strong economies of scale or with large potential advantages related to specialization, cooperation projects may bring benefits to the countries.

The multicountry framework in which cooperation projects are implemented and operated needs to be conducive to the continued operation of such projects. The more participating countries are likely to lose from withdrawal, the more stable the scheme is likely to be; or in other words, the larger the joint benefits of cooperation projects and the fairer their distribution among countries, the more likely it is that the scheme will survive in the long run. These conditions, once more, can only be fulfilled by careful project planning.

A Final Note

This chapter has reviewed the scope for cooperation projects, their potential costs and benefits, and the problems associated with their establishment and operation. In the following chapters, we shall formulate and apply a planning methodology for a subset of activities that are susceptible to the cooperation project approach, namely, a number of industrial activities that exhibit economies of scale. It should be stressed from the start, however, that the models to be used, by nature simplified representations of reality, cannot capture all problems and complications arising in cooperation project planning. In practice, many issues will remain to be resolved on the basis of judgment, while others cannot and need not be modeled. The main point we shall attempt to make while illustrating the use of programming models for this approach is that such methods provide efficient tools for the identification of opportunities for such projects, *not* that they in themselves form a panacea for the complex problems that arise in their negotiation, establishment, and operation.

3

Investment Analysis under Economies of Scale

THE PURPOSE of this chapter is to introduce the reader to a planning method that can be used for investment analysis in the presence of economies of scale; the next chapter will adapt this general approach to one that may be specifically useful for investment analysis in a multicountry context. The reader who is familiar with mathematical programming or who has read other volumes in this series[1] may wish to proceed immediately to chapter 4.

A Statement of the Problem

For activities that exhibit economies of scale, the selection of the optimal size, timing, and location of projects is a difficult planning problem. The fact that average costs of production fall as scale of production increases tends to favor large units; however, because a large production unit usually serves a large geographic area, depending on the dispersion of the market, the average transport cost per unit of output tends to increase as the scale of production expands. Because the importance of transport cost varies from one area or type of production to

---

1. In particular, David Kendrick and Ardy J. Stoutjesdijk, *The Planning of Industrial Investment Programs: A Methodology*, The Planning of Investment Programs, vol. 1 (Baltimore, Md.: Johns Hopkins University Press, 1978).

another, one cannot generalize about the most efficient size for any activity that has economies of scale. A steel mill with an annual capacity of 100,000 tons in one specific context may be efficient, while a steel mill of double that size in a different context may be inefficient, where relative efficiency is measured in terms of delivered costs of the product to the user from alternative sources.

If the activity subject to economies of scale can be considered in isolation from the rest of the economy, the optimal project may not be too difficult to determine, even though the problems of size, timing, and location need to be tackled.[2] However, very few economic activities exhibit such convenient characteristics, and in most cases varying degrees of interdependence with other activities need to be taken into account. The hypothetical example described below will illustrate this problem. To solve such combinational problems, we developed special screening techniques, which will be described in the following sections.

Assume the planning problem is to select an investment program, relating to two interdependent activities, each subject to economies of scale, which leads to the lowest cost of meeting requirements for their output. The set of activities may relate to the production of two phosphatic fertilizers, single and triple superphosphate, requiring the intermediate inputs of processed phosphate rock, sulfuric acid, and phosphoric acid. All products may be imported from abroad. The projects can be established at two possible locations, either at once or, say, five years hence. This relatively simple industrial planning problem, if solved by complete enumeration of all project combinations, involves the solution of more than 1 million linear programs.[3]

Fortunately, in recent years, more efficient mathematical programming techniques have been developed to handle this category of planning problems. As a result an increasing number of gradually more complex problems has been analyzed and, although cost in terms of

2. See Hollis B. Chenery, "Overcapacity and the Acceleration Principle," *Econometrica*, vol. 20, no. 1 (January 1952), pp. 1–28; Hollis B. Chenery, "The Interdependence of Investment Decisions," in M. Abramovitz and others, eds., *The Allocation of Economic Resources* (Stanford, Calif.: Stanford University Press, 1959); and Alan S. Manne, ed., *Investments for Capacity Expansion: Size, Location, and Time-Phasing* (London: Allen and Unwin, 1967).

3. The number of possible projects or zero-one variables is 5 times 2 times 2, which equals 20. The number of patterns of investment to be inspected, or linear programs to be solved, equals 2^{20} equals 1,048,576.

manpower and computer time remains substantial, considerable experience with their use has been gained.[4]

The Methodology in General Terms

Essentially, the approach involves the formulation of a mathematical model, the collection and organization of a great deal of numerical information, and the use of a large computer to process this information following instructions that are contained in the model. To many sector planners, this statement of the approach has strong doomsday connotations. This is justified in some but not in all respects, and it may be useful to deal with this aspect briefly first. The analysis of economic problems is always carried out on the basis of a varying degree of simplification. Some analysts are better than others at reducing a real-life economic problem to one that captures its essential aspects and yet is analytically manageable. If, furthermore, the analyst restricts himself to a particular technique of analysis, rather than letting the nature of the problem dictate the most appropriate analytic approach, one should be particularly careful in accepting the conclusions.[5] A fairly relevant example is the current fascination of many economic planners with linear programming. There is no doubt that linear programming techniques are very powerful for certain classes of problems. And, in fact, our approach itself will be based on a variant of this technique as stated before. However, it requires a very strong simplification: the assumption that all relationships in the economic problem are linear. This may be a correct or nearly correct assumption in some cases. In many cases, however, it is simply not an acceptable approximation, and the nature of the problem should in such cases dictate the use of a different analytic technique. We shall return to this issue shortly.

The second point that needs to be made with considerable emphasis is that the complexity of problems in economics varies considerably; in

4. For the most recent overview of completed work of this nature, see Larry E. Westphal, "Planning with Economies of Scale," in Charles R. Blitzer, Peter B. Clark, and Lance Taylor, eds., *Economy-Wide Models and Development Planning* (London: Oxford University Press, 1975); and Kendrick and Stoutjesdijk, *Planning of Industrial Investment Programs*, ch. 1.

5. It should be noted here that more conventional techniques of analysis must be under close scrutiny, too, in this respect, because they impose very strict limitations on the number of alternatives that can be considered.

some cases the interaction of the analyst with sector specialists is absolutely crucial to both the simplification process and the interpretation of the results.

Let us now begin to focus these more general observations on industrial sector analysis. The typical industrial subsector comprises many different products, which can be produced with many different raw materials, through many different industrial processes. It is difficult to conceive of circumstances where it will be necessary to evaluate all possible alternatives, and many can be rejected out of hand. However, it is desirable to base the selection of products and processes on the judgment of the sector specialist to ensure that all relevant possibilities are included in the analysis.

Consideration of all plausible alternatives in investment or project planning is also of the utmost importance for a subsequent phase of the project cycle—appraisal. Searching for alternatives is essential for determining correctly a number of shadow prices, such as those for land and natural resources.

Similar reasoning applies to other aspects of the problem specification. Which alternative potential plant sites should be considered? Which means of transport appear relevant? Should imports and exports from and to world markets be taken into account? How long a time period should be considered? How detailed a regional breakdown of the planning area is necessary to obtain insight in questions of location of productive facilities?

Once the problem specification has been completed and has been accepted as satisfactory by all relevant specialists (from the industrial sector, the agricultural sector, and the transport sector) and the analyst considers the problem as specified analytically manageable, the next phase in the study begins, namely, that of collecting and estimating the necessary numerical information. Again, the judgment of sector specialists is crucial, and it is imperative that the inevitable assumptions to be made are clearly specified. At what rate will the demand for final products increase during the planning period? What is most likely to happen to world market prices? What are the appropriate production costs for the various products and processes in the problem? What assumptions should be made about future transport costs?

In practice, there is frequently more than one set of estimates, reflecting varying judgments and assumptions. Consequently, the analysis focuses on the implications of such alternative estimates for production, investment, and trade, because the analyst cannot assume the authority to select a single set of estimates.

Let us now return to the observations made previously regarding the choice of analytic technique. Many of the relationships that characterize industrial production are linear or nearly linear over a relevant range. In the fertilizer industry, for example, the amount of phosphate rock needed per ton of single superphosphate remains identical regardless of whether one produces 1 or 100 tons of that product. In turn, it would appear acceptable to assume that input prices as well as transport cost per unit of product remain constant, independent of quantity involved, for the likely range of quantities that will be relevant. The major exception to the linearity assumption is with respect to investment cost. In fact, most industrial activities exhibit economies of scale, mainly because, up to a point, the investment cost per ton of capacity declines. This is illustrated in figure 3-1, where the concave curve OA represents some hypothetical investment cost function subject to economies of scale.

It will be clear that the linear approximation OB, which is the one that would be required to analyze the problem in the conventional linear programming format, is not particularly close to the original, especially at the lower part of curve, where OA is totally fictitious because plant

Figure 3-1.   *The Investment Cost Function Subject to Economies of Scale*

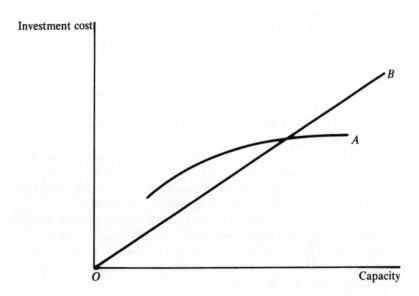

scales at very low levels do not exist. Another approach thus appears necessary; it will be discussed in detail in the following section, which is devoted to the outline of a planning model that incorporates economies of scale.

The Formulation of a Model with Economies of Scale

Our investment planning model is first stated as a simple linear programming transport problem and then slowly made more complicated by introducing multiple products, multiple processes, interplant shipments, exports, imports, and investment activities. This is followed by a statement of the complete model.

One can gradually develop an investment planning model by starting with the plants and markets that produce and consume a specific commodity. Any plant can serve any market, but one ordinarily observes that plants tend to serve nearby markets. This may be due either to competitive forces or to the desire for efficiency in a centrally planned economy. One may model this phenomenon by seeking to find which plants would serve which markets if total transport costs were minimized and if no plant was permitted to ship more than its capacity to produce and no market to receive less than it requires.

Let

$i =$ an individual plant in the set of plants I

$j =$ an individual market in the set of markets J

$x_{ij} =$ the amount of the good shipped from plant i to market j

$k_i =$ the capacity of plant i.

Then the logical necessity that no plant can ship more than its capacity can be written as

$$(3.1) \qquad\qquad \sum_{j \in J} x_{ij} \leq k_i, \qquad\qquad i \in I$$

that is, the sum of shipments from each plant i to all markets must be less than or equal to the capacity of plant i. In (3.1), the following apply.

- the symbol $\in$ indicates membership in a set
- the summation (Σ) for $j \in J$ indicates that one should add over the indexes contained in the set J (in this case markets)
- the symbol $\leq$ indicates less than or equal to

- the symbols $i \in I$ on the right indicate that we must have a constraint of type (3.1) for each plant i.

Consider an example with three marketing centers and two plants. Then the sets J and I can be written as $J = 1, 2, 3$ and $I = 1, 2$, so that (3.1) is written as

$$x_{11} + x_{12} + x_{13} \leq k_1$$

$$x_{21} + x_{22} + x_{23} \leq k_2.$$

This requires that the total of shipments from plant 1 to markets 1, 2, and 3 be less than or equal to the capacity of plant 1 and that shipments from plant 2 to markets 1, 2, and 3 be less than or equal to the capacity of plant 2.

The other constraint of the transport model is that each market should receive at least as much as it wants to purchase at current price and income levels. Let d_j equal the requirement of market j. Then the market requirement constraint may be written as

(3.2) $$\sum_{i \in I} x_{ij} \geq d_j, \qquad\qquad j \in J$$

that is, the summation of shipments from *all* plants i to *each* market j must be equal to or greater than the product requirement of market j.[6] For the example above with three markets and two plants, these constraints are written as

$$x_{11} + x_{21} \geq d_1$$

$$x_{12} + x_{22} \geq d_2$$

$$x_{13} + x_{23} \geq d_3.$$

Finally, shipments x_{ij} cannot assume negative values. This is formally stated in the mathematical structure of the model by nonnegativity constraints:

(3.3) $$x_{ij} \geq 0.$$

---

6. Normally, this constraint may be thought of as an equality as it would obviously not be consistent with the cost-minimizing objective to supply more to any market than its requirements. However, sometimes oversupply is inevitable for technical reasons, as in the case of goods that are produced and shipped in fixed proportions. For example, several chemical fertilizers contain both nitrogen and phosphorus nutrients. If market requirements are stated in terms of nutrients, it is obviously not always possible to meet requirements for both nutrients exactly, and oversupply of one of them often occurs. The general formulation of (3.2) anticipates such situations.

The objective or criterion of this problem is to minimize the transport costs while satisfying the sets of constraints (3.1), (3.2), and (3.3). Let μ_{ij} equal the constant unit transport cost for shipping the product from plant i to market j. Then the cost of transport of shipment x_{ij}, from plant i to market j is equal to $\mu_{ij}x_{ij}$, and the criterion of minimizing total cost may be stated as minimizing ξ, where

(3.4) $$\xi = \sum_{i \in I} \sum_{j \in J} \mu_{ij}x_{ij}.$$

This term represents the sum of the transport costs associated with all shipments from plants i to markets j. For the three market, two plant example, (3.4) would be written as

$$\min \xi = (\mu_{11}x_{11} + \mu_{12}x_{12} + \mu_{13}x_{13}) + (\mu_{21}x_{21} + \mu_{22}x_{22} + \mu_{23}x_{23}).$$

So, in summary, the simple transport model is to select x_{ij} to minimize total transport costs:

$$\min \xi = \sum_{i \in I} \sum_{j \in J} \mu_{ij}x_{ij},$$

subject to the constraints described in (3.5), (3.6), and (3.7).

CAPACITY CONSTRAINTS

(3.5) $$\sum_{j \in J} x_{ij} \leq k_i \qquad\qquad i \in I$$

MARKET REQUIREMENTS

(3.6) $$\sum_{i \in I} x_{ij} \geq d_j \qquad\qquad j \in J$$

NONNEGATIVITY CONSTRAINTS

(3.7) $$x_{ij} \geq 0 \qquad\qquad \begin{matrix} i \in I \\ j \in J \end{matrix}$$

At this point, it is helpful to introduce the notion of production as related to the activity level of a process z_{pi}, where z_{pi} indicates the activity level of process p at plant i. There are two reasons for introducing the notion of a process. First, it permits the description of production methods which create more than one product or by-product. An example is the industrial process of ionizing sodium chloride, which produces both sodium and chlorine gas. Second, it enables one to introduce alternative processes for producing the same good, namely, the production of pig iron with either regular ore, sinter, or pellets, or the production of electric power with either coal, natural gas, or petroleum. By explicitly representing alternative processes in the model one can use the model to analyze the shift in resource utilization in response to changes in relative prices.

Furthermore, since not all plants will have the same set of production processes, it is necessary to specify P as equal to the set of processes in use at plant i. For example, the set of processes in a textile mill might be spinning, weaving, and dyeing. To specify processes, let a_{cpi} equal the input $(-)$ or output $(+)$ of commodity c by process p at plant i per unit level of activity of process p.

For example, consider the process of producing the chemical fertilizer single superphosphate. Such a process has phosphate rock, sulfuric acid, and labor as its main inputs, and electric power and unspecified supplies as miscellaneous inputs. In such a case, one could have

$a_{cpi} = 1.0$ ton $\qquad\qquad$ $c =$ single superphosphate

$a_{cpi} = -0.6$ ton $\qquad\qquad$ $c =$ phosphate rock

$a_{cpi} = -0.36$ ton $\qquad\qquad$ $c =$ sulfuric acid

$a_{cpi} = -0.4$ manhours $\qquad\quad$ $c =$ labor

$a_{cpi} = -\$0.50$ $\qquad\qquad\quad$ $c =$ miscellaneous material inputs

that is, the process combines 0.6 tons of phosphate rock, 0.36 tons of sulfuric acid, 0.4 manhours, and \$0.50 worth of miscellaneous material inputs to produce 1 ton of single superphosphate.

In order to specify the process model, it is necessary to divide the commodities used or produced in the plant into five groups: (a) final commodities which are shipped from plants to markets, (b) intermediate commodities which are either produced within the plant or shipped among other plants, (c) raw materials which are purchased by the plant from outside sources, (d) raw materials or intermediates for which no separate specification is deemed necessary, referred to below as "miscellaneous material inputs," and (e) inputs of different types of labor. For the time being, the inputs of raw materials, other material inputs and all labor types are considered directly variable with output. Accordingly, the set of inputs and outputs C is divided into three subsets:

$CF =$ final commodities

$CI =$ intermediate commodities

$CR =$ raw materials, miscellaneous material inputs, and labor inputs.

In the example above, the sets would be specified as follows:

CF = single superphosphate

CI = sulfuric acid

CR = phosphate rock, electricity, miscellaneous supplies, and labor.

Since cost is no longer defined as attached to a final commodity but rather to the various input categories, one must define p_{ci} as the price of input c delivered to (or purchased at) plant i, and u_{ci} as the amount of purchases of input c delivered to (or purchased at) plant i, so that the cost of inputs to plant i is

$$(3.8) \qquad \sum_{c \in CR} p_{ci} u_{ci}.$$

With this notation, one may specify the process model as select z_{pi}, x_{cij}, and d_{ci} so as to minimize the sum of total shipment costs and the total cost of raw materials, labor, and miscellaneous material inputs:

$$(3.9) \qquad \min \xi = \sum_{c \in C_f} \sum_{i \in I} \sum_{j \in J} \mu_{cij} x_{cij} + \sum_{c \in CR} \sum_{i \in I} p_{ci} u_{ci},$$

subject to the following constraints.

MATERIAL BALANCE CONSTRAINTS ON FINAL COMMODITIES

$$(3.10) \qquad \sum_{p \in P} a_{cpi} z_{pi} \geq \sum_{j \in J} x_{cij}. \qquad\qquad \begin{array}{l} c \in CF \\ i \in I \end{array}$$

The production of commodity c by all processes p at plant i must at least equal the shipments of commodity c from plant i to all markets j. The typical process p which provides final commodities can be assigned a coefficient a_{cpi} equal to 1.0 in the final commodities constraint (3.10) because the unit of capacity can be arbitrarily defined in terms of one of the inputs or outputs.

MATERIAL BALANCE CONSTRAINTS ON INTERMEDIATE COMMODITIES

$$(3.11) \qquad \sum_{p \in P} a_{cpi} z_{pi} \geq 0 \qquad\qquad \begin{array}{l} c \in CI \\ i \in I \end{array}$$

The production of final products and some intermediate products by processes p at plant i requires the use of intermediate products. At least one process p in each constraint (3.11) will therefore have a negative coefficient a_{cpi}, while there has to be at least one process for producing an intermediate good which has a positive coefficient in the intermediate product constraint for the latter to hold. Note that this assumes, for the time being, that there are no interplant shipments of intermediates.

MATERIAL BALANCE CONSTRAINTS ON RAW MATERIALS, MISCELLANEOUS INPUTS, AND LABOR

$$(3.12) \qquad \sum_{p \in P} a_{cpi} z_{pi} + u_{ci} \geq 0 \qquad\qquad \begin{matrix} c \in CR \\ i \in I \end{matrix}$$

The production of intermediate and final products requires raw materials, miscellaneous inputs, and labor. The coefficient a_{cpi} in constraint (3.12) will therefore normally be negative. The purchases of raw material and miscellaneous inputs and the hiring of labor d_{ci} in turn will have to be positive for the constraint to hold.

CAPACITY CONSTRAINTS

$$(3.13) \qquad \sum_{p \in P} b_{mpi} z_{pi} \leq k_{mi} \qquad\qquad \begin{matrix} m \in M \\ i \in I \end{matrix}$$

where b_{mpi} is the number of units of capacity used on machine or productive unit m per unit of output of process p at plant i.

MARKET REQUIREMENTS

$$(3.14) \qquad \sum_{i \in I} x_{cij} \geq d_{cj} \qquad\qquad \begin{matrix} c \in CF \\ j \in J \end{matrix}$$

NONNEGATIVITY CONSTRAINTS

$$(3.15) \qquad x_{cij}, z_{pi}, u_{ci} \geq 0 \qquad\qquad \begin{matrix} i \in I \\ j \in J \\ c \in C \\ p \in P \end{matrix}$$

The difference between final, intermediate, and raw material commodities is clearly shown in the material balance constraints (3.10), (3.11), and (3.12). Final goods are shipped to markets, intermediate goods production and use must be balanced within the plant, and raw materials must be purchased outside the plant in sufficient quantities to at least equal their use in producing intermediate and final goods. Miscellaneous material inputs are by definition assumed to be available in sufficient quantities, and they appear consequently in the criterion function only as a component of the set CR.

Interplant Shipments, Exports, and Imports

Interplant shipments of intermediate materials are a common practice in a variety of industries. These shipments enter the balance equation for intermediate commodities, and they add a transportation cost element to the criterion function. These shipments are defined with the notation

$x_{cii'}$ = shipments of commodity c from plant i to plant i'

$\mu_{cii'}$ = unit cost of shipment for commodity c from plant i to plant i'.

Exports and imports also play a substantial role in most industries. The definition of exports and imports depends on the construction of the model, but they may generally be defined as shipments to or from sources outside the plant, markets, and raw material sources explicitly defined in the model. Thus for a model of a single company with several plants, export and import shipments would be to or from other companies. For a national model, the conventional definition of imports and exports would hold. For a multinational (or common market) model, imports and exports would constitute shipments to or from the set of countries not explicitly included in the model (see chapter 4).

The model includes imports of raw materials and intermediate commodities to plants and of final products to markets. It also includes exports of intermediate and final commodities from plants. The notation used for these flows is as follows:

m_{ci} = imports of commodity c to plant i (raw materials and intermediates)

m_{cj} = imports of commodity c to market j (final commodities)

e_{cil} = exports of commodity c from plant i to export areas l

L = set of export markets

μ_{ci} = unit transport costs for shipping imported commodity c from the appropriate port of entry to plant i

μ_{cj} = unit transport costs for shipping imported commodity c from the appropriate port of entry to market j

μ_{cil} = unit transport costs for shipping commodity c from plant i to the appropriate port of exit when the commodity is bound for export market l

p_{ci}^{v} = import price of commodity c at the appropriate entry port when bound for plant i

p_{cj}^{v} = import price of commodity c at the appropriate entry port when bound for market j

p_{cil}^{e} = export price of commodity c at the appropriate exit port when bound from plant i to export market area l.

Exports are labeled by destination l in order to permit the model to include discriminatory pricing.

At any stage in the development above, one could have added a time subscript to all the variables and coefficients and attached a discount factor. However, the essential element of the dynamics enters only when one introduces investment activities. These activities link the time periods together because an investment project installed in any time period will be available for use in a number of subsequent time periods as well.

Economies of Scale

Economies of scale in investment cost are modeled here through a so-called fixed charge linear approximation to the nonlinear cost function. Consider the investment (capital) cost function $\phi_{\kappa} = f(h)$ shown in figure 3-2. Here the total investment cost rises with the size h of the unit installed, but at a decreasing rate, so that the marginal cost of each increment of capacity is declining. This cost function often takes the form of a constant elasticity cost function, $\phi_{\kappa} = ah^{\beta}$, where the exponent β represents the constant elasticity. It was already said that β is in many cases in the range of 0.6 to 0.8. The true investment cost function $f(h)$ is approximated by the fixed-cost plus linear segment function, $\hat{f}(h)$. This approximation may be written

(3.16) $\phi_{\kappa} = \omega y + vh.$

If no investment is made, then y and h are both zero, and no cost is incurred. However, if any capacity is added so that h is greater than zero then y must be one, and the full fixed charge must be incurred. The mechanism that forces y to assume the appropriate value will be described later. It should be noted that the best linear approximation to the nonlinear investment cost function depends on the capacity range that is appropriate for the planning problem at hand. Inspection of figure 3-2 makes clear that the wider the relevant capacity range, the

Figure 3-2. *The Investment Cost Function*

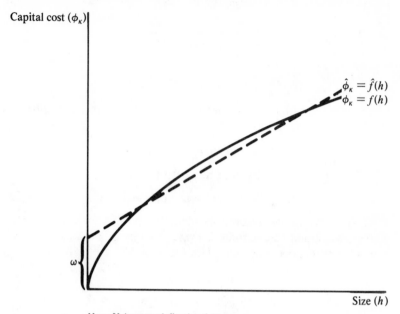

Capital cost (ϕ_κ)

$\hat{\phi}_\kappa = \hat{f}(h)$
$\phi_\kappa = f(h)$

ω

Size (h)

Note: Values are defined as follows:
$\hat{\phi}_\kappa$ = approximate capital cost for a productive unit of size h
ω = fixed charge portion of investment cost
h = size of productive unit to be installed.

higher the fixed charge ω and the smaller the slope ν of the linear approximation that provides the closest fit to the original investment cost function.

If the entire capital costs for a given period were charged in the period the project was installed, distortions would result in the timing of investments that the model would recommend. Clearly, investments in the latter part of the planning period would be discouraged, as the capacity installed is likely to generate greater costs than the benefits observed during the planning period. Furthermore, this treatment of capital costs would be a poor representation of reality, where normally investments are financed from loans that are periodically repaid. To convert the capital costs associated with capacity expansion in the model to an even stream of payments that are sufficient to cover the original cost plus interest charges for the productive unit over the period of its useful life, a capital recovery factor is applied to each investment. The capital recovery factor for productive unit m may be written as

$$(3.17) \qquad \sigma_m = \frac{(1 + \rho)^{\zeta_m}}{(1 + \rho)^{\zeta_m} - 1}$$

$$= \frac{\rho}{1 - (1 + \rho)^{-\zeta_m}},$$

which is the familiar formula for computing an annuity with present value equal to one, where

$$\sigma_m = \text{capital recovery factor}$$

$$\rho = \text{discount rate per time interval}$$

$$\zeta_m = \text{life of productive unit } m.[7]$$

Applying the capital recovery factor to the investment cost approximation, we obtain the periodical investment charge on a capacity increase for productive unit m at plant i as

$$\sigma_m(\omega_m y_m + \nu_m h_m).$$

The model should not begin to incur this periodical investment charge (which may also be interpreted as a rental payment) on an investment until the period in which the project is installed but should incur the rental in each time period after the unit is placed in operation. This is accomplished by computing the capital cost for each time period as follows:

$$(3.18) \qquad \phi_{\kappa\tau} = \sum_{\tau=1}^{t} \sum_{i \in I} \sum_{m \in M_i} \sigma_m(\omega_{mi\tau} y_{mi\tau} + \nu_{mi\tau} h_{mi\tau}),$$

where

$$\phi_{\kappa t} = \text{the capital charges incurred in each period}$$

$$\sigma_m = \text{capital recovery factor for productive unit } m$$

$$\omega_{mi\tau} = \text{fixed charge for investment in productive unit } m \text{ at plant } i \text{ in period } \tau$$

---

7. In an appendix to chapter 3 of Kendrick and Stoutjesdijk, *Planning of Industrial Investment Programs*, there is a derivation of the capital recovery factor, as well as a number of typical values of the capital recovery factor for different discount rates and plant and equipment lifetimes.

$y_{mi\tau}$ = zero-one investment variable for productive unit m at plant i in period τ

$v_{mi\tau}$ = linear portion of investment cost for productive unit m at plant i in period τ

$h_{mi\tau}$ = size of new productive unit m installed at plant i in period τ.

To see exactly how this works one may consider an example of a steel shop. In period 1 no capacity is added. In period 2 a new basic oxygen furnace converter is installed with a capacity of 200,000 metric tons of steel a year. In period 3 no new capacity is installed. In this case (subscripts refer to time):

$$y_1 = 0, \qquad h_1 = 0$$
$$y_2 = 1, \qquad h_2 = 200$$
$$y_3 = 0, \qquad h_3 = 0.$$

Then dropping the m and i subscripts on (3.18), since we are considering a single productive unit and plant, we may rewrite (3.18) as

(3.19) $$\phi_{\kappa t} = \sum_{\tau=1}^{t} \sigma(\omega_\tau y_\tau + v_\tau h_\tau).$$

Then, for time periods 1, 2, and 3 we have

$$\phi_{\kappa 1} = \sigma(\omega_1 y_1 + v_1 h_1) = 0$$
$$\phi_{\kappa 2} = \sigma(\omega_1 y_1 + v_1 h_1 + \omega_2 y_2 + v_2 h_2) = \sigma(\omega_2 + 200\, v_2)$$
$$\phi_{\kappa 3} = \sigma(\omega_1 y_1 + v_1 h_1 + \omega_2 y_2 + v_2 h_2 + \omega_3 y_3 + v_3 h_3) = \sigma(\omega_2 + 200\, v_2).$$

Thus, in both periods 2 and 3 the model incurs rental charges on the new capacity installed in period 2, but no payment is made in period 1.

This specification also results in the modification of the capacity constraint from the form (3.13) used in the previous model to

(3.20) $$\sum_{p \in P} b_{mpi} z_{pit} \leq k_{mi} + \sum_{\tau=1}^{t} (h_{mi\tau} - s_{mi\tau})$$

where $s_{mi\tau}$ is the expected retirement of capacity in productive unit m at plant i in time period τ. Recall also that k_{mi} is the initial capacity of productive unit m at plant i.

The s variables are chosen exogenously to the model. For example, if the productive unit m were the steel shop, the initial capacity might include a number of open hearth furnaces that were slated for retirement during the period covered by the model. Then $s_{mi\tau}$ would represent the capacity to be retired in each time period t. The effect of the summation over τ for τ less than or equal to t in (3.20) is to permit all capacity installed in previous periods to be available for use in period t.

Two additional constraints are needed to complete the specification of investment in the model. These two constraints introduce directly into the model the side condition

$$(3.21) \qquad\qquad y = 0 \quad \text{when} \quad h = 0$$

$$y = 1 \quad \text{when} \quad h \neq 0.$$

which was used in specifying the approximation to the investment cost function. These constraints are

$$(3.22) \qquad\qquad h_{mit} \leq \bar{h}_{mit} y_{mit} \qquad\qquad \begin{array}{l} m \in M \\ i \in I \\ t \in T \end{array}$$

and

$$(3.23) \qquad\qquad y_{mit} = 0 \quad \text{or} \quad 1 \qquad\qquad \begin{array}{l} m \in M \\ i \in I \\ t \in T \end{array}$$

where

$\bar{h}_{mit}$ = an upper bound on the size of capacity unit which can be added to productive unit m at plant i in period t

T = the set of time periods covered by the model.

The effect of (3.22) and (3.23) is to prohibit any addition to capacity unless the fixed charge is incurred, where it should be recalled that the fixed charge is only incurred if y_{mit} is equal to one. From (3.22) it follows that y_{mit} must be placed at one if h_{mit} is positive for the constraint to hold. If h_{mit} is zero, y_{mit} will be forced to zero by the model as the cost minimization objective of the model leads to a preference for not incurring the fixed charge.

A Statement of the Complete Model

The symbols used in the model can be categorized as the sets and indexes, the variables, and the parameters, as follows.

SET AND INDEXES

$$c \in C = \text{set of commodities used or produced in the industry}$$
$$CF = \text{final products}$$
$$CI = \text{intermediate products}$$
$$CR = \text{raw materials, miscellaneous material inputs,}$$
$$\text{and labor types}$$
$$i, i', \in I = \text{plant sites}$$
$$j \in J = \text{marketing centers}$$
$$m \in M = \text{productive units}$$
$$p \in P = \text{processes}$$
$$l \in L = \text{export regions}$$
$$T, t, t' \in T = \text{time periods}$$

PARAMETERS

a = process inputs ($-$) or outputs ($+$)
b = units of capacity required
k = initial capacity
s = retirements of capacity
d = market requirements
$\bar{e}$ = export bound
$\bar{h}$ = maximum capacity expansion
θ = number of years per time period
ρ = discount rate per year
δ = discount factor per time period
σ = capital recovery factor

$$= \frac{\rho(1 + \rho)^{\zeta_m}}{(1 + \rho)^{\zeta_m} - 1}$$

ζ_m = life of productive unit m
ω = fixed charge portion of investment cost
u = linear portion of investment cost
μ = unit transport cost
p = prices
p^d = domestic price
p^v = import price
p^e = export price

VARIABLES

z = process level
x = domestic shipments

e = exports
v = imports
u = domestic purchases
y = zero-one investment variable
h = capacity expansion
ξ = total cost
ϕ = cost groups
ϕ_κ = capital cost
ϕ_ψ = domestic raw materials, miscellaneous material inputs, and labor costs
ϕ_λ = transport costs
ϕ_π = import costs
ϕ_ϵ = export revenue

The model may now formally be restated as select z_{pit} (process levels), x_{cijt} (shipments of final goods), $x_{cii't}$ (shipments of intermediate goods), e_{ciet} (exports), m_{cit} (imports of raw materials and intermediates), m_{cjt} (imports of final goods), and u_{cit} (purchases of domestic inputs), so as to minimize ξ:

(3.24)
$$\min \xi = \sum_{t \in T} \delta_t(\phi_{\kappa t} + \phi_{\psi t}$$

$$\begin{bmatrix} Discounted \\ net\ cost \end{bmatrix} = \begin{bmatrix} \begin{array}{c} Total \\ capital \\ cost\ at \\ time\ period \\ t \end{array} + \begin{array}{c} Total\ domestic \\ recurrent \\ cost\ at \\ time\ period \\ t \end{array} \end{bmatrix}$$

$$+ \phi_{\lambda t} + \phi_{\pi t} - \phi_{\epsilon t})$$

$$\begin{array}{ccc} \begin{array}{c} Total \\ transport \\ + \quad cost\ at \\ time \\ period\ t \end{array} & \begin{array}{c} Total \\ import \\ + \quad cost \\ at\ time \\ period\ t \end{array} & \begin{array}{c} Total \\ export \\ - \quad revenue \\ at\ time \\ period\ t \end{array} \end{array}$$

where

$$\delta_t = \sum_{\tau=1}^{\theta} (1 + \rho)^{-\theta(t-1)-\tau}.$$

$$\begin{bmatrix} Discount \\ factor \end{bmatrix}$$

$$(3.25) \qquad \phi_{\kappa t} = \sum_{\substack{\tau \in T \\ \tau \leq t}}^{t} \sum_{i \in I} \sum_{m \in M} \sigma_m (\omega_{mi\tau} y_{mi\tau}$$

$$
\begin{bmatrix} Total\ capital \\ cost\ during \\ time\ period\ t \end{bmatrix} = \begin{bmatrix} Capital \\ recovery \\ factor \end{bmatrix} \begin{bmatrix} Total\ fixed\ charge \\ for\ all\ productive \\ units\ installed\ at\ all \\ plant\ locations\ up\ to \\ time\ period\ t \end{bmatrix}
$$

$$+ \ \nu_{mi\tau} h_{mi\tau})$$

$$
+ \begin{bmatrix} Total\ of\ the\ variable \\ portion\ of\ the\ capital \\ cost\ for\ all\ productive \\ units\ installed\ at\ all \\ plant\ locations\ up\ to \\ time\ period\ t \end{bmatrix}
$$

$$(3.26) \qquad \phi_{\psi t} = \sum_{c \in CR} \sum_{i \in I} p_{cit}^d u_{cit}$$

$$
\begin{bmatrix} Total\ domestic\ recurrent \\ cost\ during \\ time\ period\ t \end{bmatrix} = \begin{bmatrix} Cost\ of\ domestic\ raw\ material \\ labor\ and\ miscellaneous\ inputs \\ purchased\ at\ all\ plant\ locations \\ during\ time\ period\ t \end{bmatrix}
$$

$$(3.27) \qquad \phi_{\lambda t} = \sum_{c \in CF} \left\{ \sum_{i \in I} \sum_{j \in J} \mu_{cijt} x_{cijt} \right.$$

$$
\begin{bmatrix} Total \\ transport \\ costs\ during \\ time\ period\ t \end{bmatrix} = \begin{bmatrix} Cost\ of\ shipping\ all \\ final\ products\ from\ all \\ plant\ locations\ to\ all \\ domestic\ markets\ during \\ time\ period\ t \end{bmatrix}
$$

$$+ \sum_{j \in J} \mu_{cjt} v_{cjt} + \sum_{i \in I} \sum_{l \in L} \mu_{cilt} e_{cilt} \Big\}$$

$$
+ \begin{bmatrix} Cost\ of\ transporting \\ all\ imported\ final \\ products\ from\ the \\ border\ to\ all\ domestic \\ markets\ during\ time \\ period\ t \end{bmatrix} + \begin{bmatrix} Cost\ of\ transporting\ all \\ final\ products\ exported \\ from\ all\ plant\ locations \\ to\ the\ border\ for\ all \\ export\ regions\ during \\ time\ period\ t \end{bmatrix}
$$

$$+ \sum_{c \in CI} \left\{ \sum_{i \in I} \sum_{\substack{i' \in I \\ i' \neq i}} \mu_{cii't} x_{cii't} + \sum_{i \in I} \mu_{cit} v_{cit} \right.$$

$$+ \begin{bmatrix} \textit{Cost of all interplant} \\ \textit{location shipments of} \\ \textit{all intermediate} \\ \textit{products during time} \\ \textit{period t} \end{bmatrix} + \begin{array}{c} \textit{Cost of transporting all} \\ \textit{imported intermediate products} \\ \textit{from the border to all plant} \\ \textit{locations during time period t} \end{array}$$

$$\left. + \sum_{i \in I} \sum_{l \in L} \mu_{cilt} e_{cilt} \right\} + \sum_{c \in CR} \left\{ \sum_{i \in I} \mu_{cit} v_{cit} \right\}$$

$$+ \begin{bmatrix} \textit{Cost of transporting} \\ \textit{all intermediate} \\ \textit{products exported} \\ \textit{from all plant locations} \\ \textit{to all export regions} \\ \textit{during time period t} \end{bmatrix} + \begin{bmatrix} \textit{Cost of transporting all} \\ \textit{imported raw materials and} \\ \textit{labor to all plant locations} \\ \textit{during time period t} \end{bmatrix}$$

(3.28)
$$\phi_{\pi t} = \sum_{c \in CF} \sum_{j \in J} p^v_{cjt} v_{cjt}$$

$$\begin{bmatrix} \textit{Total import} \\ \textit{cost during} \\ \textit{time period} \\ \textit{t} \end{bmatrix} = \begin{bmatrix} \textit{Cost of importing all} \\ \textit{final products sold in} \\ \textit{all market areas during} \\ \textit{time period t} \end{bmatrix}$$

$$+ \sum_{c \in CI \cup CR} \sum_{i \in I} p^v_{cit} v_{cit}$$

$$+ \begin{bmatrix} \textit{Cost of importing all} \\ \textit{intermediate products,} \\ \textit{raw materials and labor} \\ \textit{used at all plant locations} \\ \textit{during time period t} \end{bmatrix}$$

(3.29)
$$\phi_{\epsilon t} = \sum_{c \in CF \cup CI} \sum_{i \in I} \sum_{l \in L} p^e_{cilt} e_{cilt}$$

$$\begin{bmatrix} \textit{Total export} \\ \textit{revenue during} \\ \textit{time period} \\ \textit{t} \end{bmatrix} = \begin{bmatrix} \textit{Revenue from the export of all} \\ \textit{final and intermediate products} \\ \textit{from all plant locations to all} \\ \textit{export regions during time} \\ \textit{period t} \end{bmatrix}$$

The constraints on the model are as follows.

MATERIAL BALANCE CONSTRAINTS ON FINAL PRODUCTS

(3.30)
$$\sum_{p \in P} a_{cpi} z_{pit} \geq \sum_{j \in J} x_{cijt}$$

$$\begin{bmatrix} \textit{Total production of ferti-} \\ \textit{lizer c from all processes} \\ \textit{at plant location i and time} \\ \textit{period t} \end{bmatrix} \geq \begin{bmatrix} \textit{Quantity of fertilizer c} \\ \textit{shipped to all market areas} \\ \textit{from plant location i at} \\ \textit{time period t} \end{bmatrix}$$

$$+ \sum_{l \in L} e_{cilt} \qquad\qquad c \in CF$$
$$i \in I$$
$$t \in T$$

$$+ \begin{bmatrix} \textit{Quantity of fertilizer} \\ \textit{c exported from plant} \\ \textit{location i to all export} \\ \textit{regions at time period t} \end{bmatrix}$$

MATERIAL BALANCE CONSTRAINTS ON INTERMEDIATE PRODUCTS

(3.31)
$$\sum_{p \in P} a_{cpi} z_{pit} + \sum_{\substack{i' \in I \\ i' \neq i}} x_{ci'it}$$

$$\begin{bmatrix} \textit{Total production of inter-} \\ \textit{mediate product c from all} \\ \textit{processes at plant location} \\ \textit{i and time period t} \end{bmatrix} + \begin{bmatrix} \textit{Quantity of intermediate} \\ \textit{product c shipped from} \\ \textit{plant location i' to} \\ \textit{plant location i at time} \\ \textit{period t} \end{bmatrix}$$

$$+ \; v_{cit} \geq \sum_{\substack{i' \in I \\ i' \neq i}} x_{cii't}$$

$$+ \begin{bmatrix} \textit{Quantity of intermediate} \\ \textit{product c imported to} \\ \textit{plant location i at time} \\ \textit{period t} \end{bmatrix} \geq \begin{bmatrix} \textit{Quantity of intermediate} \\ \textit{product c shipped from} \\ \textit{plant location i to} \\ \textit{plant location i' at} \\ \textit{time period t} \end{bmatrix}$$

$$+ \sum_{l \in L} e_{cilt} + w_{cit} \qquad\qquad c \in CI$$
$$i \in I$$
$$t \in T$$

$$+ \begin{bmatrix} \textit{Quantity of intermediate} \\ \textit{product c exported from} \\ \textit{plant location i to all} \\ \textit{export regions at time} \\ \textit{period t} \end{bmatrix} + \begin{bmatrix} \textit{Domestic sales of} \\ \textit{by-product c at} \\ \textit{plant i in time} \\ \textit{period t} \end{bmatrix}$$

MATERIAL BALANCE CONSTRAINTS ON RAW MATERIALS, LABOR, AND MISCELLANEOUS INPUTS

$$(3.32) \qquad \sum_{p \in P} a_{cpi} z_{pit} + u_{cit} + v_{cit} \geq 0 \qquad\qquad c \in CR$$
$$i \in I$$
$$t \in T$$

$$\left[\begin{array}{c} \textit{Raw} \\ \textit{materials or} \\ \textit{labor or miscel-} \\ \textit{laneous inputs} \\ \textit{used in all pro-} \\ \textit{cesses at plant} \\ \textit{location i at} \\ \textit{time period t} \end{array} \right] + \left[\begin{array}{c} \textit{Raw materials} \\ \textit{or labor or} \\ \textit{miscellaneous} \\ \textit{inputs domes-} \\ \textit{tically pur-} \\ \textit{chased (or} \\ \textit{hired) at} \\ \textit{plant location} \\ \textit{i and time} \\ \textit{period t} \end{array} \right] + \left[\begin{array}{c} \textit{Raw materials} \\ \textit{or labor or} \\ \textit{miscellaneous} \\ \textit{inputs imported} \\ \textit{to plant loca-} \\ \textit{tion i at time} \\ \textit{period t} \end{array} \right] \geq 0$$

CAPACITY CONSTRAINTS

$$(3.33) \qquad\qquad \sum_{p \in P} b_{mpi} z_{pit} \leq k_{mi}$$

$$\left[\begin{array}{c} \textit{Capacity of productive unit} \\ \textit{m for all processes at plant} \\ \textit{location i and time period t} \end{array} \right] \leq \left[\begin{array}{c} \textit{Initial capacity of} \\ \textit{productive unit m} \\ \textit{at plant location i} \end{array} \right]$$

$$+ \sum_{\substack{\tau \in T \\ \tau \leq t}} (h_{mi\tau} - s_{mi\tau}) \qquad\qquad i \in I$$
$$m \in M$$
$$t \in T$$

$$+ \left[\begin{array}{c} \textit{Total capacity expansion} \\ \textit{of productive unit m at} \\ \textit{plant location i up to} \\ \textit{time period t} \end{array} \right] - \left[\begin{array}{c} \textit{Total capacity} \\ \textit{retirement of} \\ \textit{productive unit m} \\ \textit{at plant location i} \\ \textit{up to time period t} \end{array} \right]$$

MARKET REQUIREMENT CONSTRAINTS

$$(3.34) \qquad\qquad \sum_{i \in I} x_{cijt} + v_{cjt} \geq d_{cjt} \qquad\qquad j \in J$$
$$c \in CF$$
$$t \in T$$

$$\left[\begin{array}{c} \textit{Shipment of final} \\ \textit{product c from} \\ \textit{all plants i to} \\ \textit{marketing center} \\ \textit{j in time period} \\ \textit{t} \end{array} \right] + \left[\begin{array}{c} \textit{Imports of final} \\ \textit{product c for} \\ \textit{marketing center} \\ \textit{j in time period} \\ \textit{t} \end{array} \right] \geq \left[\begin{array}{c} \textit{Market} \\ \textit{requirements} \\ \textit{for final} \\ \textit{product c} \\ \textit{in marketing} \\ \textit{center j} \\ \textit{in time} \\ \textit{period t} \end{array} \right]$$

EXPORT CONSTRAINTS

$$(3.35) \qquad \sum_{i \in I} e_{cilt} \leq \bar{e}_{clt} \qquad\qquad c \in (CF \cup C)$$
$$l \in L$$
$$t \in T$$

$$\begin{bmatrix} \text{Quantity of final or} \\ \text{intermediate prod-} \\ \text{uct c exported} \\ \text{from all plant} \\ \text{locations to ex-} \\ \text{port region l} \\ \text{at time period t} \end{bmatrix} \leq \begin{bmatrix} \text{Maximum quantity of} \\ \text{exports of product} \\ \text{c to export region} \\ \text{l at time period t} \end{bmatrix}$$

MAXIMUM CAPACITY EXPANSION CONSTRAINTS

$$(3.36) \qquad h_{mit} \leq \bar{h}_{mit} y_{mit} \qquad\qquad i \in I$$
$$m \in M$$
$$t \in T$$

$$\begin{bmatrix} \text{Increment to} \\ \text{capacity of} \\ \text{productive} \\ \text{unit m at} \\ \text{plant loca-} \\ \text{tion i and} \\ \text{time period t} \end{bmatrix} \leq \begin{bmatrix} \text{Upper bound} \\ \text{on capacity} \\ \text{of productive} \\ \text{unit m at plant} \\ \text{location i and} \\ \text{time period t} \end{bmatrix} \begin{bmatrix} \text{Zero-one} \\ \text{investment} \\ \text{variable} \end{bmatrix}$$

ZERO-ONE CAPACITY EXPANSION CONSTRAINTS

$$(3.37) \qquad y_{mit} = 0 \quad \text{or} \quad 1 \qquad\qquad i \in I$$
$$m \in M$$
$$t \in T$$

NONNEGATIVITY CONSTRAINTS

$$(3.38) \qquad z_{pit} \geq 0 \qquad\qquad p \in P, i \in I, t \in T$$
$$x_{cijt} \geq 0 \qquad\qquad c \in CF, i \in I, j \in J, t \in T$$
$$x_{cii't} \geq 0 \qquad\qquad c \in CI, i \in I, i' \in I, i' \neq i, t \in T$$
$$v_{cit} \geq 0 \qquad\qquad c \in (CI \cup CR), i \in I, t \in T$$
$$v_{cjt} \geq 0 \qquad\qquad c \in CF, j \in J, t \in T$$
$$e_{cilt} \geq 0 \qquad\qquad c \in (CF \cup CI), i \in I, l \in L, t \in T$$
$$u_{cit} \geq 0 \qquad\qquad c \in CR, i \in I, t \in T$$

$$h_{mit} \geq 0 \qquad\qquad m \in M, i \in I, t \in T$$

$$y_{mit} \geq 0 \qquad\qquad m \in M, i \in I, t \in T$$

$$w_{cit} \geq 0 \qquad\qquad c \in CI, i \in I, t \in T$$

This completes a formal statement of a dynamic investment planning model that can be used for detailed sectoral project analysis. In the next chapter, we shall discuss the modifications that may be introduced to make the model more suitable for investment analysis in a multicountry framework.

4
Models for Multicountry Planning

THE BRIEF SURVEY that will be presented here of previous work on multi-country investment planning indicates that developments in both model-ing and computer capability have permitted the analysis of planning problems in increasingly realistic terms. Undoubtedly, further progress will continue to be made in both respects. This appears to be a reasonably good moment, however, to take stock of the most promising approaches. Moreover, a candid statement of the limitations of the present state of the art will serve two purposes: first, it will alert potential users that the re-sults must be interpreted with care and that the use of the model is no sub-stitute for the use of sound judgment; second, the statement of limita-tions will provide an agenda for further research.

A Survey of Previous Work

The first planning model that was formulated in the mixed-integer for-mat to capture the impact of economies of scale was the model of the Latin American fertilizer industry by Vietorisz and Manne, published in 1963.[1] Theirs is a static model, designed to determine the investment plan that will minimize the cost of supplying a specified amount of final products to twelve regions in Latin America. Five different production locations were considered as potential sites. The production problem relates to ammo-

1. T. Vietorisz and A. S. Manne, "Chemical Processes, Plant Location, and Economies of Scale," in A. S. Manne and H. M. Markowitz, eds., *Studies in Process Analysis, Economy-wide Production Capabilities* (New York: John Wiley and Sons, 1963).

nia, on the one hand, and a composite product consisting of nitric acid, sulfuric acid, ammonium nitrate, and ammonium sulfate, on the other. The latter two are final products and need to be supplied in the fixed proportion of 60:40 in each demand region. The composite product represents an all-or-nothing case: either all component parts are produced domestically, at the same location, or both ammonium nitrate and ammonium sulfate are imported in the required proportion. Ammonia can be imported or domestically produced at any of the five locations, whether the composite product is produced at the same location or not. This formulation kept the model small, as one would wish for a first experiment, with no more than ten zero-one variables, or 2^{10} (that is, 1,024) project combinations. A special computer code was written for the IBM 650 computer, and the model was solved by complete enumeration of all project combinations and then selection of the least costly one, which took four hours of computer time.[2] The authors found that substantial gains could be derived from economic integration within Latin America, in the sense that requirements could be met much more cheaply by an integrated investment plan than by nationalistic supply patterns. Their estimate of gain amounted to 38 percent of total cost; however, they cautioned that the numerical precision of their results was limited.

In 1963 several major Latin American research institutes began a joint research effort, called the Program of Joint Studies in Latin American Economic Integration, better known under its Spanish acronym ECIEL. The first study carried out under this program, which was coordinated by the Brookings Institution, focused on the effects of a Latin American common market on several selected industries. The results of this study were summarized by Martin Carnoy and published in 1972.[3]

The objectives of the research were to determine least-cost locations and plant scales in 1975 for six selected industrial product groups for all members of the Latin American Free Trade Association (LAFTA) and to

2. The authors realized later that they could have halved the solution time of their model by stating explicitly that it never pays to construct a greater number of ammonia plants than fertilizer plants. Elsewhere, one of us has reported on several additional computer-time saving procedures that could have shortened solution time; it is also reported there, however, that none of these has as dramatic an effect as the advance in computer technology that has been made. See Ardy J. Stoutjesdijk and Larry E. Westphal, eds., *Industrial Investment Analysis under Increasing Returns* (London: Oxford University Press, forthcoming).

3. Martin Carnoy, *Industrialization in a Latin American Common Market* (Washington, D.C.: Brookings Institution, 1972).

estimate the benefits to be derived from the regional integration of these industries. The industrial product groups analyzed were nitrogenous fertilizers; methanol and formaldehyde; kraft pulp, kraft paper, and newsprint; agricultural tractors; universal parallel lathes; and powdered milk and cheese. Each participating institute made an estimate of the likely demand in its own country in 1975 for all products studied within the six product groups, fourteen products in total. With the help of technical consultants, the institutes then made cost projections for each country for those products that the institutes considered reasonable candidates for production in that country. Finally, transport costs were estimated between plants or ports and representative consumption points in each country.

Given these data and projections, a mixed-integer programming model was formulated following Vietorisz and Manne, which was used to determine the least-cost location of new plants. Solutions were obtained for each product group independently, under varying assumptions relating to exchange rates and transport cost. The solution method, like Vietorisz and Manne's was complete enumeration. This implies that each product group model must have been very small.

The model solutions were used to obtain insight into the benefits that can be derived from project collaboration, by comparing alternative investment strategies. A nationalistic investment strategy was taken to be one where each country that made cost estimates for a particular product group—and was thereby assumed to be a reasonable candidate for production of that product group—met its own requirements only, with the exception of the one with the lowest production cost, which supplied everyone else. Comparing the cost to each country with that emerging if a fully cooperative investment strategy were adopted in the region gave at least the correct order of magnitude to estimates of gains.

The third study that should be mentioned in this brief selective survey of previous work is that by Gately on the electric power sector.[4] Although, strictly speaking, not concerned with multicountry investment planning, Gately's study deals with the problem of investment planning of the electric power industry in four adjacent Indian states, thereby encountering a variety of issues of efficiency and equity that are relevant to our topic.

---

4. D. I. Gately, "Investment Planning for the Electric Power Industry: A Mixed-Integer Programming Approach, with Application to Southern India," Ph.D. dissertation, Princeton University, 1971.

The problem being addressed in his study is the following. The four states of Andhra Pradesh, Kerala, Madras (Tamil Nadu), and Mysore form one of five electricity regions in India, established for the purpose of coordinating investment planning. The planning problem is complicated for several reasons. First, there is a variety of technological options that have to be considered (hydroelectric plants, nuclear plants, conventional thermal plants based on coal, and lignite thermal plants); each state has a different resource endowment, which influences technology choice. Electric power production is subject to economies of scale under all technological options, to a varying degree. As long as production costs decline faster than distribution costs increase, concentration of power production in a limited number of sites is desirable. However, since investment decisions are made independently by the four State Electricity Boards, the coordination of investments is difficult. Although policies of self-sufficiency for each state lead to higher cost than the cost associated with a regional plan, such cooperation will not result unless it is in each state's interest to cooperate. The problem addressed by Gately is how to use a formal model—of the mixed-integer variety—to determine the magnitude of intraregional compensation payments that ensure that each state is better off with cooperation than without.

To this end, Gately formulated a mixed-integer programming model of the electric power sector, extending the linear programming model developed by the Electricité de France to incorporate economies of scale. This model was used first to determine the cost of self-sufficiency in the four states, combining Kerala and Mysore to simplify the computations. Subsequently, the lowest-cost regional investment plan was determined, and the cost of this plan to each state was estimated by assuming that the costs of plant construction and operation are incurred in the state where the plant is located and that costs of building interstate transmission lines were divided evenly between the states concerned. Overall, the gain of regional collaboration as compared with self-sufficiency was quite substantial, roughly 20 percent of total costs. However, this gain was very unevenly distributed among the states, some states being worse off than under self-sufficiency, others being much better off.

In order to achieve his objective of finding a strategy that made every state better off with collaboration, Gately proceeded to determine the payoffs that would be necessary among states to ensure that an equitable sharing in regional benefits would emerge, using a game-theoretic approach. For that purpose, he evaluated the implications of each possible coalition among the four states, retaining Kerala and Mysore as one "state." Including full cooperation and complete self-sufficiency, five alternative coalitions are possible, necessitating the solution of seven programming problems (three single-state models, three two-state models, and one three-state model).[5]

The solutions to the various models permit the determination of the costs to each state, under each coalition, of meeting electric power requirements and, therefore, the costs of each coalition to the region. Taking the costs associating with self-sufficiency in each state to be the point of zero payoff to that state, one can determine the payoff of each coalition to each state. The payoff is positive if the state is better off; it is negative when the state is not. The sum of the payoffs of each coalition is always positive, because on balance cooperation in each case was always superior to self-sufficiency. This information provides the range within which transfer payments among states can take place, in the sense that the losing state will not be interested in collaboration unless it is compensated for its loss as compared with self-sufficiency, and the gaining state will not be prepared to compensate for more than its gain from collaboration. Moreover, the sum of the payments to any two states should be no less than what they could obtain without the third state. These restrictions narrow the range within which side payments can be negotiated. They are not sufficiently strong to result in uniquely determined magnitudes for such transfer payments. For further details, the reader is referred to Gately's study, which to our knowledge was the first one to consider the matter of equity in detail.

During the early 1970s a mixed-integer programming model of the East African fertilizer industry was formulated by Stoutjesdijk, Frank, and Meeraus as the starting point for a long-term research program at the World Bank focused on investment planning under economies of scale.[6] Although it followed in the footsteps of its predecessors, the model was much larger than what had been attempted before, including 360 zero-one variables, permitting a much more realistic representation of the planning problem than had been possible hitherto. However, the study remained largely an experimental one, in the first place undertaken to assess the feasibility of solving such large mixed-integer programming problems at reasonable costs. In the process, a careful analysis was car-

5. Gately reports that, in view of the computational costs, the two-state models were never solved as mixed-integer programming models, and only the continuous solutions were found. This underestimates the cost of the investment strategy.

6. Ardy J. Stoutjesdijk, Charles Frank, Jr., and Alexander Meeraus, "Planning in the Chemical Sector," in Stoutjesdijk and Westphal, *Industrial Investment Analysis under Increasing Returns.*

ried out of the benefits that could be derived from regional investment planning in East Africa, under a large number of alternative assumptions regarding the growth of regional demand and future import prices.

Under the most likely set of assumptions the gain of regional cooperation in the East African fertilizer industry was estimated at 4 to 7 percent of total cost. This is much less than what others have estimated elsewhere. A number of reasons can explain this modest gain, among which are the very low levels of demand in East Africa and the large distances to be covered, eliminating much of the potential benefits to be derived from economies of scale in production.

This study also considered various ways in which the benefits of collaboration could be allocated among partner countries. First, as Gately had done, the range of lump-sum transfer payments was determined. However, in the East African case the feasibility of a scheme for transfer payments was considered to be extremely limited, given the severe budgetary difficulties of the three countries. Two alternatives were, therefore, suggested. One was the incorporation of the side payment in the transfer price of exports of the sector to collaborating countries, such that the export revenues (or import cost) of the losing countries would increase (decrease) by an amount equal to what lump-sum transfer payments would otherwise have been, properly discounted. If indeed trade flows occurred in the right direction and of sufficient magnitude, this mechanism for compensation would be easier to implement than lump-sum side payments. However, if such trade flows did not emerge, an alternative would be to explore to what extent a more equitable allocation of investment in the area could be recommended. The study looked into several different locational patterns for new production facilities and concluded that this approach to equitable development in the regional fertilizer industry may be the easiest to attain.

The formulation of planning models for economic cooperation among developing countries was the subject of a study by Mennes in 1972.[7] The method of analysis in this study is essentially a comparison of two sets of results calculated through medium-term planning models. One set corresponds to single-country planning models, drawn up for each of the individual countries that were envisaging participation in a cooperation scheme, on the assumption that such a scheme would not materialize. The other set corresponds to a planning model for the cooperation area as

7. L. B. M. Mennes, *Planning Economic Integration among Developing Countries* (Rotterdam: Rotterdam University Press, 1973).

a whole, on the assumption that economic cooperation would actually take place.

The planning models are in fact multisector programming models where, given an income-increase target, the use of scarce resources, particularly capital, during the plan period is minimized. The proposed planning models were used for analyzing the benefits and costs of a customs union and a common market as well as for determining the benefits and costs to individual partners in the cooperation scheme.

Special attention was given to the planning of a partial customs union, as an investment plan; the analysis was in terms of projects characterized by economies of scale. A numerical example was worked out with the aid of a programming model which distinguished between sectors or industries, commodities, projects, and productive activities and in which economies of scale were represented by fixed requirement investment cost functions. This zero-one integer programming model was solved by complete enumeration, which was feasible because the number of projects and their possible locations was limited.

During the same period Bos and Enos, in *Asian Industrial Survey for Regional Co-operation*, attempted to employ the mixed-integer programming methodology to select efficient and equitable packages of projects from among ten industrial subsectors for ten countries in Southeast Asia.[8] This led to the formulation of a planning problem that was too large to handle with the computer technology available at that time, and they were forced to assemble attractive packages of projects by approximate hand calculations. A feasible alternative might have been to formulate separate planning models for each subsector and to address the objectives of efficiency and equity sequentially.

Following the East African study mentioned earlier, a number of increasingly operational investment analyses were carried out by the World Bank research team, mostly of different industrial subsectors in specific countries. Some of these studies are reported as case studies in companion volumes in this series. Three more multicountry studies were undertaken, all of the fertilizer industry. The first of these was a study of the world fertilizer industry, designed to determine where future production capacity for fertilizers should be established worldwide if the objective of minimization of production and transport costs is to be met; what the resulting trade flows might be; and what total capital requirements would

---

8. United Nations, Economic Commission for Asia and the Far East, *Asian Industrial Survey for Regional Co-operation* (New York: UN, 1975).

be. The study was never published, but served as a background to a confidential World Bank document that was discussed by the Bank's Board of Directors and led to the periodic review of the world fertilizer situation by that organization.[9]

The two other studies are more relevant for our present purpose. The first is a study of the fertilizer sector of the countries that form the Association of South East Asian Nations (ASEAN), by Choksi and Meeraus;[10] the second is an analysis of the prospects for collaboration in fertilizer production and distribution among the countries of the Andean Pact, by Stoutjesdijk and staff of the Andean secretariat.[11] The latter study is the subject of the case study of this volume and will be discussed in detail in part two.

The study of ASEAN focused on the nitrogen industry in that region and evaluated the advantages of different degrees of collaboration during the period 1980–90. Using available demand forecasts for the countries in the region during the planning period, a planning model was formulated to determine the least-cost production and trade pattern that would meet demand for nitrogen in the form of urea. The area was subdivided into sixteen demand regions, which could be supplied from fourteen plant locations as well as by imports from outside the region. The planning period spans from 1982 to 1990; it is subdivided into eight annual periods. Because of a prior decision by the ASEAN countries, only one size is considered for the nitrogen complex: a 1,725 ton per day urea plant, associated with a 1,000 ton per day ammonia plant.

Within this framework, the model was used to evaluate the implications of six alternative scenarios. Four of the scenarios included the possibility of regional trade and varied the freedom of choice in the number and timing of specific projects. At one extreme, no capacity expansion was permitted, so that the model had as its objective the selection of the least-cost supply pattern, given existing production capacity and the possibility of imports from outside the region. At the other extreme, the model was free to determine the least-cost supply pattern, including the possibility of capacity expansion. The two remaining scenarios did not permit regional

9. This line of inquiry was continued in A. Dammert, "A World Copper Model for Project Design," Ph.D. dissertation, University of Texas at Austin, May 1977, and A. Dammert, "A World Aluminum Model," World Bank, 1978 (processed).

10. A Choksi and A. Meeraus, "The Coordination of Investments in the ASEAN Fertilizer Sector," World Bank, November 1977 (processed).

11. Acuerdo de Cartagena, "Evaluacion de los Effectos de las Principales Estrategias de Desarrollo del Sector de Fertilizantes," Lima, Peru, October 1980 (processed).

trade. The first of these allowed capacity expansion; the second one did not.

On the basis of these scenarios, detailed calculations could be made of the relative benefits of different degrees of cooperation. If full cooperation among the countries were to be agreed on, four new nitrogen plants could be constructed in the region during the planning period, one to be located in Indonesia at Aceh in 1982, and three in East Malaysia at Miri in 1982, 1985, and 1988, respectively. If agreement could be reached on only one ASEAN fertilizer project, this project could be located at either Aceh or Miri, the cost difference between the two locations being marginal.

Cooperation among the ASEAN countries was found to be very beneficial. Compared with a policy of national autarky, the total gain, expressed as the discounted value in constant 1977 U.S. dollars, amounted to $300 million, or 13 percent, over the planning period when four projects were to be established. Even if agreement could be reached on only one project, the gain was sizable: $80 million, or 3.5 percent, below the cost of nationalistic policies.

The nationalistic supply pattern is very different from the optimal regional one. No new capacity expansion would be needed in Indonesia, existing capacity being sufficient to meet domestic demand until 1990. However, Malaysia, the Philippines, and Thailand would require new capacity.

In 1978, the United Nations Industrial Development Organization (UNIDO) published a report by Kuyvenhoven and Mennes devoted to the various stages of analysis of projects for regional cooperation.[12] No formal methods for project formulation were proposed in their study, but special attention was paid to the appraisal and selection of those projects from within a well-defined set that should be considered as attractive projects for regional cooperation. Furthermore, they proposed procedures to assemble equitable packages of efficient projects.

Adopting the Little-Mirrlees project appraisal method and terminology,[13] they proposed the following appraisal and selection procedure. For each project that needs to be considered, the social internal rate of return (IRR) is computed, defined as the rate of interest at which the sum of the

12. Arie Kuyvenhoven and L. B. M. Mennes, "Projects for Regional Cooperation: Identification, Selection, Evaluation and Location," United Nations Industrial Development Organization, Industry and Development, no. 1, (New York: United Nations, 1978).

13. I. M. D. Little and J. A. Mirrlees, *Project Appraisal and Planning in Developing Countries* (London: Heinemann Educational Books, 1974).

discounted present value of each year's net social profit becomes zero. When the same project can be located in different countries, the location with the highest IRR will be called the efficient location of the project. In addition, they assumed that for each country the accounting rate of interest (ARI) can be computed; ARI is defined as the interest rate for which the number of projects undertaken without cooperation just exhausts the national investment resources. In the case of complete cooperation, the ARI is defined as the interest rate for which the total number of projects undertaken in all participating member countries exhausts the combined investment resources.

Using these concepts, they proposed two criteria for the selection of projects for regional cooperation. First, a cooperation project's social internal rate of return for its efficient location when serving the regional market (IRR_{max}) must exceed the internal rate of return of a comparable project in that country without cooperation:

$$IRR_{max} > \text{comparable IRR without cooperation.}$$

Second, a cooperation project's social internal return for its efficient location should exceed the average accounting rate of interest for the region, as well as the accounting rate of interest of the country in which it is to be located:

$$IRR_{max} > \text{average regional ARI}$$

and

$$IRR_{max} > \text{ARI for the country of efficient location.}$$

Having selected the projects that should be of interest as cooperation projects, the problem remains of finding an equitable allocation of projects among the collaborating countries. The guiding principle proposed by Kuyvenhoven and Mennes is that projects should be allocated such that the benefits accruing to each country should at all times be larger with cooperation than without. Unless the number of projects is very small, this assignment problem may be quite complex, and the authors proposed the use of integer programming techniques to find the most efficient allocation. Once more, the reader is referred to the study itself for further details.

In 1980 ter Wengel published a study on the allocation of industry among the same group of countries that is the subject of the case study in the second part of this book: the Andean Common Market.[14] In ter Wen-

---

14. Jan ter Wengel, *Allocation of Industry in the Andean Common Market*, Studies in Development and Planning 11 (Boston: Martinus Nijhoff, 1980).

gel's study a planning model was developed that used the domestic resource cost of foreign exchange as the appropriate criterion for allocation
of a multicountry situation. What made this criterion practicable for the
allocation of a large number of industries in several countries was its vir-
tual identity to the Corden measure of effective protection. The Corden
measure of effective protection, which is equal to the domestic resource
cost minus one, is given by the ratio of the domestic value added and the
international value added minus one. Taking domestic prices to be equal
to international prices plus tariffs, the domestic value added per unit of
output evaluated at domestic prices is given by the difference between the
value of output and the value of tradable inputs. The international value
added is given by the difference between the value of output and the value
of inputs evaluated at international prices. Both the domestic value added
and the international value added measures are corrected for imported
capital charges and for the returns accruing to foreign investors.

The model developed for the allocation of industries was once again an
integer programming model. The objective function of the model was to
minimize the weighted sum of the domestic resource costs for all industries in all countries; the weights were given by the ratio of the international value added in the industry and the total international value added
in all the assigned industries. The minimization was affected by three
types of constraints: first, those ensuring that all industries are allocated;
second, those determining monopolistic allocations of industries; and
third, those designed to ensure that the countries are assigned industries
according to predetermined distributional objectives. Since it was not
clear what benefits the member countries expect from the assignment of
industries, several types of distributional constraints were formulated.
First, constraints were designed to allocate industries as identical entities
to the countries: the number of industries assigned to each country was
determined by the country's income relative to the area's income in one
case and by the country's population relative to the population of the area
in a second case. Second, distributional constraints were formulated with
respect to values added, sales values, and investment requirements, and
the countries were assigned amounts of value added, sales values, and investment requirements according to the minimum country requirements
equal to the minimum accruing to the countries on the basis of either income or population.

The model was utilized to design industry allocations that minimize
the cost of supplying the area with the products of the industries of the
petrochemical program of the Andean Common Market. It was assumed
that the industries would be designed to satisfy the projected 1985
demands of the area and that these demands were completely inelastic.

The costs of the various industry allocations designed with the model were always less than the costs of supplying the area, given the industry allocations designed by the technical body of the agreement among the member countries, the Junta del Acuerdo de Cartagena. This was due to two factors. First, the ter Wengel model exploited economies of scale to a greater extent than the original allocation, reducing the number of projects from fifty-six to twenty-two. Second, subject to the distributional constraints, the model ensured that for each allocation, each country's comparative advantage was fully taken into account. Depending on the distributional constraints imposed and the assumptions made about the opportunity costs of capital, the cost reductions amounted to between 8 and 25 percent. Costs were found to be lowest when the allocations were constrained by numerical distribution constraints based on either population or income, because it was thus possible to satisfy the industry demands of the high-cost countries with the relatively small industries, while the relatively large industries were assigned to the lower-cost countries.

An Assessment of the Basic Approach

The foregoing survey of previous work suggests that, in principle, the structure of a model for investment analysis in a multicountry context need not differ from one useful for a single country. In particular, if the focus of analysis is on efficiency, the cooperation area can be treated as a single country, and the only difference may be in terms of size, in the sense that more production locations, marketing centers, import and export points, and transport links may have to be considered.

In such circumstances, the approach presented in chapter 3 is perfectly adequate to analyze a multicountry investment planning problem with economies of scale. More often than not, however, efficiency cannot serve as the only criterion for the identification and selection of an attractive multicountry investment program, and other factors will have to be taken into account.

Thus, additional restrictions ensuring equity and fairness, political acceptability, and stability may be required. But such restrictions can be difficult to express objectively. It may be possible to measure political acceptability and stability in terms of benefits received compared with the bargaining strength of countries or pressure groups within countries; it is nearly impossible to come up with a proper definition of equity and fairness.

The notion of fairness was rigorously introduced in mathematical studies on the division problem—the problem of dividing an object among a finite number of agents so that each agent is satisfied, with respect to his preferences, with the portion he receives. In this context, Schmeidler and Vind showed that in an economy with a finite number of agents, each owning an initial allocation of a finite number of commodities, assuming no production and a given price and preference system, an optimal equilibrium results if the agents choose the net trade that, according to their preferences, is maximal in the budget set. The equilibrium has the property that the net trade for any agent is at least as good as the net trade for any other agent (fair net trades).[15]

Multicountry investment analysis with economies of scale involves two additional problems. First, the analysis has to be extended to include more than one country and, therefore, different prices.[16] Second, the effect of including indivisibles in an economy has to be analyzed, in particular with respect to fairness and the existence of price equilibrium.[17]

As discussed below, when acceptability constraints are introduced in our models, we will deal with these problems in a rather pragmatic way. In addition, a cooperation project package that is considered more equitable than another by most criteria may be more unstable or politically unfeasible.

For our purposes here, equity and fairness may be defined as minimum shares in the value added, investment, employment, or number of projects resulting from the cooperation scheme. Political acceptability has to do with the probability that a country will join a cooperation scheme, if the allocation of projects in such a scheme would financially harm any individual, family, or group that holds political power. When those with political influence are already producing some good at a cost higher than the price a favored foreigner could charge, the cooperation effort is likely to meet with stiff resistance. The stability of an integration scheme depends on the extent to which a country or group of countries finds it more profitable to join the scheme than to develop the industries concerned in isolation. Game theory can be used to derive necessary or sufficient conditions for stability.

15. David Schmeidler and Karl Vind, "Fair Net Trades," *Econometrica*, vol. 40, no. 2 (July 1972), pp. 637–42.

16. Schmeidler and Vind, p. 642.

17. Lars-Gunnar Svensson, "Large Indivisibles: An Analysis with Respect to Price Equilibrium and Fairness," *Econometrica*, vol. 51, no. 4 (July 1983), pp. 939–54.

Bergendorff has shown that with the aid of the concepts of individual rationality (namely, that each country in the cooperation scheme obtains more than it would in isolation) and group rationality (namely, that total cooperation gains have to be disbursed) it is possible to derive rules for allocating projects to countries in such a way that the propensity to disrupt the prospective cooperation scheme is minimized.[18] We will not pursue this matter further here. It must be emphasized, however, that when, in the remainder of this book, we use the expression "acceptability," we refer to a condition that the distribution of the net benefits of cooperation over the various countries is such that the proposed scheme is acceptable to all partners. Usually, this will imply a distribution different from one based on efficiency criteria alone.

There are essentially two ways in which the equity or acceptability issue can be addressed in a multicountry framework. One is to introduce equity formally into the model, by adding constraints to the model of a "satisficing" nature, that is, lower bounds that need to be satisfied for the solution to be feasible. For example, such a constraint might specify that no country may be allocated two projects unless all other countries have at least one project. This approach is relatively easy to implement and may in fact reduce the computational complexity of the programming problem.

The second possibility is to use the model as a framework for the appraisal of specific investment strategies that have been designed with varying degrees of equity in mind. This approach should ideally be used in conjunction with optimization dominated by efficiency criteria, so as not to lose sight of the costs associated with greater equity.

With this background, we shall now turn to the formulation of planning models relevant to multicountry investment planning, starting with the simplest case and proceeding to more complex ones, as much as possible following the order of chapter 3.

A Cooperation Model: Simplest Version

One can conceive of circumstances in which two or more countries are interested in investigating to what extent their existing production units could meet market requirements more efficiently—that is, with lower transport and distribution costs—if trade barriers among the countries

---

18. Hans G. Bergendorff, "Multi-country Planning with Economies of Scale," World Bank, 1974 (processed).

were abolished. Capacity expansion is explicitly not taken into consideration in this simple case.

We shall first state the problem for a single regional good, in which by definition normally no overseas trade is possible (see chapter 2). In addition, we assume that there are no economies of scale in production and that production costs of the commodity concerned are approximately the same at all locations. The planning problem is thus to identify a supply pattern that minimizes transport and distribution costs and meets market requirements in all marketing centers without requiring a level of supply from any existing production location that exceeds its capacity to produce.

For those familiar with the literature on linear programming, it is not difficult to see that this problem is identical to the well-known transportation problem. The cost coefficients of the transport flows between the production and marketing centers are equal to the unit costs of shipping, that is, transport and distribution costs per unit. The special structure of transportation models substantially reduces the computational burden of the simplex algorithm. We will, however, not deal with the corresponding solution method here, but rather refer the reader to the existing literature in this field.[19] Nor will we present the mathematical formulation of this simple model.

As soon as we recognize that the planning problem at hand boils down to a transportation problem, it will be clear that we can drop the assumption of approximately equal production costs without losing the attractive features of that type of linear programming problem. If the unit cost of producing an item differs from plant to plant, then this cost is simply included in the determination of the cost coefficients of the various transport flows.

What happens if we modify the model to a multiproduct format? In fact, not very much changes in that case. If we distinguish n commodities, we will have to draw up and solve n independent transportation problems.

If we drop the assumption of constant production cost, however, the convenient format of a transportation problem can no longer be maintained. We shall postpone the discussion of how to deal with economies of scale until later on in this chapter, when we consider the case of capacity expansion. The assumption of constant production cost is, however, normally justified if the analysis focuses on the scope for cooperation, given

19. See, for instance, Harvey M. Wagner, *Principles of Operations Research*, 2d ed. (London: Prentice-Hall International, 1975), ch. 6.

specific production capacities. In that case, past investments no longer have decision value and can be considered as sunk cost, so that marginal production costs only play a role. These will often be constant or near constant over a wide range of output levels.

Finally, we extend the analysis to so-called international goods and services, that is, products that are normally traded in world markets. The main implication of this extension is that a given country will have three options to meet market requirements for a given product: produce domestically, import from a partner country in a cooperative trading system, and import from the world market. The introduction of sources of supply from outside the cooperation area leaves us with a planning problem identical to a transportation problem, as long as we continue to assume constant production cost.

A Multiproduct Process Model with Imports

Most industries use raw materials and intermediates to produce final products. The scope for specialization among countries in the earlier production phases may be as large as for final products, and for that purpose the model should be expanded to permit analysis of such possibilities. Although we shall state a general model of this type below, we will limit its discussion to essentials so as to avoid undue repetition of the process model described in chapter 3. The only difference between that model and the one stated below is that here the possibility of imports from world markets is included and several formulations of possible acceptability constraints for international goods and services are added.

The process model employs the following notations:

SETS AND INDEXES

$c \in C$ = set of commodities
  CF = final products
  CI = intermediate products
  CR = raw material, miscellaneous material inputs, and labor inputs
$i \in I = I1 \cup I2 \cup \ldots$
  = set of plants, where $I1$ is the subset of plants in country 1, $I2$ is the subset of plants in country 2, etc.
$j \in J = J1 \cup J2 \cup \ldots$
  = set of markets, where $J1$ is the subset of markets in country 1, $J2$ the subset of markets in country 2, etc.

$m \in M$ = set of productive units
$p \in P$ = set of production processes

VARIABLES

u = purchases of inputs from within the planning area
x = shipments
z = process levels
v = imports from world markets
ϕ = cost groups
ϕ_ψ = raw materials, miscellaneous material inputs, and labor costs
ϕ_λ = transport cost
ϕ_π = import cost

PARAMETERS

a = process inputs ($-$) and outputs ($+$)
b = capacity utilization coefficient
k = capacity
p = prices
d = market requirements
μ = unit transport cost

The process model has the following structure:

(4.1) $$\min \xi = \phi_\psi + \phi_\lambda + \phi_\pi$$

where

(4.1a) $$\phi_\psi = \sum_{c \in CR} \sum_{i \in I} p_{ci}^d u_{ci}$$

$$\begin{bmatrix} Input \\ costs \end{bmatrix} = \begin{bmatrix} Total\ costs\ of\ raw\ materials,\ labor,\ and \\ miscellaneous\ inputs\ at\ all\ plant\ sites \end{bmatrix}$$

(4.1b) $$\phi_\lambda = \sum_{c \in CF} \left(\sum_{i \in I} \sum_{j \in J} \mu_{cij} x_{cij} + \sum_{j \in J} \mu_{cj} v_{cj} \right)$$

$$\begin{bmatrix} Transport \\ costs \end{bmatrix} = \begin{bmatrix} Transport\ costs\ of\ all\ regionally\ produced \\ and\ imported\ final\ products\ of\ all\ markets \end{bmatrix}$$

$$+ \sum_{c \in CI} \left(\sum_{i \in I} \sum_{\substack{i' \in I \\ i \neq i'}} \mu_{cii'} x_{cii'} + \sum_{i \in I} \mu_{ci} v_{ci} \right)$$

$$+ \begin{bmatrix} Transport\ cost\ for\ all\ interplant\ shipments\ of \\ intermediates\ and\ all\ imported\ intermediates\ to \\ all\ plant\ sites \end{bmatrix}$$

$$+ \sum_{c \in CR} \left(\sum_{i \in I} \mu_{ci} v_{ci} \right)$$

$$+ \left[\begin{array}{c} \textit{Transport cost for all imported raw materials to all} \\ \textit{plants; domestically purchased raw materials are priced} \\ \textit{inclusive of transport costs} \end{array} \right]$$

(4.1c) $$\phi_\pi = \sum_{c \in CF} \sum_{j \in J} p_{cj}^v + \sum_{c \in CI \cup CR} \sum_{i \in I} p_{ci}^v v_{ci}$$

$$\left[\begin{array}{c} \textit{Import} \\ \textit{costs} \end{array} \right] = \left[\begin{array}{c} \textit{Import cost of} \\ \textit{final products} \end{array} \right] + \left[\begin{array}{c} \textit{Import cost of intermediates} \\ \textit{and raw materials} \end{array} \right]$$

The model is subject to the following constraints:

MATERIAL BALANCE CONSTRAINTS ON FINAL PRODUCTS

(4.2) $$\sum_{p \in P} a_{cpi} z_{pi} \geq \sum_{j \in J} x_{cij} \qquad \begin{array}{c} c \in CF \\ i \in I \end{array}$$

$$\left[\begin{array}{c} \textit{Production of} \\ \textit{product c at plant} \\ \textit{i by all processes p} \end{array} \right] \geq \left[\begin{array}{c} \textit{All shipments from} \\ \textit{plant i of product} \\ \textit{c to all markets j} \end{array} \right]$$

MATERIAL BALANCE CONSTRAINTS ON INTERMEDIATE PRODUCTS

(4.3) $$\sum_{p \in P} a_{cpi} z_{pi} + \sum_{\substack{i' \in I \\ i \neq i'}} (x_{ci'i} - x_{cii'}) + v_{ci} \geq 0 \qquad \begin{array}{c} c \in CI \\ i \in I \end{array}$$

$$\left[\begin{array}{c} \textit{Production of} \\ \textit{intermediates at} \\ \textit{plant i by all} \\ \textit{processes p} \end{array} \right] + \left[\begin{array}{c} \textit{Balance of} \\ \textit{interplant ship-} \\ \textit{ments from and} \\ \textit{to plant i} \end{array} \right] + \left[\begin{array}{c} \textit{Imports of} \\ \textit{interme-} \\ \textit{diate c at} \\ \textit{plant i} \end{array} \right] \geq 0$$

MATERIAL BALANCE CONSTRAINTS ON RAW MATERIALS, MISCELLANEOUS INPUTS, AND LABOR

(4.4) $$\sum_{p \in P} a_{cpi} z_{pi} + v_{ci} + u_{ci} \geq 0 \qquad \begin{array}{c} c \in CR \\ i \in I \end{array}$$

$$\left[\begin{array}{c} \textit{Use of raw material,} \\ \textit{miscellaneous input, or} \\ \textit{labor type c at plant i} \\ \textit{by all processes p} \end{array} \right] + \left[\begin{array}{c} \textit{Import} \\ \textit{of c at} \\ \textit{plant i} \end{array} \right] + \left[\begin{array}{c} \textit{Local} \\ \textit{purchase} \\ \textit{of c at} \\ \textit{plant i} \end{array} \right] \geq 0$$

CAPACITY CONSTRAINTS

(4.5) $$\sum_{p \in P} b_{mpi} z_{pi} \leq k_{mi} \qquad \begin{array}{c} m \in M \\ i \in I \end{array}$$

$$\begin{bmatrix} Capacity\ requirements \\ for\ all\ processes\ at \\ plant\ i \end{bmatrix} \leq \begin{bmatrix} Available\ capacity \\ for\ productive \\ unit\ m\ at\ plant\ i \end{bmatrix}$$

MARKET REQUIREMENTS

(4.6) $$\sum_{i \in I} x_{cij} + v_{cj} \geq d_{cj} \qquad\qquad c \in CF$$
$$J \in J$$

$$\begin{bmatrix} Shipments\ of \\ product\ c\ from\ all \\ plants\ i\ to\ market\ j \end{bmatrix} + \begin{bmatrix} Imports\ of \\ product\ c \\ for\ market\ j \end{bmatrix} \geq \begin{bmatrix} Demand\ for \\ product\ c \\ in\ market\ j \end{bmatrix}$$

NONNEGATIVITY CONSTRAINTS

(4.7) $$z_{pi},\ x_{cij},\ x_{ci'i},\ x_{cii'},\ v_{ci'},\ v_{cj},\ \geq 0$$

This completes the formal statement of the process model suited to analyze the benefits of economic cooperation among several countries in a multiproduct framework that permits imports from world markets. At this point, we have not yet discussed the treatment of exports to world markets, nor has the possibility of capacity expansion been incorporated. Before addressing these complications, we shall discuss several acceptability constraints that may be added to the efficiency model.

As a first step toward the introduction of acceptability constraints, we shall in each case identify and define the outcomes of the efficiency model to which acceptability conditions may, in principle, apply.

Acceptability Constraints Relating to the Level of Production

The first relevant result in this respect is the production level at existing plants. It is conceivable that a country's decisionmakers insist that capacity utilization rates at existing production facilities do not deteriorate following a cooperation agreement. The efficiency model yields the production level for each productive unit at each plant site, by selecting an optimal level of z_{pi} as stated in constraint (4.5). The acceptability constraint that may have to be added could be of the following form:

(4.8) $$\sum_{p \in P} b_{mpi} z_{pi} \geq \beta_{mi} k_{mi} \qquad\qquad m \in M$$
$$i \in I$$

where β_{mi} is an exogenously specified capacity utilization constraint.

Alternatively, the acceptability constraint may be relaxed somewhat by specifying it for all of a country's relevant productive capacity collectively:

$$(4.9) \qquad \sum_{i \in I1} \sum_{p \in P} \sum_{m \in M} b_{mpi} z_{pi} \geq \beta_1 \sum_{i \in I1} \sum_{m \in M} k_{mi}$$

$$\begin{bmatrix} \textit{Production of all productive} \\ \textit{units at all plants in} \\ \textit{country 1} \end{bmatrix} \geq \begin{bmatrix} \textit{A specified level of production} \\ \textit{of all plants in country 1} \end{bmatrix}$$

Acceptability Constraints Relating to Intraregional Trade

A second set of results to which acceptability conditions may apply relates to intraregional trade flows. In fact, in practice such trade balances are often regarded as a proxy for the distribution of gains of economic cooperation. Even though it is now widely realized that this measure of gain can be highly misleading, we shall assume that there are other good reasons why a cooperative investment or production program with fairly balanced intraregional trade may be preferable to one with highly skewed trade accounts. If the planning problem relates to a single commodity, problems of evaluation of trade flows do not occur, and the desired balance can be specified by volume. In a multiproduct framework, trade flows within the cooperation area need to be stated by value. Unfortunately, at the outset, supply prices at the various marketing centers are not known; moreover, the prices at which intraregional trade will eventually take place are policy variables within a certain range, set by negotiations, or the subject of decisions by entrepreneurs based upon profit maximization. How, therefore, can trade balance constraints be specified ex ante?

Our proposal is simply to use world market prices inclusive of delivery costs to all marketing centers. In that case, the intraregional trade flow for final goods, in world market prices, from one country to another resulting from the efficiency model is:

$$(4.10) \qquad \sum_{c \in CF} \sum_{i \in I1} \sum_{j \in J2} x_{cij}(p_{cj}^v + \mu_{cj})$$

and, vice versa,

$$(4.11) \qquad \sum_{c \in CF} \sum_{i \in I2} \sum_{j \in J1} x_{cij}(p_{cj}^v + \mu_{cj})$$

where $p_{cj}^v + \mu_{cj}$ is equal to the delivered cost at marketing center j if requirements were to be met by imports from abroad. If trade in intermediate and raw materials may take place, similar expressions should be added covering these product groups.

The acceptability constraint on intraregional trade flows may now take the form of a relationship between any two countries' regional exports that is bound by an exogenously specified margin, say Δ, where Δ may not exceed or be smaller than a specified percentage. Similar treatment may be extended to intraregional trade in intermediates and raw materials.

Acceptability Constraints Relating to International Trade

Acceptability constraints with regard to international trade may take a variety of forms. For example, no country may want to experience a deterioration of its net trade position in relation to the rest of the world. While it is straightforward to formulate such a constraint, it should be borne in mind that trade with prospective partner countries should be netted out, as such trade flows now are classified as intraregional trade.

A second possible acceptability constraint on international trade may reflect a desire by some or all of the countries of the region to become self-sufficient over time. Although self-sufficiency would not normally be an advisable policy to impose upon the investment program and may lead to inefficiency in the production structure, it is often a consideration.

Finally, a range of external tariff policies may be incorporated in the model. For example, a gradual abolition or lowering of trade restrictions may be specified. A simple way to do so is to specify world market prices for specific periods, which incorporate the product-specific impact of particular trade restrictions, and to solve the model within this framework.

The Treatment of Exports

A regional cooperation agreement can be considered a special case of an export-oriented investment strategy, with the risk somewhat reduced by an explicit agreement on products, quantities, or prices. However, regional trade need not be a complete substitute for trade in world markets, and often countries may wish to leave open the option of trade with the outside world. It should be noted that the scope for such exports may be enhanced by regional cooperation to the extent that plants established on the basis of the regional markets will usually be larger than national plants and therefore will have lower production costs.

The cost minimization formulation of the model necessitates the specification of final demand. This applies as much to domestic and regional market requirements as it does to export demand. In practice, therefore, the procedure that has so far been used to incorporate export demand into the model is by the specification of export targets, usually in the form of maximum constraints, with attainable export prices that are equal to a fixed proportion of corresponding c.i.f. import prices (which represent cost plus insurance and freight charges). In principle, a downward-sloping demand curve for exports can be approximated within a linear programming format, but no computational experience with this formulation exists for this class of models.[20]

The specification of exports to world markets requires the following notation:

$l \in L$ = set of export markets

e_{cil} = exports of commodity c from plant i to export area l

$\bar{e}_{cil}$ = export target (upper bound) commodity c from plant i to export area l

$\bar{e}_{cl}$ = export target (upper bound) for commodity c to export area for all plants combined

p^e_{cil} = export price for commodity c from plant i to export area l.

The structure of the model is now modified by the addition of the export activity in the material balance constraints for final and intermediate products, the addition of an export upper bound reflecting the postulated target, and the addition of a term representing export revenue in the objective function.[21]

The possibility of exports to the rest of the world does not require special attention with respect to determining the benefits of cooperation and their distribution over the partner countries. Such exports take place only if more than marginal production cost plus transport cost are covered by the attainable export price.

Given that the incorporation of exports to world markets in a multi-country model does not require special modifications of the general model, we refer the reader to chapter 3, or to the subsequent models in this chapter, for the specific formulation of the relevant export constraints.

---

20. See, however, John H. Duloy and Roger D. Norton, "CHAC, A Programming Model of Mexican Agriculture," in Louis M. Goreux and Alan S. Manne, eds., *Multi-Level Planning: Case Studies in Mexico* (Amsterdam: North-Holland, 1973).

21. Note once more that exports to partner countries were treated as international exports before the cooperation agreement, but subsequently have become intraregional exports.

Capacity Expansion

We shall now turn to the complications arising as a result of the consideration of capacity expansion in a multicountry context. Once more, if the guiding principle is the identification of the least-cost investment, production, and trade pattern in the cooperation area, the building blocks provided in chapter 3 are sufficient to formulate a multiperiod, multiproduct investment planning model that can be used to formulate efficient supply programs. By simply deleting activities that denote imports and exports from and to the rest of the world, we have a model that focuses on regional goods and services; by including these activities, we transform the model to one that is used to analyze international goods and services. However, as a rule, equity or acceptability considerations will play an important role when capacity expansion is considered in a multicountry framework, and the models below will incorporate specific constraints that reflect such considerations.

The Static Process Model

Assume two countries seek to minimize the cost of meeting market requirements for a set of regional products, that is, products that cannot be imported from outside the cooperation area, for a given target year in the future.[22] The products in question are produced with economies of scale, and ex-plant production costs depend on whether production takes place in single facilities for the entire regional market or in production units that are designed to meet market requirements for country 1 and country 2 separately. For simplicity, assume also that inputs into the production of the regional good cannot be imported from world markets either.

To formulate a model that can analyze the various options, we need to introduce some additional notation:[23]

h = new capacity

$\bar{h}$ = maximum capacity expansion

y = zero-one variable

---

22. The case for international products is given in the next section, which describes the dynamic process model.

23. See chapter 3 for a detailed explanation of new elements in the model.

σ_m = capital recovery factor[24] for productive unit m

$$= \frac{\rho(1 + \rho)^{\xi_m}}{(1 + \rho)^{\xi_m} - 1}$$

ω = fixed charge portion of investment costs

ν = linear portion of investment costs

ϕ_κ = capital costs.

Then the static capacity expansion model has the following structure:

(4.12) $$\min \xi = \phi_\kappa + \phi_\psi + \phi_\lambda$$

where

(4.12a) $$\phi_\kappa = \sum_{i \in I} \sum_{m \in M} \sigma_m(\omega_{mi} y_{mi} + \nu_{mi} h_{mi})$$

$$\begin{bmatrix} Capital \\ cost \end{bmatrix} = \begin{bmatrix} Proportion\ of\ investment\ costs\ to \\ be\ charged\ during\ the\ target\ year \end{bmatrix}$$

(4.12b) $$\phi_\psi = \sum_{c \in CR} \sum_{i \in I} p^d_{ci} u_{ci}$$

$$\begin{bmatrix} Domestic \\ input \\ costs \end{bmatrix} = \begin{bmatrix} Local\ purchases\ of\ raw\ materials, \\ miscellaneous\ inputs,\ and\ labor \end{bmatrix}$$

(4.12c) $$\phi_\lambda = \sum_{c \in CF} \sum_{i \in I} \sum_{j \in J} \mu_{cij}$$

$$\begin{bmatrix} Transport \\ cost^{25} \end{bmatrix} = \begin{bmatrix} Transport\ cost\ of\ the \\ final\ product \end{bmatrix}$$

The model is subject to the following constraints.

MATERIAL BALANCE CONSTRAINTS ON FINAL PRODUCTS

(4.13) $$\sum_{p \in P} a_{cpi} z_{pi} \geq \sum_{j \in J} x_{cij} \qquad \begin{matrix} c \in CF \\ i \in I \end{matrix}$$

$$\begin{bmatrix} Production \\ of\ final\ prod- \\ uct\ c\ at \\ plant\ i \end{bmatrix} \geq \begin{bmatrix} Shipments\ of\ product \\ c\ from\ plant\ i\ to \\ all\ markets\ j \end{bmatrix}$$

24. It is assumed here that the cooperating countries all have the same discount rate. Clearly, this need not be the case, and the capital recovery factor may be country-specific.
25. We assume no regional trade in intermediates and raw materials.

MATERIAL BALANCE CONSTRAINTS ON INTERMEDIATE PRODUCTS

$$(4.14) \qquad \sum_{p \in P} a_{cpi} z_{pi} \geq 0 \qquad\qquad \begin{array}{l} c \in CI \\ i \in I \end{array}$$

$$\begin{bmatrix} \textit{Production and use of} \\ \textit{intermediate } c \textit{ at plant } i \\ \textit{must at least balance} \end{bmatrix} \geq 0$$

MATERIAL BALANCE CONSTRAINTS ON RAW MATERIALS

$$(4.15) \qquad \sum_{p \in P} a_{cpi} z_{pi} + u_{ci} \geq 0 \qquad\qquad \begin{array}{l} c \in CR \\ i \in I \end{array}$$

$$\begin{bmatrix} \textit{Use of raw material} \\ c \textit{ at plant } i \end{bmatrix} + \begin{bmatrix} \textit{Purchase of} \\ \textit{raw material} \\ \textit{for plant } i \end{bmatrix} \geq 0$$

CAPACITY CONSTRAINTS

$$(4.16) \qquad \sum_{p \in P} b_{mpi} z_{pi} \leq k_{mi} + h_{mi} \qquad\qquad \begin{array}{l} m \in M \\ i \in I \end{array}$$

$$[\textit{Capacity utilization}] \leq \begin{bmatrix} \textit{Initial} \\ \textit{capacity} \end{bmatrix}\begin{bmatrix} \textit{Capacity} \\ \textit{expansion} \end{bmatrix}$$

INVESTMENT CONSTRAINTS

$$(4.17) \qquad h_{mi} \leq \bar{h}_{mi} y_{mi}$$

$$\begin{bmatrix} \textit{Capacity} \\ \textit{expansion} \end{bmatrix} \leq \begin{bmatrix} \textit{Maximum} \\ \textit{capacity} \end{bmatrix}\begin{bmatrix} \textit{Zero or} \\ \textit{one} \end{bmatrix}$$

$$(4.18) \qquad y_{mi} = 0 \quad \text{or} \quad 1$$

MARKET REQUIREMENTS

$$(4.19) \qquad \sum_{i \in I} x_{cij} \leq d_{cj} \qquad\qquad \begin{array}{l} c \in CF \\ j \in J \end{array}$$

$$\begin{bmatrix} \textit{Shipments from all} \\ \textit{plants } c \textit{ to} \\ \textit{market } j \end{bmatrix} \leq \begin{bmatrix} \textit{Market requirements for} \\ \textit{product } c \textit{ in market } j \end{bmatrix}$$

NONNEGATIVITY CONSTRAINTS

$$(4.20) \qquad x_{cij}, y_{mi}, h_{mi}, z_{pi}, u_{ci} \geq 0 \qquad \begin{array}{l} c \in CF \\ i \in I \\ m \in M \\ j \in J \\ p \in P \end{array}$$

Acceptability requirements in the static capacity expansion model for regional goods and services may relate to a variety of characteristics of the emerging supply pattern. As before, they may focus on intraregional trade balances or on the production level of existing or of newly established production facilities. The formulation of this type of equity constraint has been dealt with before (see constraints [4.8] to [4.11]) and will not be repeated here.

One new concern may arise, namely, the distribution of new capacity among the cooperating countries. Often this concern may be expressed in the form of a requirement that each country shares in the number of new plants; for example, no country might be allocated a second plant until all countries have at least one plant. Obviously, other related concerns may be important, too, such as the distribution of investment, employment, and value added. Incorporation of these concerns in the model in the form of acceptability constraints is fairly straightforward; examples of how it might be done will be presented for the dynamic capacity expansion model with international trade in the following section.

The Dynamic Process Model

The dynamic process model for international goods and services uses the building blocks explained in chapter 3 and the previous sections in this chapter. As before, we shall first formulate the efficiency version of the model and then add several acceptability constraints. The constraints may be used in case the efficient investment strategy entails perceived inequities in the regional supply pattern that make agreement among the countries impossible.

SETS AND INDEXES

$i, i' \in I$ = plant sites
    $I1$ = plant sites in country 1
    $I2$ = plant sites in country 2, etc.
   $j \in J$ = market areas

$J1$ = market areas in country 1
$J2$ = market areas in country 2, etc.
$l \in L$ = export areas outside the cooperation area
$m \in M$ = productive units
$p \in P$ = production processes
$t \in T$ = time intervals and time periods
$c \in C$ = commodities used or produced in the section
CF = final products
CI = intermediate products
CR = raw materials, miscellaneous inputs, and labor

VARIABLES

z = process levels (production levels)
x = regional shipments
e = exports outside the cooperation area
v = imports from outside the cooperation area
u = domestic purchases
y = zero-one investment decisions
h = capacity expansion
ϕ = cost or revenue groups
ξ = total costs
ϕ_{χ} = capital costs
ϕ_{ψ} = recurrent costs
ϕ_{λ} = transportation costs
ϕ_{π} = import costs
ϕ_{ϵ} = export revenues

PARAMETERS

a = process inputs $(-)$ or outputs $(+)$
b = capacity utilization
k = initial capacity
s = retirements of capacity
α = market requirements
$\bar{e}$ = export bounds
$\bar{h}$ = maximum capacity expansion
θ = number of time intervals per time period
ρ = discount rate per time interval
δ = discount factor
σ_m = capital recovery factor per productive unit m

$$= \frac{\rho(1 + \rho)^{\zeta_m}}{(1 + \rho)^{\zeta_m} - 1}$$

ζ_m = life of productive unit m

ω = fixed-charge portion of investment cost

ν = linear portion of investment cost

p = prices

pd = regional price

pv = import price from rest of the world

pe = export price to rest of the world

μ = unit transport cost

The model may now formally be stated as select z_{pit} (process levels), x_{cijt} (shipments of final goods), $x_{cii't}$ (shipments of intermediate goods), l_{cilt} (exports), v_{cit} (imports of raw materials and intermediates), v_{cjt} (imports of final goods), and u_{cit} (purchases of domestic inputs j), so as to minimize costs, as follows:

(4.21)
$$\min \xi = \sum_{t \in T} \delta_t (\phi \kappa_t + \phi_{\psi t}$$

$$\begin{bmatrix} Discounted \\ net\ cost \end{bmatrix} = \begin{bmatrix} Discount \\ factor \end{bmatrix} \begin{bmatrix} Total\ capital \\ cost\ at\ time \\ period\ t \end{bmatrix} + \begin{matrix} Total\ domestic \\ recurrent\ cost \\ at\ time\ period \\ t \end{matrix}$$

$$+ \phi_{\lambda t} + \phi_{\pi t} - \phi_{\epsilon t})$$

$$+ \begin{matrix} Total \\ transport \\ cost\ at \\ time\ period\ t \end{matrix} + \begin{matrix} Total\ import \\ cost\ at\ time \\ period\ t \end{matrix} - \begin{matrix} Total\ export \\ revenue\ at \\ time\ period \\ t \end{matrix} \Bigg]$$

where the discount factor[26] is

(4.21a)
$$\delta_t = \sum_{\tau=1}^{\theta} (1 + \rho)^{-\theta(t-1)-\tau}$$

and where

(4.21b)
$$\phi_{\kappa t} = \sum_{\tau=1}^{t} \sum_{i \in I} \sum_{m \in M} \sigma_m (\omega_{mi\tau} y_{mi\tau})$$

---

26. Note again that the discount factor may be country-specific, reflecting differences in discount rates.

$$\begin{bmatrix} Total \\ capital \\ cost\ dur\text{-} \\ ing\ time \\ period\ \mathrm{t} \end{bmatrix} = \begin{bmatrix} Capital \\ recovery \\ factor \end{bmatrix} \begin{bmatrix} Total\ fixed\ charge \\ for\ all\ productive \\ units\ installed\ at \\ all\ plant\ locations \\ up\ to\ time\ period\ \mathrm{t} \end{bmatrix}$$

$$+\ v_{mi\tau}h_{mi\tau})$$

$$+ \begin{bmatrix} Total\ of\ the\ variable \\ portion\ of\ the\ capital \\ cost\ for\ all\ productive \\ units\ installed\ at\ all \\ plant\ locations\ up\ to \\ time\ period\ \mathrm{t} \end{bmatrix}$$

(4.21c)
$$\phi_{\psi t} = \sum_{c \in CR} \sum_{i \in I} p_{cit}^d u_{cit}$$

$$\begin{bmatrix} Total\ domestic \\ recurrent\ cost \\ during\ time \\ period\ \mathrm{t} \end{bmatrix} = \begin{bmatrix} Cost\ of\ domestic\ raw\ material, \\ labor,\ and\ miscellaneous\ inputs \\ purchased\ at\ all\ plant\ loca\text{-} \\ tions\ during\ time\ period\ \mathrm{t} \end{bmatrix}$$

(4.21d)
$$\phi_{\lambda t} = \sum_{c \in CF} \left\{ \sum_{i \in I} \sum_{j \in J} \mu_{cijt} x_{cijt} \right.$$

$$\begin{bmatrix} Total \\ transport \\ costs\ during \\ time\ period\ \mathrm{t} \end{bmatrix} = \begin{bmatrix} Cost\ of\ shipping\ all\ final\ prod\text{-} \\ ucts\ from\ all\ plant\ locations \\ to\ all\ domestic\ markets\ during \\ time\ period\ \mathrm{t} \end{bmatrix}$$

$$+ \sum_{j \in J} \mu_{cjt} v_{cjt} + \sum_{i \in I} \sum_{l \in L} \mu_{cilt} e_{cilt} \Bigg\}$$

$$+ \begin{bmatrix} Cost\ of\ transporting \\ all\ imported\ final \\ products\ from\ the \\ border\ to\ all\ domestic \\ markets\ during\ time \\ period\ \mathrm{t} \end{bmatrix} + \begin{bmatrix} Cost\ of\ transporting\ all \\ final\ products\ exported \\ from\ all\ plant\ locations \\ to\ the\ border\ for\ all \\ export\ regions\ during \\ time\ period\ \mathrm{t} \end{bmatrix}$$

$$+ \sum_{c \in CI} \left\{ \sum_{i \in I} \sum_{\substack{i' \in I \\ i' \neq i}} \mu_{cii't} x_{cii't} + \sum_{i \in I} \mu_{cit} v_{cit} \right.$$

$$+ \begin{bmatrix} \textit{Cost of all interplant} \\ \textit{location shipments of} \\ \textit{all intermediate} \\ \textit{products during time} \\ \textit{period t} \end{bmatrix} + \begin{array}{c} \textit{Cost of transporting all} \\ \textit{imported intermediate products} \\ \textit{from the border to all plant} \\ \textit{locations during time period t} \end{array}$$

$$+ \sum_{i \in I} \sum_{l \in L} \mu_{cilt} e_{cilt} \Big\} + \sum_{c \in CR} \Big\{ \sum_{i \in I} \mu_{cit} v_{cit} \Big\}$$

$$+ \begin{bmatrix} \textit{Cost of transporting} \\ \textit{all intermediate} \\ \textit{products exported} \\ \textit{from all plant locations} \\ \textit{to all export regions} \\ \textit{during time period t} \end{bmatrix} + \begin{bmatrix} \textit{Cost of transporting all} \\ \textit{imported raw materials and} \\ \textit{labor to all plant locations} \\ \textit{during time period t} \end{bmatrix}$$

$$(4.21e) \qquad \phi_{\pi t} = \sum_{c \in CF} \sum_{j \in J} p^{v}_{cjt} v_{cjt}$$

$$\begin{bmatrix} \textit{Total import} \\ \textit{cost during} \\ \textit{time period} \\ \textit{t} \end{bmatrix} = \begin{bmatrix} \textit{Cost of importing all} \\ \textit{final products sold in} \\ \textit{all market areas during} \\ \textit{time period t} \end{bmatrix}$$

$$+ \sum_{c \in CI \cup CR} \sum_{i \in I} p^{v}_{cit} v_{cit}$$

$$+ \begin{bmatrix} \textit{Cost of importing all} \\ \textit{intermediate products,} \\ \textit{raw materials, and labor} \\ \textit{used at all plant locations} \\ \textit{during time period t} \end{bmatrix}$$

$$(4.21f) \qquad \phi_{et} = \sum_{c \in CF \cup CI} \sum_{i \in I} \sum_{l \in L} p^{e}_{cilt} e_{cilt}$$

$$\begin{bmatrix} \textit{Total export} \\ \textit{revenue during} \\ \textit{time period} \\ \textit{t} \end{bmatrix} = \begin{bmatrix} \textit{Revenue from the export of all} \\ \textit{final and intermediate products} \\ \textit{from all plant locations to all} \\ \textit{export regions during time} \\ \textit{period t} \end{bmatrix}$$

The model is subject to the following constraints.

MATERIAL BALANCE CONSTRAINTS ON FINAL PRODUCTS

$$(4.22) \qquad \sum_{p \in P} a_{cpi} z_{pit} \geq \sum_{j \in J} x_{cijt}$$

$$\begin{bmatrix} \text{\textit{Total production of ferti-}} \\ \text{\textit{lizer c from all processes}} \\ \text{\textit{at plant location i and time}} \\ \text{\textit{period t}} \end{bmatrix} \geq \begin{bmatrix} \text{\textit{Quantity of fertilizer c}} \\ \text{\textit{shipped to all market areas}} \\ \text{\textit{from plant location i at}} \\ \text{\textit{time period t}} \end{bmatrix}$$

$$+ \sum_{l \in L} e_{cilt} \qquad\qquad\qquad \begin{aligned} c &\in CF \\ i &\in I \\ t &\in T \end{aligned}$$

$$+ \begin{bmatrix} \text{\textit{Quantity of fertilizer}} \\ \text{\textit{c exported from plant}} \\ \text{\textit{location i to all export}} \\ \text{\textit{regions at time period t}} \end{bmatrix}$$

MATERIAL BALANCE CONSTRAINTS ON INTERMEDIATE PRODUCTS

(4.23)
$$\sum_{p \in P} a_{cpi} z_{pit} + \sum_{\substack{i' \in I \\ i' \neq i}} x_{ci'it}$$

$$\begin{bmatrix} \text{\textit{Total production of inter-}} \\ \text{\textit{mediate product c from all}} \\ \text{\textit{processes at plant location}} \\ \text{\textit{i and time period t}} \end{bmatrix} + \begin{bmatrix} \text{\textit{Quantity of intermediate}} \\ \text{\textit{product c shipped from}} \\ \text{\textit{plant location i' to}} \\ \text{\textit{plant location i at time}} \\ \text{\textit{period t}} \end{bmatrix}$$

$$+ v_{cit} \geq \sum_{\substack{i' \in I \\ i' \neq i}} x_{cii't}$$

$$+ \begin{bmatrix} \text{\textit{Quantity of intermediate}} \\ \text{\textit{product c imported to}} \\ \text{\textit{plant location i at time}} \\ \text{\textit{period t}} \end{bmatrix} \geq \begin{bmatrix} \text{\textit{Quantity of intermediate}} \\ \text{\textit{product c shipped from}} \\ \text{\textit{plant location i to}} \\ \text{\textit{plant location i' at}} \\ \text{\textit{time period t}} \end{bmatrix}$$

$$+ \sum_{l \in L} e_{cilt} \qquad\qquad\qquad \begin{aligned} c &\in CI \\ i &\in I \\ t &\in T \end{aligned}$$

$$+ \begin{bmatrix} \text{\textit{Quantity of intermediate}} \\ \text{\textit{product c exported from}} \\ \text{\textit{plant location i to all}} \\ \text{\textit{export regions at time}} \\ \text{\textit{period t}} \end{bmatrix}$$

MATERIAL BALANCE CONSTRAINTS ON RAW MATERIALS, LABOR, AND MISCELLANEOUS INPUTS

$$(4.24) \qquad \sum_{p \in P} a_{cpi} z_{pit} + u_{cit} + v_{cit} \geq 0. \qquad \begin{matrix} c \in CR \\ i \in I \\ t \in T \end{matrix}$$

$$\begin{bmatrix} Raw \\ materials\ or \\ labor\ or\ miscel \\ laneous\ inputs \\ used\ in\ all\ pro \\ cesses\ at\ plant \\ location\ \mathrm{i}\ at \\ time\ period\ \mathrm{t} \end{bmatrix} + \begin{bmatrix} Raw\ materials \\ or\ labor\ or \\ miscellaneous \\ inputs\ domes \\ tically\ pur \\ chased\ (or \\ hired)\ at \\ plant\ location \\ \mathrm{i}\ and\ time \\ period\ \mathrm{t} \end{bmatrix} + \begin{bmatrix} Raw\ materials \\ or\ labor\ or \\ miscellaneous \\ inputs\ imported \\ to\ plant\ loca \\ tion\ \mathrm{i}\ at\ time \\ period\ \mathrm{t} \end{bmatrix} \geq 0.$$

CAPACITY CONSTRAINTS

$$(4.25) \qquad \sum_{p \in P} b_{mpi} z_{pit} \leq k_{mi}$$

$$\begin{bmatrix} Capacity\ of\ productive\ unit \\ \mathrm{m}\ for\ all\ processes\ at\ plant \\ location\ \mathrm{i}\ and\ time\ period\ \mathrm{t} \end{bmatrix} \leq \begin{bmatrix} Initial\ capacity\ of \\ productive\ unit\ \mathrm{m} \\ at\ plant\ location\ \mathrm{i} \end{bmatrix}$$

$$+ \sum_{\substack{\tau \in T \\ \tau \leq t}} (h_{mi\tau} - s_{mi\tau}) \qquad \begin{matrix} i \in I \\ m \in M \\ t \in T \end{matrix}$$

$$+ \begin{bmatrix} Total\ capacity\ expansion \\ of\ productive\ unit\ \mathrm{m}\ at \\ plant\ location\ \mathrm{i}\ up\ to \\ time\ period\ \mathrm{t} \end{bmatrix} - \begin{bmatrix} Total\ capacity \\ retirement\ of \\ productive\ unit\ \mathrm{m} \\ at\ plant\ location\ \mathrm{i} \\ up\ to\ time\ period\ \mathrm{t} \end{bmatrix}$$

MARKET REQUIREMENTS CONSTRAINTS

$$(4.26) \qquad \sum_{i \in I} x_{cijt} + v_{cjt} \geq d_{cjt} \qquad \begin{matrix} c \in CF \\ j \in J \\ t \in T \end{matrix}$$

$$\begin{bmatrix} Shipment\ of\ final \\ product\ \mathrm{c}\ from \\ all\ plants\ \mathrm{i}\ to \\ marketing\ center \\ \mathrm{j}\ in\ time\ period \\ \mathrm{t} \end{bmatrix} + \begin{bmatrix} Imports\ of\ final \\ product\ \mathrm{c}\ for \\ marketing\ center \\ \mathrm{j}\ in\ time\ period \\ \mathrm{t} \end{bmatrix} \geq \begin{bmatrix} Market \\ requirements \\ for\ final \\ product\ \mathrm{c} \\ in\ marketing \\ center\ \mathrm{j} \\ in\ time \\ period\ \mathrm{t} \end{bmatrix}$$

EXPORT CONSTRAINTS

(4.27)
$$\sum_{i \in I} e_{cilt} \leq \bar{e}_{clt}$$

$$c \in (CF \cup CI)$$
$$l \in L$$
$$t \in T$$

$$\begin{bmatrix} \text{Quantity of final or} \\ \text{intermediate prod-} \\ \text{uct c exported} \\ \text{from all plant} \\ \text{locations to ex-} \\ \text{port region } l \\ \text{at time period } t \end{bmatrix} \leq \begin{bmatrix} \text{Maximum quantity of} \\ \text{exports of product} \\ \text{c to export region} \\ l \text{ at time period } t \end{bmatrix}$$

MAXIMUM CAPACITY EXPANSION CONSTRAINTS

(4.28)
$$h_{mit} \leq \bar{h}_{mit} y_{mit}$$

$$m \in M$$
$$i \in I$$
$$t \in T$$

$$\begin{bmatrix} \text{Increment to} \\ \text{capacity of} \\ \text{productive} \\ \text{unit m at} \\ \text{plant loca-} \\ \text{tion i and} \\ \text{time period } t \end{bmatrix} \leq \begin{bmatrix} \text{Upper bound} \\ \text{on capacity} \\ \text{of productive} \\ \text{unit m at plant} \\ \text{location i and} \\ \text{time period } t \end{bmatrix} \begin{bmatrix} \text{Zero-one} \\ \text{investment} \\ \text{variable} \end{bmatrix}$$

ZERO-ONE CAPACITY EXPANSION CONSTRAINTS

(4.29)
$$y_{mit} = 0 \quad \text{or} \quad 1.$$

$$i \in I$$
$$m \in M$$
$$t \in T$$

NONNEGATIVITY CONSTRAINTS

(4.30)
$$z_{pit} \geq 0 \qquad\qquad p \in P, i \in I, t \in T$$
$$x_{cijt} \geq 0 \qquad\qquad c \in CF, i \in I, j \in J, t \in T$$
$$x_{cii't} \geq 0 \qquad\qquad c \in CI, i \in I, i' \in I, i' \neq i, t \in T$$
$$v_{cit} \geq 0 \qquad\qquad c \in (CI \cup CR), i \in I, t \in T$$
$$v_{cjt} \geq 0 \qquad\qquad c \in CF, j \in J, t \in T$$
$$e_{cilt} \geq 0 \qquad\qquad c \in (CF \cup CI), i \in I, l \in L, t \in T$$
$$u_{cit} \geq 0 \qquad\qquad c \in CR, i \in I, t \in T$$

$$h_{mit} \geq 0 \qquad\qquad m \in M, i \in I, t \in T$$

$$y_{mit} \geq 0 \qquad\qquad m \in M, i \in I, t \in T$$

This completes the statement of a dynamic investment planning model that can be used to analyze sectorwide investment programs within a multicountry context, as long as the analysis focuses exclusively on efficiency aspects. If acceptability considerations must be brought to bear upon the investment problem, the model can be expanded in a variety of ways to deal with these complications. To this expansion we shall now turn.

We have already dealt with examples of acceptability constraints on international and intraregional trade flows. For that reason we will consider here only the sorts of constraints that can be measured as more or less equal shares in the benefits of the investment program.

Distributional Constraints

To introduce several types of distributional constraints, it is convenient to define sets that group plants or markets by country. Let $w \in W$ represent the set of countries. Then, $(w, i) \in EI$ is the set of plant sites i in country w, and $(w, j) \in WJ$ is the set of markets j in country w.

With this notation, we can, for example, express the number of fertilizer projects by country as follows:

$$\hat{Y}_{wt} = \sum_{\substack{i \in I \\ (w,i) \in WI}} \sum_{m \in M} Y_{mit}.$$

Similarly, capacity built in each country for producing fertilizer nutrients can now be expressed as

$$\bar{h} = \sum_{\substack{i \in I \\ (w,i) \in WI}} \sum_{m \in M} \alpha_{m,n} h_{mit}$$

where h is the capacity expansion variable, and $\alpha_{m,n}$ is the nutrient content of type n for each productive unit m. Similar aggregations can be made for other relevant aspects of the investment program and expressed in acceptability constraints, as described below.

A relatively trivial constraint is to add to the optimization problem an upper or lower bound on the number of projects in each country.

$$\text{low}_w \leq \sum_t \hat{Y}_{wt} \hat{\delta}_t \leq \text{up}_w$$

where $\hat{\delta}_t$ is a discount factor that may be added to account for the time preference countries may have with regard to project implementation.

Table 4-1. *Hypothetical Values for Measures of Acceptable Inequality between Countries* $\hat{Y}_A$ *and* $\hat{Y}_B$

$\hat{Y}_A$	$\hat{Y}_B$	$\hat{Y}_A - \hat{Y}_B$	$\Delta = 1$
0	0	0	—
	1	−1	Possible
	2	−2	Not possible
1	0	1	Possible
	1	0	—
	2	−1	Possible
2	0	2	Not possible
	1	1	Possible
	2	0	—

Alternatively, one may want to introduce an absolute measure of acceptable inequality between countries:

$$\Delta_{low} \leq \hat{Y}_w - \hat{Y}_{\hat{w}} \leq \Delta_{up}. \qquad\qquad \begin{matrix} w \in W \\ \hat{w} \in W \\ w \neq \hat{w} \end{matrix}$$

For example, assume Δ_{low} equals Δ_{up} equals 1, meaning that the difference in the number of projects in each country and any other partner country cannot exceed one.[27] Hypothetical values under such an assumption are shown in table 4-1.

Relative measures of equality within the region may also be introduced. Let $\phi_{k,w}$ stand for the total investment charges by country.[28] Then

$$\phi_{k,w} \geq \alpha_w \sum \phi_{k,w}$$

where

$$\sum_w \alpha_w < 1.$$

This means that, for a cooperative plan to be acceptable to country w, a minimum proportion of all regional investment charges needs to be incurred by plants located in country w.

Alternatively, a maximum constraint can be formulated

$$\phi_{k,w} \leq \beta_w \sum \phi_{kw}$$

---

27. The value Y_w can be substituted for any other measure of project impact, if desired.
28. Once more, ϕ can stand for any other project element.

where

$$\sum_w \beta_w > 1.$$

Here, a country wishes to incur no more than a specific proportion of total regional investment charges.

Finally, acceptability constraints with regard to project impact can be expressed relative to partner countries:

$$\phi_w - \phi_{\hat{w}} \le \alpha_{w,\hat{w}} \sum_{\hat{w}} \phi_w \qquad \begin{matrix} w \in W \\ \hat{w} \in W \\ w \ne \hat{w} \end{matrix}$$

where

$$0 < \alpha_{w,\hat{w}} < 1.$$

The two extreme situations that may emerge with this constraint are (a) $\alpha_{w,\hat{w}}$ equals zero, in which case the shares in country w and $\hat{w}$ are equal, and (b) $\alpha_{w,\hat{w}}$ equals one, in which case country w is allocated all benefits associated with ϕ.

5

Uses and Limitations
of the Models

A FORMAL FRAMEWORK for investment analysis, such as the models proposed in this book, has several advantages, regardless of whether the planning area encompasses several countries, a single country, a region within a country, or, for that matter, a single company. Such models, which were described in general terms in the first volume in this series,[1] permit a full accounting of the interdependencies among a specified set of activities, even if these activities exhibit economies of scale. When domestic production is considered as an alternative to imports, the model is instrumental in determining the optimal size of capacity construction or expansion. Moreover, and simultaneously, the model can be used to determine an efficient timetable for constructing or expanding capacities, the optimal location and output mix, and the cost-minimizing transport patterns for raw materials, intermediates, and final products.

In practice, the model is often used less as an optimization framework than as a simulation device. As such, it may check the internal consistency of a specific investment program and determine the ranking of alternative programs or projects in relation to those identified with the use of the model. Although a very large number of project combinations are possible, particularly if scale, location, and timing are allowed to vary, the use of the model to evaluate the implications of specific project proposals

---

1. David A. Kendrick and Ardy J. Stoutjesdijk, *The Planning of Industrial Investment Programs: A Methodology*, The Planning of Investment Programs, vol. 1 (Baltimore, Md.: Johns Hopkins University Press, 1978).

is computationally much simpler than full-fledged optimization. For multicountry investment planning, the model is particularly helpful in analyzing alternative locations for investment projects. Often the trade-offs that may have to be made between efficiency and equity are greatly affected by the localization characteristics of the investment program under consideration.

Efficiency and Equity

In most analyses of international project cooperation, considerations of both efficiency and equity usually play a role. However, no specific attention to equity would be necessary if the correct social prices were used to value output and all the inputs. Project cooperation would then boil down to the removal of nonoptimal trade policies, and all trading partners would gain.

Let us analyze the gains of project cooperation, and their distribution, for two countries and for a good that can be traded between them, but not with the rest of the world (a so-called regional good), for which both countries have installed production capacity. The least-cost supply pattern that may emerge following the abolition of trade barriers could take the form of a modified production level in the two countries, involving expanded production in, say, country 1 and contracted production in country 2. In that case, trade flows between the two countries would change as well. This result could be achieved by a combination of production and transport cost advantages of a production location in country 1 in relation to a marketing center in country 2.

In the absence of cooperation, the original production levels and trade flows could only have been maintained with the aid of tariffs or subsidies in country 2. Is there any difference in effect between removing tariffs and removing production subsidies? It is well known from the theory of protection that abolishing a tariff involves a welfare gain to the overall economy which is (apart from the sign) equal to the sum of the so-called production and consumption cost of a tariff.[2] A subsidy, in contrast, relates only to a production cost; it follows that abolishing a subsidy implies a welfare gain amounting to no more than the corresponding production cost (except for the sign).

In the models presented in this book, demand is assumed to be fixed. Under that assumption, we have a vertical demand curve, which implies

---

2. See, for instance, Melvyn B. Kraus, *The New Protectionism* (Oxford: Basil Blackwell, 1979), pp. 32–33.

that the consumption cost of a tariff is equal to zero.[3] Thus, in the case of fixed demand requirements, the total welfare effects are the same for removing a tariff or removing a subsidy.

For our two-country case, we will try to determine in detail the welfare effects of this cooperation scheme. Although the structure of our models is such that the welfare effects in country 2 are the same, whether protection consists of tariffs or production subsidies, it may be useful to continue to distinguish between these two forms of protectionism.

In the case of a tariff, its removal leads to a lower price of the commodity concerned in country 2. The welfare effects are an increase in consumer surplus that is larger than the decrease in producer surplus and government revenues. It is also assumed that the removal of the tariff is fully reflected in the domestic price in country 2. If not, part of the consumer surplus in country 2 does not materialize, and country 1 will experience a producer surplus.

In contrast, the removal of a production subsidy leaves the domestic price in country 2 unchanged. The government's welfare increases by an amount equal to the per unit subsidy times domestic output. The latter amount is larger than the reduction in producer surplus. In this case there is no possibility that a part of the overall welfare gain in country 2 is transferred to country 1.

If we suppose that in country 2, before cooperation, no tariffs on imports or subsidies on production of the commodity concerned existed, we obviously cannot expect any welfare changes related to domestic protection. There is a benefit to the producers in country 1, however, due to higher utilization of hitherto excess capacity. This gain is at the cost of the producers in country 2, who experience an increase in excess capacity.

All the welfare changes mentioned thus far are efficiency implications of the optimal solution of our simple cooperation model. In other words, we deal here with the welfare gains and losses of the various parties in the cooperation area, which are implied in the optimal solution of our cooperation model, formulated as an efficiency problem. Before we can discuss equity, we will have to evaluate these welfare effects corresponding to the efficiency problem, so as to obtain an estimate of the net benefits of cooperation.

In order to obtain an economically correct estimate of these net benefits, we will have to move from a financial to an economic analysis. In

---

3. At least, if consumers and the government, which receives the tariff revenues, value the welfare changes identically.

Figure 5-1.   *A Simple Cooperation Model*

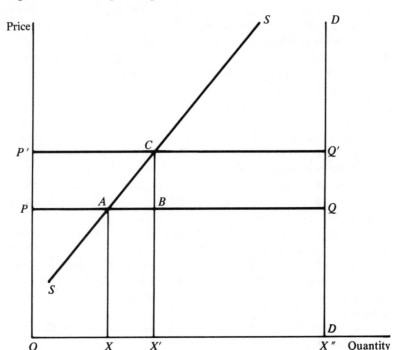

other words, instead of using market prices, we will have to use efficiency or, possibly, social prices.[4] If we then value the output (demand) and all the inputs in both countries at accounting prices, it is clear that in the present case project cooperation amounts to the removal of nonoptimal trade policies. We use the term trade policies, although the good in question is only partly tradable, because if the cost at accounting prices of producing the good independently in country 2 is higher than the accounting price attainable through cooperation, the good should be imported from country 1.

Let us assume that we have obtained, by means of the transport method, an optimal solution of our simple cooperation model, which is presented in figure 5-1. In this figure, P is the accounting price of the

4. We follow the terminology used by Lyn Squire and Herman G. van der Tak, *Economic Analysis of Projects* (Baltimore, Md.: Johns Hopkins University Press, 1975), pp. 5-6.

good concerned in country 2. In the case of a partly tradable good the accounting price is interpreted as the marginal social benefit, which is equal to the domestic price times the standard conversion factor. The domestic supply curve is represented by SS; the domestic demand curve DD is depicted as a vertical line, because the price elasticity of demand is assumed to be zero. The supply from country 1 is represented by the curve PQ. Before cooperation there exists a tariff in country 2 which raises the domestic price to P'. In that situation the optimal solution of our precooperation transport problem implies that, of the total amount consumed in country 2 (OX''), OX' is produced domestically and $X'X''$ is imported from country 1. Once a cooperation agreement is reached and the corresponding tariff in country 2 removed, the optimal solution of the cooperation model implies that only OX is produced domestically, whereas imports from country 1 amount to XX''.

For country 2 the gain from cooperation is equal to the triangle ACB in figure 5-1, that is, the increase in consumer surplus $PP'Q'Q$ minus the reduction in producer surplus $PP'CA$ and minus the loss of government revenue $BCQ'Q$. It is important to note that in calculating this gain account is taken of the increase in excess capacity and unemployment in country 2 due to increased imports from country 1. The cost coefficients corresponding to production in country 2 are based on accounting prices; that is, they fully reflect the economic and social cost of increased excess capacity and unemployment. If it turns out that, nevertheless, increased imports from country 1 involve net benefits for country 2, this is shown in the corresponding optimal solution of our simple cooperation model in figure 5-1.

What are the benefits from cooperation for country 1? These benefits are not depicted in figure 5-1, but they can easily be determined. They are equal to the increase in exports to country 2 (XX'), multiplied by the difference between the accounting price P and the marginal social costs in country 1. The latter supply curve is not represented in figure 5-1.

When this analysis is formulated in terms of mathematical programming, it is not difficult to prove that the gains from cooperation—ACB for country 2 and XX' times P minus marginal social cost for country 1— are equal to the following expression: the objective function value of the simple cooperation model explained in chapter 4 minus the sum of the optimal objective function values of the two transport models for the two countries in isolation, that is, assuming no cooperation, which is reflected in a protective tariff in country 2. The objective functions are the same: to minimize the supply cost at accounting prices for satisfying fixed domestic demand. The analysis can easily be extended to international goods and services by increasing the number of possible suppliers and by setting the accounting price equal to the border price.

What conclusions can be drawn from the preceding analysis? The main point is that when outputs and inputs are valued at accounting prices, there will be gains from cooperation for each prospective partner. In other words, the use of accounting prices means that in fact equity cannot be considered a relevant issue in cooperation. Rather, aiming at maximum efficiency by means of cooperation involves net benefits for each participating country which would otherwise not have been obtained.

It follows that accounting prices are the correct basis for making decisions on production and trade in a cooperation scheme. No equity constraints should be incorporated in the corresponding cooperation model. An equitable distribution of net benefits is implied in the optimal solution of the cooperation model based on efficiency considerations, once inputs and outputs are valued at accounting prices.

In practice, we cannot adopt the above reasoning as the single leading principle for our planning models for project cooperation, because many economic policy decisions are not made on the basis of accounting prices. Nor are policymakers accustomed or inclined to employ such prices for negotiations or decisions.

For that reason we will have to take into account considerations with respect to, for instance, the balance of payments or existing production capacity. Such considerations lead to additional constraints in our cooperation planning models. It seems to be more appropriate to name such constraints acceptability constraints, as we did in chapter 4, rather than equity constraints. It must be emphasized, however, that when acceptability constraints of some form or other are introduced, account should be taken of their relative cost in lost efficiency.

There is a final point to be discussed, which has to do with equity within each of the partner countries. The Stolper-Samuelson theorem tells us that when protection is diminished or abolished, leading to a lower domestic relative price of the good concerned, the real wage of the factor intensively used in the production of that good is reduced.[5] In the case of project cooperation, it is likely that most of the industries concerned will be capital intensive. This would mean that a scheme of project cooperation would lead to a change in income distribution in favor of labor and at the cost of capital in those partner countries where protection is reduced. This matter will not be pursued any further in our analysis.

5. W. F. Stolper and P. A. Samuelson, "Protection and Real Wages," *Review of Economic Studies*, vol. 9 (1971), pp. 58–73.

Acceptability Constraints, Compensation, and Differential Pricing

Acceptability constraints, in whatever form, serve the useful purpose of increasing the stability of the planned cooperation scheme. That is, the constraints increase the probability that the cooperation scheme will be realized and will remain intact during the planning period. In chapter 4 we proposed, for example, acceptability constraints relating to capacity utilization, intraregional trade flows, international trade flows, and capacity allocation. There may be still other types of acceptability constraints. One set of such constraints could, for example, involve an allocation of investment projects so that each prospective partner would be assigned at least one project producing regional goods and services. The investment projects producing international commodities would then be allocated in conformity with the optimal solution of this partly constrained efficiency model. In this way, each partner would have a guaranteed minimum share in the benefits, and it would be hard for any of the partner countries to withdraw from the cooperation scheme during the planning period.

Which of these constraints would be preferred in an actual situation will depend, in particular, on the extent that one or more of the prospective partners considers the optimal solution of the efficiency model to involve an inequitable distribution of benefits. The numerical values of these constraints will be an outcome of negotiations among the prospective partners. Political and power factors will play an important part in this regard.

We may add that, independent of the system of prices used, the benefits of cooperation and their resulting distribution over the partner countries can in principle be determined as follows. The benefits of cooperation for the area as a whole are equal to the difference between the optimal objective function value of the multicountry model and the sum of the optimal objective function values of the single-country models. The cooperation benefits for each partner country can be determined by again comparing the optimal solutions of the single-country models with the one of the multicountry model. The cooperation benefits of any of the prospective partner countries are equal to the minimum costs of production, transport, and investment, that is, the optimal objective function value of the country's single-country model minus the share in total minimum costs, according to the optimal objective function value of the multicountry model, to be attributed to that country. The latter share can be determined by identifying in the optimal solution of the multicountry model all variables corresponding to satisfying the fixed demand requirements in the country concerned (domestic shipments, shipments from the partner countries, and other imports), as well as the variables corresponding to the country's exports to world markets and sales of by-products. The optimal amounts of these two sets of variables have to be multiplied by their corresponding direct cost coefficients. This still leaves out the fixed-charge part of total investment costs, which also partly has to be allocated to the country concerned. The simplest way of doing this is to allocate the fixed charges in proportion to the share of domestic production used for domestic shipments and exports to world markets.

Related to the stability of the planned cooperation scheme is the question of the robustness of the investment pattern, that is, the extent to which the optimal investment pattern is modified in response to changes in crucial parameters. This matter can best be dealt with by means of sensitivity analysis, which will be demonstrated in the case study later.

Compensation

If one or more of the prospective partners in a cooperation scheme believe that the distribution of the benefits will be unequal, they may reject the scheme altogether, even though they would be worse off without cooperation. Acceptability constraints, such as the ones mentioned above, may make the cooperation scheme acceptable to all prospective partners, but such constraints have disadvantages as well. The main drawback is that the optimal solution of the model with acceptability constraints is less efficient than the optimal solution without them: the efficiency model.

For this reason it might be useful to devise a compensation scheme, so as to attain the maximum possible benefits of cooperation for the cooperation area as a whole. In this respect we refer again to the work by Gately discussed in chapter 4.

Such compensation schemes play a considerable role in some cooperation schemes like the Southern African Customs Union, the Communauté Economique de l'Afrique de l'Ouest (CEAO), and the Union Douanière et Economique de l'Afrique-Centrale (UDEAC). In these cases, however, the criterion advocated for such compensation is the net tariff revenue forgone as a result of buying the products concerned from other partner countries. A rationale for transfers of this kind can be derived from classical customs union theory, inasmuch as this loss of revenue corresponds to a loss of welfare that a country suffers from trade diversion.

The investment planning models formulated in this book, however, are stated in terms of minimizing the costs to be incurred for satisfying demand in each of the prospective partner countries. This implies that if imports from third countries are cheaper than domestic production or imports from partner countries, the former imports will be selected in the optimal solution of the planning model. In other words, trade diversion and compensation schemes are not relevant for our present analysis. We will return to this issue in the section on external tariffs.

Nevertheless, compensation may be a useful instrument in negotiating a cooperation scheme. Once the distribution of net benefits over the partner countries has been estimated along the lines set out above, the amounts to be compensated depend solely on the negotiating power of the various prospective partners.

Differential Pricing

Would differential pricing be a good system for bringing about compensation among partner countries? In a somewhat different context Pursell and Snape have considered the optimal policy toward an exporting industry subject to economies of scale where the export price covers marginal, but not average, costs.[6] They find that net social gains are maximized when the domestic price is reduced to the export price where there may be a case for a subsidy to enable the domestic firm to set up and export.

We have doubts, however, about whether, according to the assumptions of our models, differential pricing can be considered a means for redistributing cooperation benefits over the partner countries. In principle it seems possible for a plant to charge a higher delivery price for shipments to destinations in different countries. In practice, however, such a system would require a tariff between the cooperation partners so as to prevent the lower priced commodities with destination to, for instance, country 1 to flow to country 2. This would not be at all in compliance with the assumptions of the cooperation schemes dealt with in this book, which imply a partial customs union among the partner countries. For this reason we will not pursue this matter any further.

---

6. G. Pursell and R. H. Snape, "Economies of Scale, Price Discrimination and Exporting," *Journal of International Economics*, vol. 3, no. 1 (February 1973), pp. 85–91.

The Package Approach, Financing, and External Tariffs

The package approach has already been discussed in some detail in chapter 2. Its purpose is to enhance the durability and stability of the co-operation scheme by ensuring that each participating country obtains at least one cooperation project. This approach may be distinguished from two other approaches to economic cooperation. The first is selective trade liberalization, which implies a gradual step-by-step and item-by-item approach with a policy of progressive advance toward the long-run aim of a free-trade area. The second approach consists of industrial complementary agreements, to be negotiated by representatives of the private sector in a specific industry in each partner country, for specialization and an exchange of products within the industry. The package approach involves a number of problems related to methodology as well as policy, which are dealt with later in this chapter.

Financing

Besides these problems, there is the matter of financing the cooperation projects. In this respect one could formulate as a leading principle that each country should finance the projects that are allocated to it, according to the optimal solution of the multicountry investment model.

It is not difficult to understand the logic on which this principle rests. For this purpose it is good to remember that the planning models presented in this book are structured to satisfy fixed requirements as minimum costs. To put it differently, they can be described best as models for cost-effectiveness analysis. If it turns out that the optimal way of satisfying domestic—and partly foreign—requirements is by means of domestic production, it is entirely reasonable that the country concerned would finance the necessary investment itself. If not, it would opt for a more expensive solution, such as, importing from the prospective partner or third countries.

To correctly take account of the financial resources available to each prospective partner, the annual discount rate ρ, used in our models, should be the country-specific accounting rate of interest. If, according to the optimal solution of the multicountry model, a project is allocated to a country, the use of the country-specific accounting rate of interest makes sure that the capital expenditures of the project can indeed be financed by the available resources of the country concerned. The use of country-specific accounting rates of interest also renders it possible to take account of the differences in available financial resources among countries—for instance, Venezuela compared with Bolivia—and the corresponding commitments to consumption and saving.

The situation is different when a project cooperation scheme is accompanied by a common fund for financing the proposed projects. An attractive feature of such a common fund is that probably foreign sources of financing are more easily available for cooperation projects than for similar projects for individual countries. This is, for instance, the case in ASEAN, where the Japanese government has accepted a commitment in principle to provide loans on concessional terms in support of cooperation projects. This is very explicitly subject to confirmation of the economic viability of the projects and the support of each project by all ASEAN member countries. In case of such a common fund, a uniform accounting rate of interest, not a country-specific one, should be used as the annual discount rate ρ.

Another possibility for raising the finance for cooperation projects, which is not dependent on foreign participation or foreign assistance, is the pooling of international reserves of the partner countries. As the risk of abnormal demand on the reserve position would be proportionately less when spread over a number of countries, total reserves held could be reduced, or countries could benefit from an increased level of insurance coverage. The resulting savings in foreign exchange could then be utilized by the countries themselves to finance the cooperation projects. Recently, the possibilities of such a scheme for ASEAN have been analyzed.[7] Unfortunately, in that case it would appear that the potential benefits of pooling international reserves would be insufficient incentive for the countries to tackle the sensitive political problems involved, like the size of the central fund and the possibility of exploitation of the scheme by a country running a continuous deficit.

Yet another possibility for financing would be via the private rather than the public sector. In that case one may safely assume that the participation of subsidiaries of transnational corporations would be considerable. However, as was recently shown by Tironi,[8] the change in economic welfare of a group of countries forming a customs union that affects industries dominated by foreign firms is given not only by the stan-

7. J. R. Dodsworth and J. Diamond, "Monetary Cooperation as a Source of Development Finance: The ASEAN Case," *Journal of Development Economics*, vol. 7, no. 3 (September 1980), pp. 409–25.

8. Ernesto Tironi, "Customs Union Theory in the Presence of Foreign Firms," *Oxford Economic Papers*, vol. 34, no. 1 (March 1982), pp. 150–71.

dard trade creation and diversion effects but also by the foreign profit creation and diversion effects. To what extent this influences the analysis presented in this study has not been pursued.

External Tariffs

It was already said that the optimal solution of the efficiency model yields the cheapest supply pattern for satisfying demand in the cooperation area: either domestic production, or imports from the prospective partners, or imports from third countries. To put it differently, the planning models presented in this book lead to optimal investment and trade policies for the various partner countries. For this reason trade creation may occur according to the optimal solution, but trade deviation will not.

Project cooperation is sometimes considered a means of fostering industrialization in developing countries. Looking in this way at economic cooperation does mean a break with the traditional customs union theory, which views any increase in the union's national income through increased specialization as good and any negative effect on national income through trade diversion as bad. Rather, customs unions are approached through the advantages they may offer by swapping markets for the products of each participant's high-cost industries.[9] It was already mentioned in chapter 1 that such a policy may easily lead to increasingly protective barriers and may produce negative effects on competitiveness, income distribution, and so forth.

In contrast to the analysis of the preceding chapters, such an approach assumes that welfare is generated not only by satisfying demand at minimum costs, but also by the collective consumption of a specific public good, that is, a level of industrial production in excess of what would be commercially viable in the absence of protection. If that assumption is adopted, the analysis is changed considerably to the extent that common external tariffs will play an important part. In that case it is possible to determine an "efficient" common external tariff, which would provide the specified level of industrial production in the cooperation area at the lowest cost in combined national income forgone. If each partner country claims a specified level of industrial production for itself, a mutually ad-

---

9. Among the first to emphasize such an approach were: C. A. Cooper and B. F. Massell, "A New Look at Customs Union Theory," *Economic Journal*, vol. 75 (December 1965), pp. 742-47; C. A. Cooper and B. F. Massell, "Towards a General Theory of Customs Unions for Developing Countries," *Journal of Political Economy*, vol. 73, no. 5 (October 1965), pp. 461-76.

vantageous cooperation scheme is still possible. Tariffs that bring about such a scheme may be termed "quasi-efficient." The analysis can be extended to permit compensation payments from one country to another.

We will not deal with this matter any further here. Instead, in our case study we will apply sensitivity analysis to tariffs, that is, the import prices of the commodities concerned. Sensitivity analysis can be used to determine at what levels of external tariffs an investment program becomes efficient (in the sense of appearing in the optimal solution of the multicountry investment planning model).

Clearly, it is not necessary to assume a constant tariff over the whole planning period. Instead, the consequences of a tariff policy that is differentiated over time can be analyzed.

Limitations of the Approach

The limitations of the approach to cooperation projects that has been outlined here stem from two sources: methodology and policy.

Methodology

The limitations with respect to the methodology have already been mentioned in the first volume of the present series on the planning of investment programs.[10] They are the following:

- the assumption of fixed demands
- the assumption of no substitution in demand
- the assumption of fixed prices of some inputs and outputs
- the assumption of no uncertainty
- the representation of policy objectives
- the size of the programming problem.

We will confine ourselves to a brief discussion of two of these points: the assumption of fixed demands and the size of the programming problem.

The models in this book are all expressed in terms of satisfying fixed requirements at minimum costs. The assumption that requirements remain fixed when delivery costs are lowered implies either that lower costs do not lead to lower prices or that the price elasticity of demand is zero. It is clear that the former implication is not in conformity with the logic of

---

10. Kendrick and Stoutjesdijk, *Planning of Industrial Investment Programs*, ch. 7.

our cooperation model. In our model, the aim of project cooperation is to satisfy demand at lower costs than without cooperation. This implies that transport flows in a situation with cooperation will be different from those without cooperation. Different transport flows will mainly come about as a reaction of demand on price differences. In other words, lower costs must result in lower prices; otherwise in most cases demand will not react. Possibly, not the whole of the decrease in cost may be passed on to the consumer in the form of lower prices. Part of it may be retained by the (new) producer. This matter of producer and consumer surplus was discussed in detail in the section "Efficiency and Equity."

So we will have to accept the other implication: a zero price elasticity of demand or, to put it differently, a vertical demand curve. This assumption was maintained throughout our earlier analysis of the distribution of the net benefits of cooperation.

Whenever the demand for final products is price elastic, the model results may be inconsistent, in the sense that market requirements may have been estimated on the basis of prices that differ from those implied by the solution of the model. If that is the case, the best procedure may be to solve the model repeatedly until the requirements implied by the two sets of prices are more or less similar. In the case of many final products, however, this procedure may be cumbersome and costly. Nonetheless, fixed demand requirements or a vertical demand curve must be considered as a simplification that is nearly unavoidable, if the models are not to become unmanageably complicated.

As for problems related to the size of the programming model, it is well known that they are already quite considerable for a model of a single country. Clearly, these problems become even more complicated in the case of project cooperation, where more countries are involved. Finally, it may be good to emphasize that there are many other possibilities for economic cooperation among countries, a number of which were mentioned in chapter 2, which cannot be analyzed with the aid of the planning methods presented in the preceding chapters.

Policy

The limitations of our approach with respect to policy are related to the limited successes—to put it mildly—of cooperation schemes among developing countries. In chapters 1 and 2 we mentioned four reasons for the modest results of cooperation thus far: special interests at various levels hampering tariff reductions, differences in levels of development, disagreements over the distribution of benefits, and the general inclination to safeguard national sovereignty. Recent detailed studies on the specific difficulties encountered in some cooperation schemes, such as the East African Community[11] and the Andean Pact,[12] indeed confirm the validity of these four basic reasons.[13]

In another study on the role of cooperation in industrialization, Hughes and Ohlin emphasize that developing countries generally lack the physical and commercial infrastructure for high levels of trade.[14] They make the point that cooperation among countries with similar endowments but different levels of development meets with still greater difficulties than cooperation among more equal partners, because in the former case the gains from cooperation tend to be more skewed to the richer countries.

On the sort of cooperation projects that the models in this book are related to, Hughes and Ohlin remark that regional authorities have tended to plan very capital-intensive, large-scale enterprises prematurely for what were essentially still very small and poor markets by global standards. Also the effects of common external tariff formulation have usually been to raise protection quite substantially. Although the authors stress the desirability of political and economic cooperation among developing countries and point to the rapidly growing South-South trade, they believe that the project cooperation schemes that are the subject of this book are not likely to accelerate the industralization of developing countries.

Recently Arndt and Garnaut have surveyed the progress made by the ASEAN countries toward regional economic cooperation.[15] With respect to the possible contribution the establishment of large ASEAN industrial plants can make to an acceleration of the industralization of the region, Arndt and Garnaut are very cautious. To their minds the difficulties that

11. Arthur Hazelwood, "The End of the East African Community: What Are the Lessons for Regional Integration Schemes?" *Journal of Common Market Studies*, vol. 43, No. 1 (September 1979), pp. 40–58.

12. Rafael Vargas-Hidalgo, "The Crisis of the Andean Pact: Lessons for Integration among Developing Countries," *Journal of Common Market Studies*, vol. 17, no. 3 (March 1979), pp. 213–26.

13. See also Ali M. El-Agraa, ed., *International Economic Integration* (London: Macmillan, 1982), ch. 7–13.

14. Helen Hughes and Goran Ohlin, "The International Environment," in John Cody, Helen Hughes, and David Wall, eds., *Policies for Industrial Progress in Developing Countries* (Oxford: Oxford University Press, 1980).

15. H. W. Arndt and Ross Garnaut, "ASEAN and the Industrialization of East Asia," *Journal of Common Market Studies*, vol. 17, no. 3 (March 1979), pp. 191–212.

have been encountered by the first group of ASEAN industrial projects illustrate the basic dilemma of regional economic cooperation, which also hampers progress toward intra-ASEAN trade liberalization. Between industrial subsectors for which each country's market is large enough for at least one optimal-size plant and others for which such plants can be established at an efficient scale only if they can sell much of their output on the world market, there is only a narrow range of production processes for which the wider regional market makes just enough difference in cost through the economies of scale it offers. For this reason, Arndt and Garnaut emphasize that one cannot be confident that the ASEAN economies have any regional alternative to industrialization based on worldwide trade expansion.

We too are skeptical about the magnitude of potential benefits of project cooperation schemes, and we concur that regional economic cooperation should not lead to the establishment of highly protected industries unable to compete in world markets. Nevertheless, we find a bit more reason for optimism.

In the case of ASEAN there is some evidence that regional economic cooperation may lead to competitive regional plants. In a United Nations study it is estimated that nine of the twelve proposed regional projects show good prospects of being competitive at world prices, and even if it is judged wise to help them in the initial years, they are likely to be able to sell exports outside the ASEAN region if capacity permits.[16]

In a recent paper on the development of industries on a regional basis in the ASEAN countries, Staab shows that there are substantial gains to be realized by these countries from establishing the aluminum and urea fertilizer industries on a regional basis.[17] In constant mid-1973 prices the savings for the regionally integrated aluminum and urea fertilizer industries are estimated to be $374 and $84.9 a ton for aluminum metal and urea fertilizer, respectively, when compared with the most likely alternative of imports from outside the region. Furthermore, the removal of plant output constraints, other than those imposed by the availability of skilled labor and capital, results in considerable additional gains for the partner countries through the realization of economies of scale. For the aluminum industry, the additional gain amounts to $18 a ton of

16. United Nations, "Economic Cooperation among Member Countries of the Association of South East Asian Nations," *Journal of Development Planning*, no. 7 (1974), p. 129.

17. Martin J. Staab, "The Production Location Problem and the Development of Industries on a Regional Basis in the ASEAN Countries," *Developing Economies*, vol. 18, no. 1 (March 1980), pp. 65–95.

aluminum metal, and for the urea fertilizer industry, it is $4.28 a ton of urea. (All amounts are in U.S. dollars.)

In still another study, Pearson and Ingram consider the potential gains from industrial cooperation between Ghana and the Ivory Coast in seven industries, which are together a large portion of total industry in both countries.[18] They estimate that, because of trade creation, economies of scale, and offsetting domestic divergencies between private and social costs, Ghana and the Ivory Coast stand to achieve welfare gains of 33 percent and 22 percent, respectively, of gross output in world prices.

As for the prospects for efficient industries in the Andean Common Market, the reader is referred to the case study in the second part of this book.

Considering these results, we conclude that regional economic cooperation offers a viable scope for reaping the benefits of economies of scale and that it may very well serve as an intermediate step toward an outward-looking pattern of industrialization. The narrowness or breadth of this scope depends on the actual situation in the region concerned with respect to investment, production, and distribution costs. We believe that quite a number of the problems encountered in past attempts at regional cooperation are in fact problems of planning. Among these are determination of the correct mix of domestic production, imports from prospective partners, and imports from third countries; the timing and size of cooperation projects; and the distribution of benefits and costs among the partner countries. The purpose of this book is to formulate methods and models for solving precisely these planning problems and to thus enhance the feasibility of regional economic cooperation schemes.

18. Scott R. Pearson and William D. Ingram, "Economies of Scale, Domestic Divergencies, and Potential Gains from Economic Integration in Ghana and the Ivory Coast," *Journal of Political Economy*, vol. 88, no. 5 (October 1980), pp. 994–1008.

PART TWO

A Case Study of the Fertilizer Sector of the Andean Common Market

6

Introduction and Summary

As IN THE OTHER VOLUMES in this series, the case study illustrates the use of the planning methodology in an actual situation. The emphasis is on the application of the method, rather than the actual results obtained. Consequently, attention will be paid to how to collect and organize data, how to arrive at a policy-relevant formulation of the planning problem, how to construct a corresponding planning model and analyze its results, and how to communicate with technicians and policymakers at various stages of the study. Nevertheless, in order to provide the reader with sufficient background to arrive at a judgment as to the feasibility and usefulness of the approach, a comprehensive data base and highlights of the results will be provided as well.

In several regards, the analysis of investments in a multicountry context entails substantially different problems from such analysis in a national context, as was described in part one. Mainly, a careful tradeoff has to be established between efficiency and acceptability in the distribution of costs and benefits resulting from a joint investment program. To a large extent, the strengths and weaknesses of a particular investment pattern are revealed only at the time negotiations take place among the participating countries, when both preferences and criticisms are likely to be the most clearly articulated. At that time, the advantage of a fully implemented and calibrated model should be clear: new investment scenarios can be generated and evaluated rapidly, so that the negotiations need not suffer lengthy interruptions. The experience with the Andean Common Market in this regard will be described in this case study as well.

A Chronology and Summary of the Case Study

The use of chemical fertilizers in all five countries composing the Andean Common Market (Bolivia, Colombia, Ecuador, Peru, and Venezuela) is increasing rapidly and is considered an important factor in bringing about increased productivity in agriculture. Greater agricultural productivity is a high priority of government policy throughout the region in view of the projected rapid growth of population.

In recognition of this priority and rapidly rising international prices for fertilizer material, the Andean Common Market Secretariat (also called the junta) proposed to the Common Market Commission (the Comisión del Acuerdo de Cartagena) in March 1974 that an agreement be reached on fertilizers in the Andean region. The proposal did not envisage specific assignments of fertilizer production facilities; rather, the principal objective was to establish an accelerated program of trade liberalization, with a relatively low common external tariff of 5 percent on raw materials and 10 percent on final products. It was not until March 1977 that three countries (Colombia, Peru, and Venezuela) agreed in principle with the proposed strategy, while the other two (Bolivia and Ecuador) had fundamental disagreements. In light of this situation, the secretariat proposed a much more detailed study of the fertilizer sector, including an appraisal of alternative development strategies for the industry in the subregion. On the basis of this appraisal, the secretariat hoped to come up with a new proposal, technically more efficient and politically more acceptable than the original proposal. This plan of action was accepted by the commission during the same meeting in March 1977.

To carry out the study, the secretariat invited the participation of the Inter-American Development Bank and the World Bank. During the subsequent discussions among the three organizations, it was decided to carry out the study with the use of a planning model that had been developed at the World Bank for investment analysis of industrial subsectors. Until then, this analytic framework had mostly been used in connection with national investment programs. The Andean study provided an opportunity to employ the model in a multicountry setting.

The planning problem and the approach selected can be summarized as follows. Four out of the five countries (Colombia, Ecuador, Peru, and Venezuela) currently have fertilizer production facilities; all five countries have formulated detailed plans for new capacity construction. The raw material situation in all five countries is reasonably favorable, in particular for nitrogenous fertilizer production, as natural gas is available throughout the area. Phosphate rock deposits are known to exist in three countries (Colombia, Peru, and Venezuela), but only in Peru are they large enough for a major industrial development.

All fertilizer production exhibits economies of scale, in the sense that production costs are crucially dependent upon the scale of production. However, although growing rapidly, the use of fertilizers in the Andean region is still at a modest level, and implementation of the current expansion plans would result in substantial overcapacity for the foreseeable future, unless exports to world markets are possible. It would appear that the project planners in several of the countries, notably Bolivia and Venezuela, are much more optimistic in this regard than seems warranted.

Under these circumstances, the objective of the study was to formulate a number of alternative investment scenarios for the region as a whole that would meet prospective demand for fertilizer material more efficiently than would be possible by the implementation of national plans. In order to enhance the acceptability of these investment scenarios to the member countries, it was recognized that explicit attention needed to be paid to the distribution of costs and benefits associated with each scenario. The planning method should, therefore, permit the rapid determination of the tradeoff between efficiency and equity, where equity may be defined, for example, as an acceptable share in the regional investment and production program for each country or as an acceptable effect on each country's balance of payments.

The study proceeded in several phases. First, a planning model was formulated that captured the most essential features of the fertilizer sector in the five countries, of fertilizer production processes to be considered for further study, and of the world market for fertilizers. The model was designed to analyze the possibility of improvements in the operation of the existing fertilizer sector, as well as to appraise future investment strategies. The initial model formulation provided the starting point for the design of a questionnaire that served as a guideline for local sector specialists in collecting country-specific data and for industry experts from the World Bank in collecting international data.

The analytical phase in the study began following a workshop in Lima, Peru, where the data base was discussed. As stated before, the usual objective of an investment analysis that employs the planning method under discussion here is the identification of a sectoral investment program that meets specified market requirements at minimum cost. This objective may make sense in a national context. For the identification of an efficient and equitable investment program in a multicountry context, it did not appear the most desirable starting point, because all the countries involved had already drawn up national plans for the expansion of the industry. To design an analysis of a regional investment plan as if these national plans did not exist, and as if efficiency criteria alone would be sufficient to persuade governments to abandon national plans that might be at variance with regional cost minimization, was clearly unrealistic and was likely to leave the negotiators with an unmanageable task.

It was therefore decided to adopt a different approach initially. The national plans of the five countries were taken as given, as far as project scale, product mix, and location were concerned, and the parts of the planning model that would normally specify a wide range of choice in these regards were correspondingly modified. In total, ten new project complexes are currently under consideration: two in Bolivia, two in Colombia, one in Ecuador, three in Peru, and two in Venezuela. In addition, there is a Bolivian project, a large ammonia and urea plant, which is entirely dependent on an export agreement with neighboring Brazil. In this report, this project has been ignored, as it has no relevance for the Andean market. One existing plant in Peru, near Cuzco, requires investments to continue operation. The model was used to compute the implications of the earliest feasible implementation of all national plans, under restrictive but more realistic assumptions regarding the scope for exports to world markets.

As could have been expected, the implications of this strategy are quite alarming. The total discounted cost of meeting Andean fertilizer requirements over the period 1981–92, net of export revenues, amounts to approximately $3.1 billion under the national plans. Minimal intraregional trade takes place, and the capacity utilization of many plants is low, particularly in the early years of the planning period.[1]

As a first step toward determining the composition of a more efficient investment program, the restrictions imposed on the planning model were relaxed with respect to the timing of implementation of the otherwise fully defined projects. No longer was it assumed that all projects were to be implemented as soon as possible. Instead, the model was used to determine the least-cost timing for capacity expansion, including the possibility of postponing inplementation beyond 1989, that is, beyond the planning horizon of the study. The result indicates that, out of the ten possible projects, only three should be implemented during the planning period. The total discounted cost for this strategy amounts to $2.67 billion, which is 15 percent below the total cost of implementation of present national plans. Postponement of specific projects alone, there-

---

1. This applies to nitrogenous fertilizers; the region remains a deficit area for phosphate and potash.

fore, can lead to substantial cost savings to the region. Closer inspection of the composition of the investment program, however, revealed that this scenario is unlikely to be considered as acceptable to all five countries because under it neither Bolivia nor Ecuador would host an Andean project.

The model was therefore used to formulate the least-cost investment strategy from among the complete set of national projects, but under the condition that all countries would have at least one project by the end of the planning period. The resulting investment program was composed of five projects, one in each country. Although this investment scenario involves a more even distribution of projects over the countries, and can thus be expected to be a better basis for negotiations, it should be pointed out that there is a minor tradeoff between efficiency and acceptability, in the sense that the discounted cost of this scenario is $2.68 billion, or $10 million more than the previous scenario. This difference is well within the margin of error of the basic data and assumptions. Clearly, implementation of this more acceptable strategy would be more efficient than the realization of current national plans. A limited amount of sensitivity analysis was also carried out, which will be discussed in chapter 9.

The Andean Common Market Secretariat drew up a proposal for a coordinated investment strategy for the fertilizer industry, which was submitted for consideration by the governments of the Andean countries. During early 1980, staff from the secretariat visited the five countries to obtain initial reactions to the proposal and to consult on the most appropriate instruments to implement the development strategy for the fertilizer industry formulated by the secretariat. On the basis of the comments received, which included revisions of demand forecasts, changes in the characteristics of some projects under consideration, modification of some local raw material prices, and a reevaluation of the scope for improvements in capacity utilization in Peru and Venezuela, the model was rerun for all scenarios included in the analysis. Using the model to evaluate these changes, the secretariat was able to circulate a revised report to the countries in May 1980, and a technical meeting of government experts was planned for June. This meeting had to be rescheduled four times, because of differences of opinion within the secretariat with respect to the most desirable strategy to obtain approval of the proposal and because one member country (Venezuela) did not consider itself prepared to participate in detailed discussions. Eventually, staff from the secretariat visited the countries once more to provide further information on the nature of the proposed fertilizer sector strategy. In December 1980 the ministers of industry of the five countries met in Lima and formulated a position on the proposal. Underlining the strategic importance of fertilizers to the economies of the Andean Group and recognizing the potential gains to be derived from a coordinated investment strategy, they nevertheless declined to approve detailed assignments of projects by country, as contained in the proposal. Instead, the secretariat was requested to continue to analyze the scope for a coordinated development of the industry, to produce annually a report that reviews the situation in the sector, and to make nonbinding recommendations for future developments, not only for investment and production, but also for distribution and commercialization of fertilizers. At the same time, a decision was made to lower the common external tariff on fertilizers and raw materials from 10 percent and 5 percent, respectively, to a general level of 3 percent, in accordance with the policy in the region toward trade liberalization.

A realistic assessment of the situation should not render this outcome surprising. First, the proposal that emerged from the analysis was in many respects more detailed and comprehensive than any national development plan in the five countries. Under such circumstances, one must expect an initial reluctance on the part of the countries to agree to detailed recommendations. Second, the five countries are in peculiarly different circumstances as far as the fertilizer sector is concerned. Bolivia, though rich in natural resources, has a very small domestic market, and any efficient industrial development in the sector is dependent upon the scope for exports. However, because of Bolivia's location, its natural export outlets for products that have high transport cost relative to value are not in its partner countries, but rather in Argentina, Brazil, and Paraguay. An Andean market–based project in Bolivia implies by necessity a sacrifice on the part of the other four countries. Ecuador is in a better position, although in that country too the small domestic market means that transport and distribution costs will be higher than in partner countries. It is unlikely that Ecuador has a comparative advantage to Colombia, Peru, and Venezuela in the production of nitrogenous fertilizers, and an Andean project located in Ecuador may not show as good a rate of return. Moreover, it will be dependent upon continued access to the markets of neighboring countries. Peru has a major advantage in phosphate production because it has the largest known deposits of phosphate rock in South America. From Peru's point of view, it can be argued that an Andean fertilizer agreement is not essential to the development of its phosphate industry, which could very well export to world markets.[2] Simi-

---

2. In effect, Peru is among a few countries, including the Arab Republic of Egypt, Mexico, Morocco, and the United States, upon which adequate world supply of phosphate rock will be dependent until new resources are found.

larly, but less important, the scope for potash production in Peru could be argued to be comparable to that of phosphate. An agreement on phosphate and potash may well turn out to be more important to Bolivia, Colombia, Ecuador, and Venezuela than to Peru. To the extent the resource base in Colombia is known, it is clear that this country will remain dependent in part on imports. Unless firm agreement can be reached on future supply prices and such prices are lower than projected world market prices, it is of obvious advantage to Colombia to keep its options open rather than to agree to stringent Andean sources of supply. Finally, Venezuela's plan for fertilizer production, particularly in nitrogen, are so ambitious that any realistic level of exports to the Andean Group countries is marginal to the commercial success of the new projects, particularly if all other nitrogenous fertilizer projects in the region are implemented.

Transport cost and a competitive rather than complementary resource base, in particular for nitrogenous fertilizers, constitute major obstacles to efficient specialization among the five countries in the fertilizer sector. From the analysis that was carried out it is clear that substantial benefits are to be derived from coordination. This policy would lead to increased trade in fertilizer material among the countries. However, it should at the same time be realized that most of the benefits derive from a more efficient timing of project implementation. To the extent that the analysis has contributed to a better understanding of this aspect and continued reviews of future development could achieve a similar objective, a new role for the Andean Common Market Secretariat may have been identified that could be more lasting than attempts at stringent project assignments.

In the meantime, at the World Bank, it was decided to use the Andean model to carry out additional analysis, using the model as a project design tool. To obtain a benchmark for the comparison of the various investment scenarios, the least-cost investment program was determined, unhampered by constraints relating to current national plans. The results are reported in chapter 10.

The Organization of the Case Study

Following this introduction and summary, a chapter will be devoted to a brief description of the fertilizer sector in each country, and of the Andean Common Market as a whole. Next, in chapter 8, a statement of the model and the corresponding set specification will be given; in the appendix, a computer-readable data base will be provided on the basis of which all results achieved in this study can be reproduced. This chapter will also include an overview of the scenarios evaluated with the model.

Chapters 9 and 10 describe the results. The first chapter will focus on the results achieved in collaboration with the staff of the Andean secretariat, culminating in the proposal for a coordinated investment strategy submitted to the member governments. Chapter 10 reports upon further experiments conducted with the model at the World Bank. These generally take less account of the political realities in the Andean region and should therefore not be seen as "improvements" over the Andean proposals. They are meant in the first place to evaluate the importance of the constraints on project size on the distribution of projects in the region. Chapter 11 provides some general conclusions.

7

The Empirical Background

THE ANDEAN COMMON MARKET (ACM) was established in 1969 with the signing of the Cartagena Agreement by the governments of Bolivia, Chile, Colombia, Ecuador, and Peru. Venezuela joined the Andean Group in 1973, and Chile withdrew in 1976.

The combined population of the ACM in 1980 was around 73 million people, while the gross "regional" product was about $116 billion. In comparison, Brazil's population is one-and-a-half times as large and its gross national product (GNP) more than double that of the ACM countries combined. Both in population and GNP, the ACM is roughly comparable to Mexico.

The aggregate figures conceal substantial differences among the countries in the group, as measured by size of population, level of development, and growth performance. In table 7-1, several key indicators are given by country. Compared with Colombia, Peru, and Venezuela, Bolivia and Ecuador are small countries, both in population and GNP. However, income per capita in Ecuador has surpassed that of Colombia and is growing at an annual rate that is substantially higher than that in any of its partner countries, chiefly because of oil exports.

The ACM aims at the gradual abolition of all barriers to intraregional trade; this process is scheduled to be completed by 1985. Moreover, a common external tariff is to be established on all imports from abroad, but, because of disagreements among the member countries regarding the level and structure of the common external tariff, the original time schedules had to be abandoned, and it is unclear at this time whether and when agreement can be reached. In addition to measures directly ori-

Table 7-1. *Key Indicators for the ACM Countries*

Country	GNP at market prices		Per capita GNP at market prices		Population	
	Total, 1980 (millions of U.S. dollars)	*Average annual real growth, 1970–79 (percent)*	*Total, 1980 (U.S. dollars)*	*Average annual real growth, 1970–79 (percent)*	*Total, 1980 (millions)*	*Average annual growth, 1970–79 (percent)*
Bolivia	3,190	4.9	570	2.3	5.6	2.6
Colombia	31,570	6.0	1,180	3.7	26.7	2.3
Ecuador	10,230	8.7	1,220	5.4	8.4	3.3
Peru	16,470	2.9	930	0.2	17.6	2.7
Venezuela	54,220	6.1	3,630	2.7	14.9	3.4
Total or average	115,680	5.8	1,580	3.0	73.2	2.8

Source: World Bank Atlas, 1981 (1980 figures are provisional).

ented to trade, the ACM has initiated a series of sectoral programming exercises that are designed to lead to regionally coordinated investment, production, and trade policies for specific industrial subsectors. The original list of subsectors includes automobiles, metalworking, petrochemicals, steel, fertilizers, pharmochemicals, and telephone-related electronic equipment; agreement has been reached on the first three sectors.[1]

Trade within the ACM has increased very rapidly, from $96 million in 1969 to $873 million in 1977, or by an average annual rate of 32 percent. During the same period, overall exports of the Andean countries grew by just over 17 percent. Although the share of intraregional trade in total trade increased, from just 2 percent to 5.5 percent, exports to world markets continue to predominate. As far as the composition of intraregional exports is concerned, it is primarily exports of manufactured goods and of petroleum and derivatives that explain the rapid growth over the past decade, the former growing at 31.5 percent a year and the latter at 37 percent. Together, these categories account for 80 percent of intraregional trade.[2]

1. Venezuela was not a member of the ACM when the metalworking sectoral agreement was approved (1972); negotiations have taken place, and with Decision 146 Venezuela joined the agreement.
2. Data are from "Andean Group," *Newsbulletin* (Lima, Peru) no. 21 (June 1979).

The Fertilizer Sector in the Andean Common Market Countries

On the basis of a questionnaire designed for this study, country-specific consultants established a comparable data base on the fertilizer sectors of the five Andean countries.[3] This section gives a summary of their findings; a more systematic presentation of the data is provided in the next chapter.[4]

Demand

Demand for fertilizer nutrients has been growing steadily in the Andean region. From 1970 to 1975, for the region as a whole, demand increased at an annual rate of 8.5 percent. For the period 1976–82 a distinctly lower annual rate of growth of demand was estimated: 5.8 percent for the region. This lower annual rate of growth is mainly due to a more or less stagnating demand for fertilizer nutrients in Venezuela.

For the rest of the 1980s the demand for fertilizers is projected to increase more rapidly than during 1976–82: at an annual rate of growth of 7.6 percent. At that rate total consumption of fertilizer nutrients in the Andean region would reach a level of nearly 2 million metric tons by 1991.

The individual country estimates and projections of demand and the aggregate picture for the Andean region are given in table 7-2. For the countries with the lowest level of fertilizer consumption at the present time, Bolivia and Ecuador, demand is projected to grow faster: by 18.9 and 9.8 percent annually, respectively. In Venezuela, the largest user, demand for fertilizer is expected to grow considerably faster than in the recent past: by 8.6 percent annually. In the other countries the annual rate of growth of demand will be lower: 6.0 and 6.5 percent in Colombia and Peru, respectively.

The total consumption of fertilizers in the Andean region, as expressed in terms of the three major plant nutrients—N (nitrogen), P (phosphate), and K (potash)—in 1976 amounted to about 700,000 tons; approxi-

---

3. The consultants involved were Alfonso Avilés (Ecuador), Alberto Gómez (Colombia), Henry Harman (Peru), Oscar Lovera (Venezuela), and Hugo Ossío (Bolivia).

4. Readers unfamiliar with some of the technical terminology relating to fertilizers and production processes may wish to consult vol. 2 in this series: Armeane Choksi, Alexander Meeraus, and Ardy Stoutjesdijk, *The Planning of Investment Programs in the Fertilizer Industry* (Baltimore, Md.: Johns Hopkins University Press, 1980).

Table 7-2. *Demand for the Three Major Fertilizer Nutrients in the ACM Countries, 1976, 1982, and 1991*

Country and nutrient	Amount (thousands of metric tons)			Average annual growth (percent)	
	1976	*1982*	*1991*	*1976–82*	*1982–91*
Bolivia					
N	1	3	23	18.0	26.9
P	2	5	15	17.6	12.5
K	—	—	—	—	—
Total	3	8	38	17.7	18.9
Colombia					
N	108	189	324	9.7	6.2
P	69	134	232	11.7	6.3
K	42	84	132	12.3	5.1
Total	219	407	688	10.9	6.0
Ecuador					
N	20	36	83	10.3	9.7
P	17	29	67	9.5	9.6
K	10	17	40	9.7	9.8
Total	47	82	190	9.7	9.8
Peru					
N	101	123	187	3.4	4.7
P	17	34	79	12.0	10.0
K	13	20	47	7.5	9.9
Total	131	177	313	5.2	6.5
Venezuela					
N	133	138	283	1.0	8.4
P	95	102	263	1.1	11.1
K	71	65	118	−1.4	6.8
Total	299	305	664	0.3	8.6
All ACM *countries*					
N	363	489	900	5.1	7.0
P	200	304	656	7.2	8.9
K	136	187	337	5.4	6.8
Total	699	980	1,893	5.8	7.6

Note: N signifies nitrogen; P signifies phosphate; and K signifies potash.

mately one-half of this total was used in the form of N, 30 percent as P, and the remaining 20 percent as K. Fertilizer use in Bolivia is negligible at the present time, and in Ecuador it is very low, less than 7 percent of the total. Venezuela is the largest user of fertilizer (43 percent of the total); Colombia is next (31 percent), followed by Peru (19 percent). A large proportion of total demand in each country is for a variety of multinutrient fertilizers, that is, fertilizer granules that contain specific proportions of some or all of the major nutrients (referred to as NPK).

To give these projections some perspective, they may be compared with projections made by the World Bank, in an internal document, for the period 1977–88. In the case of nitrogen, consumption in all developing countries taken together is projected to increase at an annual rate of 8.2 percent; in Latin America alone, the corresponding figure is 8.9 percent. Comparing these growth rates to those in table 7-2, it appears that the two countries which start from a very low base, Bolivia and Ecuador, have higher demand growth rates, while Venezuela corresponds more or less to the average. Both Peru's and Colombia's demand projections appear on the low side. In the case of phosphate, demand in the developing countries in total, and in Latin America alone, is projected to grow at 8.1 percent a year. With the exception of Bolivia, all the ACM countries project demand to grow at a somewhat higher annual rate. Finally, for potash, the World Bank demand projections amount to 8.7 percent a year for all developing countries and 9.2 percent a year for Latin America. This is not much different from our demand projection for Peru, but higher than those for Colombia and Venezuela. It is much higher than our demand projection for Ecuador where even a decrease in the demand for potash is projected. No potassic fertilizer is expected to be consumed in Bolivia.

Part of the demand for fertilizer nutrients needs to be met by specific fertilizer types for agronomic reasons. This applies to one straight fertilizer, ammonium sulfate; moreover, each country uses specific fertilizer mixes, containing two or three nutrients. The proportion of demand to be met by such fertilizers in each country has been specified in the data used for the model. The complete data input set in chapter 8 gives detailed information.

It should be noted that the individual country projections of demand for fertilizers were extensively discussed at two workshops in Lima, Peru, and reflect a broad consensus among the participants, who represented a range of interests associated with the fertilizer sector. The projections in table 7-2 are given by country; the actual analysis was done on the basis of projected demand levels by regions within countries, eighteen for ACM in total; these more detailed projections are given in the next chapter.

Supply

All countries in the ACM, with the exception of Bolivia, have fertilizer production facilities. In net terms, the capacity to produce fertilizer nutrients in the ACM amounts to 934,600 tons annually, or over 34 percent more than the demand in 1976.[5] This figure is based on the assumption that all existing production facilities can produce during 330 days of operation at 90 percent of design capacity. Most of the theoretical excess capacity is in nitrogen, where a domestic demand level of 363,000 tons compares with a capacity to produce 665,000 tons. For phosphates, the situation is more balanced, while for potash, there is a shortage of capacity.

In actual operation, however, only a few of the existing production facilities work anywhere near to full capacity, and instead of having substantial overcapacity, or production surpluses for export outside the region, the ACM needs to *import* fertilizer material from abroad to meet demand. Precise production figures for a recent year in Venezuela are not available, although it is known that rates of capacity utilization in that country are very low. For the other countries, production estimates are available for 1976, and they reveal that the rate of capacity utilization in that year was 68 percent in Peru, 47 percent in Colombia, and 41 percent in Ecuador, assuming full capacity utilization to be reached whenever plants are operated for 330 days per year and at 90 percent of design capacity. In Venezuela, the overall rate of capacity utilization in that year was almost certainly lower, perhaps as low as 30 percent. Much of the overcapacity in the region is in NPK plants, that is, those plants that produce multinutrient fertilizers.

The individual country capacities and the total for the Andean region can be found in table 7-3, by major nutrient. These capacities refer to the year 1976, but they are the same for 1982.

Expansion Plans

Each of the ACM member countries has investment plans for fertilizer capacity expansion. Peru has a very favorable raw material situation for phosphate and potash production, at Bayovar, in the north, and major projects are under consideration. These involve the production of sul-

---

5. Multinutrient fertilizers sometimes require other fertilizers for their production. To the extent this is the case, counting production capacities for both will overstate the relevant supply capacity. For that reason, a net concept is used here.

Table 7-3. *Annual Capacities for Production of the Three Major Fertilizer Nutrients in the ACM Countries, 1976*
(thousands of metric tons)

Country	Amount
Bolivia	
N	—
P	—
K	—
Total	—
Colombia	
N	147.6
P	41.0
K	34.1
Total	222.7
Ecuador	
N	2.9
P	13.3
K	4.3
Total	20.5
Peru	
N	88.8
P	9.6
K	7.1
Total	105.5
Venezuela	
N	426.2
P	150.8
K	9.1
Total	586.1
All ACM countries	
N	665.4
P	214.6
K	54.6
Total	934.6

furic and phosphoric acid, triple superphosphate (TSP), and diammonium phosphate (DAP); the production of potassium chloride; and the production of ammonia and urea. Table 7-4 gives the design capacities for the different productive units and the projected year of operation. No other projects are being planned in Peru. However, to maintain the current production capacity of Cachimayo, near Cuzco in the south, where

Table 7-4. *Production Capacity of Fertilizer Projects*
under Consideration at Bayovar, Peru

Project	Metric tons a day	Metric tons a year[a]
Project complex 1		
Sulfuric acid	2,000	561,000
Phosphoric acid	1,334	374,200
Triple superphosphate (TSP)	1,076	301,800
Diammonium phosphate (DAP)	636	178,400
Project complex 2		
Potassium chloride	303	85,000
Project complex 3		
Ammonia	651	182,600
Urea	870	244,000

a. Assuming a rate of capacity utilization of 85 percent for 330 days a year.

nitrogenous fertilizer is produced on the basis of the electrolysis of water, electrolyzers will have to be replaced soon. Moreover, power supply would need to be increased at the local hydroelectric facility. The company concerned requires a financial participation by the fertilizer plant of $25 million in the additional investment cost needed.

In Colombia, plans exist to establish an ammonia and urea complex and a sulfuric and phosphoric acid and TSP complex at La Dorada, close to Bogota. The ammonia plant is projected to have a capacity of 1,000 metric tons a day, permitting urea production at the rate of over 1,600 tons a day. The plant will, of course, be based on natural gas from the region. The TSP plant will have a capacity of 880 metric tons a day.

A project is under consideration in Ecuador, most likely to be located at Puerto Bolivar, to produce ammonia and urea, based on locally available natural gas. The projected size of the productive units are 435 metric tons a day for the ammonia unit and 750 metric tons a day for the urea unit.

There are three fertilizer projects in Bolivia, two of which are in the nitrogenous fertilizer sector and one of which is to produce phosphatic fertilizer. First, a project under the name of Planta Pequeña is under consideration at Palmasola, 80 kilometers south of Santa Cruz, to produce 160 tons a day of ammonia and 250 tons a day of urea, on the basis of locally available natural gas. Assuming 85 percent capacity utilization, as in all new projects in this study, for 330 days a year gives an estimated annual production at this plant of 45,000 tons of ammonia and 70,000 tons of urea. A substantial part of the output of urea is expected to be exported to Paraguay and Argentina, particularly in the early years of the planning period.

Second, a project is under study to be located near the city of Potosi to produce granular triple superphosphate. Phosphate rock is to be imported, and with locally available sulfuric acid (a by-product from a nearby tin smelter), phosphoric acid will be produced in a productive unit with a planned capacity of 125 metric tons a day. The granular triple superphosphate unit, also to be established, will have a capacity of 170 metric tons a day. This is sufficient to produce annually 48,000 tons of TSP, requiring 35,000 tons of phosphoric acid. Eighty percent of the plant's output of TSP is projected to be exported.

The third and by far the most ambitious project in Bolivia is the so-called Planta Grande to produce 542 tons a day of ammonia and 942 tons a day of urea, based on natural gas. It is to be located near Puerto Suarez. Virtually the entire output of this plant is supposed to be exported to Brazil, but so far no agreement has been reached, partly because Brazil has been unwilling to provide investment capital.

Two expansion projects are under consideration in Venezuela, one to be located at Punta Caiman for the production of NPK, DAP, and TSP and the other at Caripito, to produce ammonia and urea, based upon the reserves of natural gas of the Orinoco. The capacities and productive units contemplated for these two projects are given in table 7-5. Punta Caiman is planned to obtain its ammonia from El Tablazo and its potash

Table 7-5. *Production Capacity of Fertilizer Expansion Projects in Venezuela*

Project and type	Metric tons a day	Metric tons a year[a]
Punta Caiman		
Phosphoric acid	830	232,900
Sulfuric acid	1,245	349,350
NPK (20-18-10)	2,272	637,500
DAP	561	157,361[b]
TSP	242	68,162[c]
Caripito		
Ammonia	1,500	445,000
Urea	1,030	306,000

a. Assuming a rate of capacity utilization of 85 percent for 330 days a year.
b. Of which 108,375 is needed for NPK production.
c. Of which 63,750 is needed for NPK production.

requirements through imports from abroad. Phosphate rock is obtained from the Reicito mines and by imports. At Caripito urea production at the planned level requires only 177,500 metric tons of ammonia a year. The surplus can either be sold domestically or exported.

Recapitulation

Table 7-6 presents estimates of demand and attainable supply of fertilizer nutrients in the ACM countries for 1976, 1982, and 1991. If part of the final output in a fertilizer complex is destined for multinutrient fertilizer production, total available supply capacity has been adjusted so as to avoid double counting. For our analysis we make a distinction between nitrogenous fertilizers, phosphate fertilizers, and potash. In addition, we consider only final products.[6]

In the case of nitrogenous fertilizers, the Andean Common Market as a whole, as well as the larger consumers of the member countries, could have been self-sufficient in 1976, if only capacity utilization had been higher. This situation was virtually unchanged in 1982; the Andean region as well as Venezuela could have been self-sufficient. For all the other countries attainable supply of nitrogenous fertilizers fell short of estimated demand. According to the individual national plans in 1991 attainable supply will be larger than estimated demand in each member country. For the Andean region as a whole the projected oversupply amounts to some 63 percent of projected regional demand. This overage makes clear that in the case of nitrogenous fertilizers the identification of export markets outside the Andean countries plays an important role in the current capacity expansion plans. This holds in particular for Venezuela where planned capacity of nitrogenous fertilizers is almost triple the projected demand for it in 1991.

In the case of phosphatic fertilizers the situation appears to be developing not much differently. For all countries a rapid increase in the use of phosphatic fertilizers is projected. In three countries—Colombia, Peru, and Venezuela—a very substantial increase in production capacity for phosphates is planned. In Colombia sufficient phosphate rock deposits seem to be present to justify the planned increase in capacity by 300 percent. In Peru, the planned capacity expansion is based on the Bayovar phosphate rock deposits. In Venezuela, phosphatic fertilizer production

---

6. This is correct for final products only, as insufficient capacity exists currently for intermediate products such as ammonia and phosphoric acid.

Table 7-6. *Demand for and Attainable Supply of the Three Major Fertilizer Nutrients in the ACM Countries, 1976, 1982, and 1991*
(thousands of metric tons)

Nutrient, by country	Demand			Attainable supply		
	1976	1982	1991	1976	1982	1991
Bolivia						
N	1	3	23	—	—	32
P	2	5	15	—	—	22
K	—	—	—	—	—	—
Total	3	8	38	—	—	54
Colombia						
N	108	189	324	148	148	367
P	69	134	232	41	41	164
K	42	84	132	34	34	44
Total	219	407	688	223	223	575
Ecuador						
N	20	36	83	3	3	101
P	17	29	67	13	13	16
K	10	17	40	4	4	6
Total	47	82	190	20	20	123
Peru						
N	101	123	187	89	89	233
P	17	34	79	10	10	230
K	13	20	47	7	7	58
Total	131	177	313	106	106	521
Venezuela						
N	133	138	283	426	426	729
P	95	102	263	151	151	373
K	71	65	118	9	9	75
Total	299	305	664	586	586	1,177
All ACM *countries*						
N	363	489	900	665	665	1,463
P	200	304	656	215	215	807
K	136	187	337	55	55	184
Total	699	980	1,893	935	935	2,454

will continue to be partly based on local rock complemented by imported rock. Overall, the Andean Common Market is projected to have a surplus of some 150,000 tons of phosphate nutrient production capacity by 1991, if all current plans are fully implemented.

Potash is known to exist in commercially exploitable form in Peru only. All other planned production capacity increases, as in Venezuela, are in the form of NPKs derived from imported potash. The current production plans in Peru and Venezuela notwithstanding, a very considerable deficit in production capacity of potassic fertilizer is projected to persist in the Andean region.

8

The Andean Fertilizer Model

AGAINST the empirical background provided in chapter 7, the prime objective of the case study is to formulate an investment, production, and trade strategy for the Andean region's fertilizer sector that is not only more efficient than implementation of the countries' current national plans, but also politically acceptable to each country. For that purpose, a planning model was formulated to generate efficient investment strategies, given particular sets of assumptions, and, more important in the Andean context, to quantify the implications of predetermined investment strategies. Structurally, the model corresponds closely to the dynamic multicountry process model developed in chapter 4. It was already mentioned in chapter 6 that the case study in fact consists of two parts. The first part relates to the investment strategies considered relevant by the Andean Common Market Secretariat. The second part of the study was conducted at the World Bank and contains some further experiments with the model, in particular with respect to the introduction of acceptability constraints.

Main Planning Problems and Approach

In the initial Andean application it was considered politically more expedient to take existing national investment projects in the fertilizer industry as a starting point for the analysis. As was discussed in the previous chapter, rapid implementation of all these projects, as formulated, would lead to substantial overcapacity in the region for nitrogenous fertilizer and deficits for phosphate and potash. Moreover, this strategy allows for very little intraregional trade and is based on very optimistic expectations with regard to exports of urea to world markets. The model, therefore, was used to demonstrate that substantial efficiency gains can be made by assuming gradually increasing willingness on the part of the countries to depart from national plans. In this approach, the search for *the* most efficient strategy assumes lesser importance, as it is likely that this strategy departs so much from current national plans as to be politically unacceptable.[1]

The first problem was to determine the implications of implementation of all current national plans. Given existing capacity and taking as given the size, location, and product mix of all firm projects, what are the cost implications of establishing these projects at the earliest possible date (1984–86)? We have assumed that plants cannot export more than 30 percent of production, with the exception of the plants at Palmasola and El Tablazo in Venezuela, which are allowed to export up to 70 percent of their capacities.[2] A second possible—though unlikely—scenario is that no capacity expansion occurs in the Andean fertilizer sector over the next decade and that all fertilizer demand is met by production in existing fertilizer plants and by imports.

Having determined the implications of these two strategies, which can be considered extreme options that the countries may decide to adopt, the next step was to determine a strategy that could for all practical purposes be considered the most efficient politically acceptable production strategy. It was decided that the most that would be attainable is an agreement whereby the countries are willing to consider the timing of project implementation as open to negotiation, including the possibility of postponement beyond the planning horizon of the study (1989). In this scenario, therefore, only efficient projects would be implemented; the Andean secretariat considers this the least-cost *attainable* investment strategy.[3] In this context, for a project to be called "effi-

---

1. However, see chapter 9 for an evaluation of an economically optimal strategy.

2. The large project in Bolivia at Puerto Suarez is entirely dependent on exports to Brazil. As it is, therefore, independent of the Andean Common Market, it has been ignored in most of the analysis.

3. Another option could be considered. One may argue that it may be easier to reach agreement if the possibility of alternative timing is combined with that of alternative sizing of projects. A country may be more inclined to cooperate if its original national project is modified rather than eliminated altogether from the regional investment program. However, the secretariat felt that the inclusion of this possibility would open a Pandora's box and would seriously hamper the negotiation phase. It was therefore not considered in the joint study, but during the subsequent analysis at the World Bank this option was analyzed.

cient" it suffices to have a cost-reducing impact on total cost as compared to imports or all other projects.

Within the boundaries delineated by these three strategies, it is possible to identify a very large number of variants. For example, one can explicitly vary the timing of individual projects in the program and determine the cost implications. Alternatively, one can add a specific project hitherto rejected as inefficient and determine its impact on total regional costs. Such experimentation permits the estimation of the net costs to the region of any specific constraint on the composition of the investment program.

Model Development and Set Specification

While the model formulated to analyze the scope for and benefits of project cooperation in the Andean region follows the structure of the dynamic capacity expansion model in chapter 4, several problem-specific modifications had to be made. The most important of these are the different treatment of capacity expansion, the introduction of working capital, and the use of country- and plant-specific export constraints. In describing the model, we will elaborate on these modifications.

Demand

We have divided the Andean Common Market into eighteen demand regions, each with a designated marketing center. Map 1 indicates the location of each of the marketing centers, which serve as a reference point for the determination of transport cost of final products from plants and ports. Map 2 shows the location of existing and proposed plants. A complete listing of the regions, marketing centers, and projects appears in the appendix.

In table 7-2 we presented the projected requirements of fertilizer nutrients, nitrogen (N), phosphate (P), and potash (K), for the years 1982 and 1991; the model incorporated projections for the intervening years 1985 and 1988 as well. Although the model was formulated to permit nutrient requirements to be met at lowest cost, leaving open the choice of fertilizer product, minimum levels of ammonium sulfate requirements need to be met. For the details of these projections the interested reader is referred to the complete data input presented in the appendix.

The demand requirements can be met by regional production and by imports from outside the Andean Common Market. However, several

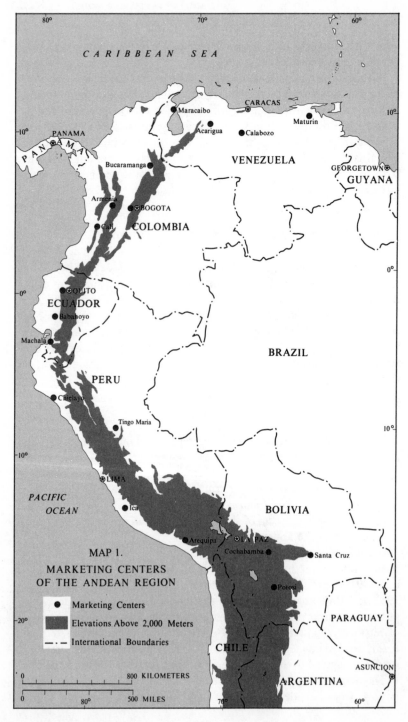

MAP 1.
MARKETING CENTERS
OF THE ANDEAN REGION

● Marketing Centers

■ Elevations Above 2,000 Meters

─ · ─ International Boundaries

0   800 KILOMETERS

0   80°   500 MILES

132

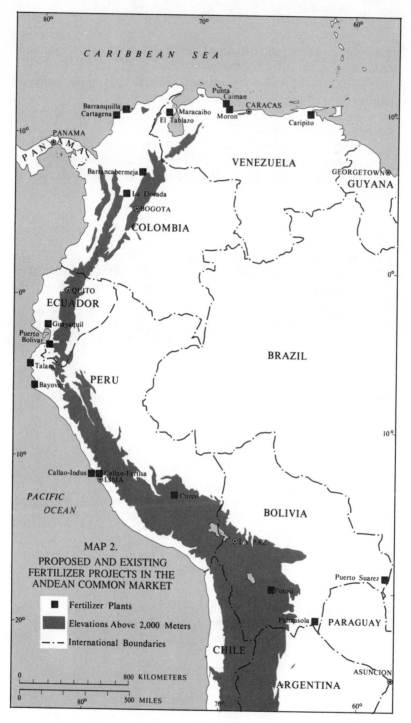

MAP 2.
PROPOSED AND EXISTING
FERTILIZER PROJECTS IN THE
ANDEAN COMMON MARKET

■ Fertilizer Plants

▨ Elevations Above 2,000 Meters

–·– International Boundaries

| 0 | | | | 800 KILOMETERS |

| 0 | | 80° | | 500 MILES |

regionally produced fertilizers (compounds and mixes) are not normally traded among countries in the region.

To formulate the demand constraints, we need to introduce some set notation.

CF = set of final products
  = urea, ammonium nitrate, ammonium sulfate, single superphosphate, triple superphosphate (TSP), potassium chloride, diammonium phosphate (DAP), and six different compounds and mixes
CQ = set of major nutrients
  = nitrogen (N), phosphate (P), and potash (K)
I = set of plant sites (see table 8-1)
J = set of marketing centers (see map 1)
MC = set of c, i, j combinations representing final products and their origin and destinations that are permissible for intraregional trade
T = set of time periods
  = 1981–83, 1984–86, 1987–89, and 1990–92.

Table 8-1. *Locations and Names of Fertilizer Plants in the Model*

Country	Site	Name
Bolivia	Palmasola	Planta Pequena
	Puerto Suarez	Planta Grande
	Potosi	ENAF
Colombia	Baranquilla	Monomeros
	Cartagena	Abocol
	Barrancabermeja	Ferticol
	La Dorada	La Dorada
Ecuador	Guayaquil	Fertisa
	Puerto Bolivar	CEPE
Peru	Callao-Fertisa	Fertisa
	Cuzco	Cachimayo
	Talara	Pertofern
	Callao-Indus	Indus
	Bayovar	Bayovar
Venezuela	Moron	IVP
	Punta Caiman	Pedevesa
	Caripito	IVP
	El Tablazo	Nitroven

Mathematically, the demand constraints can now be specified as follows.

MATERIAL BALANCE CONSTRAINTS ON DEMAND

$$(8.1) \qquad \sum_{c \in CF} \alpha_{cc'} \left[\sum_{i \in I} x_{cijt} \Big|_{(c,i,j) \in MC} \right.$$

$$\begin{bmatrix} Nutrient \\ content \end{bmatrix} \begin{bmatrix} Shipments\ of\ final \\ products\ produced \\ within\ the\ region \end{bmatrix} \begin{bmatrix} Regionally \\ traded\ to \\ the\ extent \\ allowed \end{bmatrix}$$

$$\left. + v_{cjt} \right] \geq d_{c'jt} \qquad\qquad \begin{matrix} c' \in CQ \\ j \in J \\ t \in T \end{matrix}$$

$$+ \begin{bmatrix} Imports \\ from \\ outside \\ the\ region \end{bmatrix} \geq \begin{bmatrix} Market \\ require- \\ ments\ in \\ nutrients \end{bmatrix} \begin{bmatrix} For\ each\ nutrient \\ for\ each\ marketing \\ center \\ for\ each\ time\ period \end{bmatrix}$$

where

$$x_{cijt} \Big|_{(c,i,j) \in MC}$$

is a new notation that restricts the shipment possibility x_{cijt} to the combination of products, producing sites, and marketing regions for which it is allowed, and where

$\alpha_{cc'}$ = nutrient content of each final product (see table 8-2)
x_{cijt} = shipments of final product c from plant i to marketing center j in time period t
v_{cjt} = import of final product c to marketing center j in time period t
$d_{c'jt}$ = demand requirements of nutrient c' in marketing center j in time period t.

MATERIAL BALANCE CONSTRAINTS ON AMMONIUM SULFATE
CONSUMPTION

As mentioned before, minimum levels of ammonium sulfate requirements need to be met in all countries.

$$(8.2) \qquad \sum_{i \in I} x_{cijt} + v_{cjt} \geq d_{jt} \qquad\qquad \begin{matrix} c = \text{ammonium sulfate} \\ j \in J \\ t \in T \end{matrix}$$

Table 8-2. *Nutrient Content of Final Products*
(percent)

Product	Nitrogen (N)	Phosphate (P)	Potash (K)
Ammonium nitrate	33	—	—
Ammonium sulfate	20.5	—	—
Diammonium phosphate (DAP)	18	46	—
Potassium chloride	—	—	60
Single superphosphate (SSP)	—	20	—
Triple superphosphate (TSP)	—	46	—
Urea	46	—	—
Compound 1	20	18	10
Compound 2	13	13	20
Compound 3	15	21	10
Compound 4	16	12	12
Compound 5	8	24	12
Compound 6	12	12	12

Supply

We now turn to a mathematical description of the production relationship in the model.

MATERIAL BALANCE CONSTRAINTS ON PRODUCTION

$$(8.3) \qquad \underbrace{\sum_{p \in P} \sum_{g \in G} a_{cp} z_{gpit}}_{} + \left. v_{cit} \right|_{c \in CVI}$$

$$\underbrace{\begin{bmatrix} \textit{Production of intermediate} \\ \textit{and final products, with} \\ \textit{all processes in both old} \\ \textit{and new capacity} \end{bmatrix}}_{} + \underbrace{\begin{bmatrix} \textit{Imports of products} \\ \textit{to the extent} \\ \textit{permitted} \end{bmatrix}}_{}$$

$$+ \sum_{\substack{i' \in I \\ i \neq i}} \left[x_{ci'it} - x_{cii't} \right]_{c \in CIS} + \left. u_{cit} \right|_{c \in CR}$$

$$+ \underbrace{\begin{bmatrix} \textit{Interplant shipments of} \\ \textit{products, to the extent} \\ \textit{permitted} \end{bmatrix}}_{} + \underbrace{\begin{bmatrix} \textit{Local purchases} \\ \textit{of raw material} \end{bmatrix}}_{}$$

$$\geq \left. \sum_{j \in J} x_{cijt} \right|_{(c,i,j) \in MC} + \left. e_{cit} \right|_{c \in CE} \qquad \begin{matrix} c \in C \\ i \in I \\ t \in T \end{matrix}$$

$$\geq \begin{bmatrix} \textit{Shipments of final} \\ \textit{product, including} \\ \textit{intraregional exports} \\ \textit{to the extent} \\ \textit{permitted} \end{bmatrix} + \begin{bmatrix} \textit{Exports to} \\ \textit{world markets} \\ \textit{of all} \\ \textit{exportable} \\ \textit{commodities} \end{bmatrix} \begin{bmatrix} \textit{For all} \\ \textit{commodities,} \\ \textit{plant sites,} \\ \textit{and time} \\ \textit{periods} \end{bmatrix}$$

Expression (8.3) requires the definition of much new notation.

P = set of productive processes

= ammonia, via electrolysis, natural gas, or fuel oil process; nitric acid process; ammonium nitrate process; ammonium sulfate process; urea process; single superphosphate process; triple superphosphate process; single superphosphate process on combination unit; triple superphosphate process on combination unit; phosphoric acid process; sulfuric acid process; diammonium phosphate process; diammonium phosphate on granulator unit; potassium chloride process; and compounding processes for compound 1 through compound 6

G = capacity classification index

= old capacity (that is, installed before planning period) or new capacity

CVI = set of products that can be imported from world markets

= urea, ammonium nitrate, ammonium sulfate, triple superphosphate, potassium chloride, diammonium phosphate, phosphoric acid, ammonia, phosphate rock, and elemental sulfur

CIS = set of intermediate products that can be shipped among plants

= urea, ammonium nitrate, ammonium sulfate, single superphosphate, triple superphosphate, potassium chloride, diammonium phosphate, phosphoric acid, and ammonia

CR = set of raw materials

= electricity, natural gas, fuel oil, phosphate rock, elemental sulfur, sulfuric acid, and brine

CE = set of products that can be exported

= urea, ammonium nitrate, ammonium sulfate, single superphosphate, triple superphosphate, potassium chloride, diammonium phosphate, phosphoric acid, and ammonia

Next, the parameters and variables used in (8.3) will be defined.

a_{cp} = input-output coefficient representing the input (if negative) or output (if positive) of commodity c by process p (see the appendix for a complete listing of the coefficients)

z_{gpit} = the activity level with capacity g, operated with process p at plant i in time period t

$v_{cit}\big|_{c \in CVI}$ = import of commodity c to plant i in time period t for all intermediate products that can be imported

$x_{ci'it}, x_{cii't}$ = shipments of intermediate product c between plants i and i' in time period t

u_{cit} = local purchases of raw material c for plant i in period t

$e_{cit}\big|_{c \in CE}$ = exports to world markets of commodity c from plant i in time period t for all commodities that can be exported

CONSTRAINT ON LOCAL RAW MATERIAL

(8.4) $$u_{cit} \leq 35$$ c = phosphate rock
i = Potosi (Bolivia)
$t \in T$

The availability of phosphate rock at Potosi is limited to 35,000 metric tons a year throughout the planning period.

We now turn to a discussion of the capacity constraints.

CAPACITY CONSTRAINTS ON OLD CAPACITY

(8.5) $$\sum_{p \in P} b_{mp} z_{gpit} \leq k_{mi}$$ $m \in M$
$i \in I$
$t \in T$
g = old

$$\begin{bmatrix} \text{Utilization of existing} \\ \text{capacity of productive} \\ \text{unit m at plant i in} \\ \text{time period t} \end{bmatrix} \leq \begin{bmatrix} \text{Initial} \\ \text{capacity} \end{bmatrix}$$

CAPACITY CONSTRAINTS ON NEW CAPACITY

(8.6) $$\sum_{p \in P} b_{mp} z_{gpit} \leq \sum_{\substack{\tau \in T \\ \tau \leq t}} h_{mit}$$ $m \in M$
$i \in I$
$t \in T$
g = new

$$\begin{bmatrix} \text{Utilization of new} \\ \text{capacity of productive} \\ \text{unit m at plant i in} \\ \text{period t} \end{bmatrix} \leq \begin{bmatrix} \text{Capacity installed} \\ \text{during the planning} \\ \text{period up to time} \\ \text{period t} \end{bmatrix}$$

The establishment of firm data on existing capacities in the Andean region involved a major effort, partly because of the existence of some unusually complex multiproduct plants, such as the one at Moron in Venezuela. Several plants include productive units that can be used to produce different products, giving rise to difficulties in the definition of productive capacity. Finally, halfway through the study, a plant in Colombia was destroyed as a result of an explosion, necessitating a revision of capacity estimates. The estimates of initial capacities used for the purpose of the study are given in table 8-3. Specific complications associated with some of these estimates are described in footnotes to the table.

Capacity expansion may be subject to problem-specific restrictions. Normally, our investment planning models are formulated such that any size productive unit can be constructed up to some specified maximum. In that case, the relevant constraints have the following form.

MAXIMUM CAPACITY EXPANSION CONSTRAINT

(8.7)
$$h_{mit} \leq \bar{h}_{mit} \cdot y_{mit}$$

$$m \in M$$
$$i \in I$$
$$t \in T$$

$$\begin{bmatrix} Capacity \\ expansion \end{bmatrix} \leq \begin{bmatrix} Maximum\ capacity \\ expansion\ times \\ zero\ or\ one \end{bmatrix}$$

INTEGRALITY CONSTRAINT

(8.8)
$$y_{mit} = 0 \quad \text{or} \quad 1$$

The zero-one variable, y_{mit}, is connected with the investment cost that is charged only if capacity expansion takes place or, put differently, if h_{mit} is not negative. Constraint (8.7) ensures that if capacity expansion is to take place, y_{mit} must be placed at one. This will become clear when we discuss the objective function later.

In the case of the Andean fertilizer model, the treatment of the investment function is somewhat different initially. All countries in the region have drawn up investment programs for the fertilizer industry. For particular sites, relatively well-defined investment packages have been established. The secretariat of the Andean Common Market felt that these should be taken as a starting point of our analysis. This required

Table 8-3. *Installed Capacity of Fertilizer Plants in Operation, 1980*
(tons per day)

Product	Baran-quilla	Barran-cabermeja	Callao-Fertisa	Callao-Indus	Carta-gena	Cuzco	Guay-aquil	Moron	El Tablazo	Talara
Ammonia (electricity)	—	—	—	—	—	50	—	—	—	—
Ammonia (fuel oil)	—	65	70	—	—	—	—	600	1,800	300
Ammonia (natural gas)	—	150	140	—	340	118	—	—	—	—
Ammonium nitrate	212	—	50	—	—	—	—	200	—	—
Ammonium sulfate	—	—	—	—	—	—	—	920	—	—
Granulator[a]	850	—	—	240	425	—	180	460	—	—
NPK	—	—	—	—	—	—	—	—	—	—
Nitric acid	230	85	107	—	68	90	17	88	—	—
Phosphoric acid	—	—	—	—	—	—	120	650	—	—
SSP	—	—	—	100	—	—	—	—	—	—
SSP-TSP	—	—	—	—	—	—	—	300[b]	—	—
Sulfuric acid	162	65	—	—	500[c]	—	80	1,200	—	—
Urea	—	—	—	—	—	—	—	750	2,400	510

Note: The capacity figures refer to "nameplate" capacity, that is, nominal capacity. Effective capacity is normally lower. For old plants, capacity utilization is 90 percent, except in Peru and Venezuela, where it is 75 percent. The NPK plants in Barranquilla, Guayaquil, and Moron are assumed to be able to achieve 60 percent capacity utilization in 1981–83, 65 percent in 1984–86, and 90 percent thereafter (75 percent in Venezuela's Moron). All plants are assumed to operate 300 days a year. NPK denotes compounded fertilizers of various compositions.

a. The granulator can produce DAP at 880 metric tons a day, or 920 metric tons of NPK a day, or granulate powdered TSP at 1,400 metric tons a day.

b. Can produce either SSP or TSP at this capacity level.

c. This plant was destroyed in 1980; however, it is being rebuilt with this design capacity.

an initial formulation of (8.7) which simply equated h_{mit} to these packages:

$$(8.9) \qquad h_{mit} = \sum_{n \in NF} \hat{h}_{nim} \cdot y_{nt}^P \qquad\qquad \begin{array}{l} m \in M \\ i \in I \\ t \in T \\ n \in N \end{array}$$

where

NF = set of fixed packages of projects
$\hat{h}_{nim}$ = capacity expansion of each productive unit in the package n
y_{nt}^P = integrality constraint for each package.

The integrality constraint y_{nt}^P is the usual zero-one constraint; if all packages must be implemented, in a given period, y_{nt}^P for that period is simply equated to one.

MUTUAL EXCLUSIVITY CONSTRAINT

$$(8.10) \qquad\qquad \sum_{t \in T} y_{nt}^P \leq 1 \qquad\qquad n \in N$$

which means that each package n can be implemented at most once. If the inequality in (8.10) is made into an equality, it means that each package must be implemented but the model determines the timing.

It is possible to make the size of projects within each package variable by replacing (8.9) with (8.11):

$$(8.11) \qquad h_{mit} \leq \sum_{n \in NV} \gamma \hat{h}_{nim} \cdot y_{nt}^P \qquad\qquad \begin{array}{l} m \in M \\ i \in I \\ t \in T \end{array}$$

where γ could be any positive number depending upon the degree of flexibility one wants to build into the model. If $\gamma = 2$, each productive unit could be up to twice its original size. The packages of projects currently under consideration in the Andean region are listed in table 8-4.

A significant area of controversy in the study was the prospects for exports to world markets. Most project packages were defined as they were because of relatively optimistic views regarding such projects. Regardless of one's degree of optimism in this regard, it was generally accepted that actual exports would be limited, thus necessitating the introduction of export constraints, by plant or by country:[4]

---

4. In chapter 9, only the plant-specific constraints were evaluated.

EXPORT CONSTRAINTS BY PLANT

$$(8.12) \qquad e_{cit} \le \lambda_i \sum_{g \in G} \sum_{p \in P} a_{cp} z_{gpit} \Big|_{a_{cp} > 0} \qquad \begin{array}{l} c \in CE \\ i \in I \\ t \in T \end{array}$$

$$\begin{bmatrix} Exports \\ by\ plant\ \mathrm{i} \\ in\ period\ \mathrm{t} \end{bmatrix} < \begin{bmatrix} Fixed\ proportion\ of\ output \\ of\ plant\ \mathrm{i}\ in\ period\ \mathrm{t} \end{bmatrix}$$

Table 8-4. *Project Packages Considered in the Andean Region*

Country and package	Site	Products	Nominal capacity (tons a day)
Bolivia			
BOL-1	Palmasola	Ammonia (natural gas)	160
		Urea	250
BOL-2	Potosi	TSP	170
		Phosphoric acid	125
Colombia			
COL-1	La Dorada	Ammonia (natural gas)	1,000
		Urea	1,600
COL-2	La Dorada	TSP	880
		Phosphoric acid	650
		Sulfuric acid	980
Ecuador			
ECU-1	Puerto Bolivar	Ammonia (natural gas)	435
		Urea	750
Peru			
PER-1	Bayovar	Ammonia (natural gas)	651
		Urea	870
PER-2	Bayovar	Sulfuric acid	2,000
		Phosphoric acid	1,334
		TSP	1,076
		DAP	636
PER-3	Bayovar	Potassium chloride	303
Venezuela			
VEN-1	Punta Caiman	Phosphoric acid	830
		Sulfuric acid	1,245
		NPK	2,272
		TSP	242
		DAP	561
VEN-2	Caripito	Ammonia (natural gas)	1,500
		Urea	1,030

Note: Capacity utilization for new plants is assumed to be 85 percent.

EXPORT CONSTRAINTS BY COUNTRY

$$(8.13) \qquad \sum_{i \in I} e_{cit} \Big|_{(w,i) \in WI} \leq \lambda_w \sum_{i \in I} \sum_{g \in G} \sum_{p \in P} a_{cp} z_{gpit} \Big|_{a_{cp} > 0} \qquad \begin{matrix} c \in CE \\ w \in W \\ t \in T \end{matrix}$$

The stringency of the export constraint selected will be discussed in the context of the results.

Objective Function

The objective of the model is uniformly the minimization of costs[5] to be incurred to meet demand requirements. In the aggregate, it has the following form:

$$(8.14) \qquad \min \xi = \sum_{t \in T} \delta_t \sum_{w \in W} \phi_{wt}$$

$$[Total\ cost] = \begin{bmatrix} Discount \\ factor \end{bmatrix} \begin{bmatrix} Cost\ in\ all \\ countries \end{bmatrix}$$

where the total costs are defined as the sum of the cost components minus export revenue for each country, as specified below:

$$(8.15) \qquad \phi_{wt} = \phi_{\kappa wt} + \phi_{\psi wt} + \phi_{\gamma wt} + \phi_{\mu wt}$$
$$+ \phi_{\pi wt} + \phi_{\lambda wt} - \phi_{\epsilon wt}.$$

The individual components are defined in the following.

CAPITAL COST

$$(8.16) \qquad \phi_{\kappa wt} = \sum_{\substack{\tau \in T \\ \tau \leq t}} \sum_{i \in I} \sum_{m \in M} \sigma \Bigg[\omega_{mi} \Big(y_{mi\tau} + \sum_{\substack{n \in N \\ \hat{h}_{nim} \neq 0}} y_{nt}^P \Big)$$

$$+ \nu_{mi} h_{mi\tau} \Bigg] \Bigg|_{(w,i) \in WI} \qquad \begin{matrix} w \in W \\ t \in T \end{matrix}$$

where

σ = capital recovery factor (see chapter 3 for a full explanation)[6]
ω_{mi} = fixed charge portion of the investment cost for productive unit m in site i

5. All costs are in 1977 U.S. dollars, with local costs converted to U.S. dollars at the official exchange rate.
6. The capital recovery factor incorporates a discount rate of 10 percent.

ν_{mi} = linear portion of the investment cost for productive unit m in
    site i

so that (8.16) states the capital cost in each country in period t is the
capital recovery factor times the total investment that has taken place in
that country since the beginning of the planning period. Total investment is equal to the sum of the fixed charges, for unspecified capacity
expansion (if permitted), and packages of prespecified projects, where
n is the number of projects in each package.

The packages of projects considered in the Andean model were given
in table 8-4. The linearized investment cost function is presented in table 8-5, together with the maximum capacity level for which the function was estimated.

OPERATING COST

$$(8.17) \qquad \phi_{\psi wt} = \sum_{g \in G} \sum_{i \in I} \left[\sum_{p \in P} p_{gpi}^{z} z_{gpit} \right.$$

$$\left. + \sum_{\substack{\tau \in T \\ \tau \leq t}} \sum_{m \in M} p_{m}^{h} h_{mi\tau} \right]_{(w,i) \in WI} \qquad \begin{array}{l} w \in W \\ t \in T \end{array}$$

Table 8-5. *Investment Cost for New Fertilizer Plants
in the Andean Region*

Product	Fixed portion (millions of dollars)	Proportional portion (dollars per ton per year)	Limit (thousands of tons per year)
Ammonia	84.7	185	300
Ammonium nitrate	5.4	36	200
Ammonium sulfate	4.7	48	300
DAP	8.6	63	300
NPK	8.6	63	300
Nitric acid	5.0	43	200
Phosphoric acid	17.4	100	300
Potassium chloride	10.2	153	100
SSP	10.2	35	200
Sulfuric acid	14.8	58	300
TSP	9.5	47	300
Urea	29.4	93	500

Note: Dollar amounts are expressed in 1977 U.S. dollars.

The first term on the right-hand side of (8.17) relates to operating cost items for old and new plants that are proportional to actual production levels. In the case of old plants, historical input levels have been used, and due to variations among plants, these tend to be plant-specific. For new plants, the more customary engineering estimates for input requirements were used. Note that neither raw material nor working capital is included in (8.17); they are specified separately in (8.18) and (8.19). The type of inputs that are included are electricity, water, steam, bags, and so forth.

The second term on the right in (8.17) is relevant for new projects only and relates to those operating cost items that are fixed with capacity, such as part of maintenance.

Details on operating cost for old plants can be found in the appendix. Here, we shall confine ourselves to giving the operating cost for new plants (see table 8-6).

DOMESTIC RAW MATERIAL COST

$$(8.18) \qquad \phi_{\gamma wt} = \sum_{c \in CR} \sum_{i \in I} p_{ci}^d u_{cit} \Big|_{(w,i) \in WI} \qquad\qquad \begin{aligned} w &\in W \\ t &\in T \end{aligned}$$

Table 8-6. *Operating Cost for New Plants*
(1977 U.S. dollars per ton)

Product	Cost related to capacity	Cost related to production
Ammonia (electricity)	34.5	12.3
Ammonia (fuel oil)	34.5	12.3
Ammonia (natural gas)	34.5	12.3
Ammonium nitrate	8.4	10.4
Ammonium sulfate	8.0	0.2
DAP	7.7	5.5
Granulator	9.3	1.7
NPK	6.5	2.9
Nitric acid	10.6	2.2
Phosphoric acid	16.8	9.0
Potassium chloride	13.0	22.0
SSP	9.3	1.7
SSP-TSP	9.3	1.7
Sulfuric acid	0.3	2.5
TSP	9.3	1.7
Urea	17.8	8.0

Raw materials purchased within the Andean region by the plants in each country are assumed to be available at various locations at fixed prices—although to some extent varying by location—and in quantities that do not represent a binding constraint during the planning period. The one exception applies to Potosi (Bolivia) where the annual production of local phosphate rock is limited to 35,000 metric tons.

The prices assumed for regionally available raw material, delivered to the plant, are given in table 8-7.

WORKING CAPITAL COST

$$(8.19) \qquad \phi_{\mu wt} = 0.025 \left[\phi_{\psi wt} + \phi_{\gamma wt} \right.$$

$$\left. + \sum_{c \in CR} \sum_{i \in I} (p^v_{cit} + \mu_i) v_{cit} \right]_{\Big|_{(w,i) \in WI}} \qquad \begin{matrix} w \in W \\ t \in T \end{matrix}$$

Table 8-7. *Regional Raw Material Prices by Plant Location*
(U.S. dollars per unit)

Plant location	Electricity	Natural gas[a]	Fuel oil	Phosphate rock	Sulfur	Sulfuric acid	Brine
Barrancabermeja	—	1	—	—	—	—	—
Bayovar	—	1	—	30	40	—	0.2
Callao-Fertisa	—	—	39	—	—	40	—
Callao-Indus	—	—	—	—	—	40	—
Caripito	—	1	—	—	—	—	—
Cartagena	—	1	—	—	—	—	—
Cuzco	2	—	—	—	—	—	—
La Dorada	—	1	—	—	—	—	—
Moron	—	1	—	50	45	—	—
Palmasola	—	1	—	—	—	—	—
Potosi	—	—	—	45	—	10	—
Puerto Bolivar	—	1	—	—	—	—	—
Puerto Suarez	—	1	—	—	—	—	—
Punta Caiman	—	—	—	42	45	—	—
El Tablazo	—	1	—	—	—	—	—
Talara	—	1	—	—	—	—	—

Note: Dashes indicate that input is either not available or not relevant at a specific plant location.

a. Not enough is known about the production conditions for natural gas by producing location and overtime. A uniform supply price has been chosen for all locations with natural gas, approximately representing a world market price equivalent, so that the desirability of the use of gas at each location for further processing depends on factors other than the relative supply price of natural gas.

Working capital cost is equal to 2.5 percent of the sum of operating cost and domestic and imported raw material cost. Raw material cost includes transport cost to the plant.

IMPORT COST

(8.20)
$$\phi_{\pi wt} = \sum_{c \in CF} \sum_{j \in J} p^v_{cjt} v_{cjt} \Big|_{(w,j) \in WJ}$$
$$+ \sum_{c \in CV} \sum_{i \in I} p^v_{cit} v_{cit} \Big|_{(w,i) \in WI} \qquad \begin{array}{l} w \in W \\ t \in T \end{array}$$

Total import cost for each country is equal to the cost of imports of final products to markets in the country plus the cost of imported materials to all plants in each country. The import prices assumed to prevail during the planning period for imports from outside the Andean region are given in table 8-8.

TRANSPORT COST

(8.21)
$$\phi_{\lambda wt} = \sum_{c \in CF} \sum_{j \in J} \left[\sum_{i \in I} \mu_{ij} x_{cijt} + \mu_j v_{cjt} \right]_{(w,j) \in WJ}$$

$$\begin{bmatrix} \textit{Transport cost for regionally} \\ \textit{produced and imported} \\ \textit{final products shipped to} \\ \textit{regional markets} \end{bmatrix} = \begin{bmatrix} \textit{Transport cost} \\ \textit{for exports} \end{bmatrix}$$

$$+ \left[\sum_{i \in I} \sum_{c \in CE} \mu_i e_{cit} + \sum_{c \in CV} \mu_i v_{cit} \right.$$

$$+ \begin{bmatrix} \textit{Transport cost for} \\ \textit{imported materials} \\ \textit{to plants} \end{bmatrix}$$

$$+ \sum_{\substack{i' \in I \\ i' \neq i}} \sum_{c \in CIS} \mu_{i'i} x_{ci'it} \right]_{(w,i) \in WI} \qquad \begin{array}{l} w \in W \\ t \in T \end{array}$$

$$+ \begin{bmatrix} \textit{Transport cost} \\ \textit{for interplant shipments} \end{bmatrix}$$

The transport costs for the various categories of commodities, for all relevant shipment possibilities, represent the largest single body of data

Table 8-8. *Import Prices of Fertilizer Nutrients, 1981–92*
(1977 U.S. dollars per ton)

	1981–83	1984–86	1987–89	1990–92
Ammonia	119.4	160.1	179.0	179.0
Ammonium nitrate	145.4	165.0	174.0	174.0
Ammonium sulfate	112.2	120.3	123.0	123.0
DAP	211.4	242.9	254.2	254.2
Elemental sulfur	73.3	78.3	80.0	80.0
Phosphate rock	57.4	60.3	61.3	61.3
Phosphoric acid	169.2	193.0	200.0	200.0
Potassium chloride	98.8	103.6	105.2	105.2
TSP	166.1	187.0	194.2	194.2
Urea	163.7	186.8	198.0	198.0

Note: Prices are c.i.f., that is, including cost, insurance, and freight.

required for the model. It is too voluminous to reproduce here, and the interested reader is referred to the appendix.

Whenever possible, the transport cost data requirements should be met in a way that minimizes the risk of mistakes and facilitates consistency checks. In normal circumstances, these objectives can be met by the construction of a distance matrix covering all relevant sites (markets, plants, and ports) and estimated transport cost functions that reflect the impact of, for example, loading, unloading, and distances on total cost. The geophysical characteristics of the Andean region, in particular the mountainous terrain, substantially reduced the scope for generalization of transport cost, and we were forced to estimate the relevant cost for each shipment possibility. It is one of the areas where the accuracy of our results could be improved by more detailed studies.[7]

EXPORT REVENUE

(8.22)
$$\phi_{\epsilon wt} = \sum_{c \in CE} \sum_{i \in I} p^e_{cit} e_{cit} \Big|_{(w,i) \in WI} \qquad \begin{array}{l} w \in W \\ t \in T \end{array}$$

$$\left[\begin{array}{l} \textit{Value of exports outside the} \\ \textit{Andean region for each country} \end{array} \right]$$

7. As this manuscript was being prepared, we learned that the Andean secretariat has obtained the resources to finance a detailed study of fertilizer distribution in the region.

Table 8-9. *Export Prices of Fertilizer Nutrients, 1981–92*
(1977 U.S. dollars per ton)

	1981–83	1984–86	1987–89	1990–92
Ammonia	56	88	103	103
Ammonium nitrate	96	112	119	119
Ammonium sulfate	70	76	78	78
DAP	149	174	183	183
Phosphoric acid	95	114	120	120
Potassium chloride	59	63	64	64
SSP	54	61	63	63
TSP	113	130	135	135
Urea	111	129	138	138

Note: Prices are f.o.b., that is, free on board.

Export prices are set in relation to c.i.f. import prices in the case of all exportable products contained in the set *CE*. In most cases, the export price is 80 percent of the import price minus $20 a ton. In the case of acids and ammonia, the export price is 80 percent of the import price minus $40 a ton. The resulting prices are given in table 8-9.

This completes the description of the Andean fertilizer model and the major data inputs and assumptions made. The results reported in the next chapter were obtained on the basis of this model structure and data. A complete computer-readable statement of the data is given in the appendix.

9
Results of the Andean
Fertilizer Model

THE NORMAL USE OF MODELS, such as those described in this volume and companion volumes in the series, is to design an investment program, with associated production and trade patterns, that minimizes the cost of meeting the exogenously specified market requirements for final products. In this context, "design" refers to decisions regarding the timing, location, scale, technology, and product mix of each new project that contributes to the achievement of the objective.

Our collaborating institution, the Andean Common Market Secretariat, had good reason to argue for a different approach, at least initially. All countries in the region have firm views with regard to the future development of the fertilizer sector, and to proceed with the analysis as if such plans do not exist appeared unrealistic. Consequently, the following approach was adopted. Following several workshops in Lima in which representatives of various important sectors from each country participated and which aimed at achieving a consensus regarding the main data, assumptions, and projections, the model was used to evaluate a series of scenarios starting with existing national fertilizer sector development plans. Gradually, it was assumed that the countries would be willing to be flexible, particularly with regard to the timing of the implementation of specific projects, and the efficiency gains of such flexibility were determined. Eventually, a regional investment plan was generated that left the more cost-effective national projects intact, and yet produced a regional distribution of projects that was fairly equitable among the countries, in the sense that each country would host at least one project.

Before this approach could be implemented, two sets of projections required considerable discussion. First, the countries had widely differing views of the rate of growth of domestic demand for fertilizers. Although these could be explained to some extent by differences in initial levels, it was clear that the basis for some exceedingly high projected rates of increase was very weak. In the end, reasonably uniform and realistic rates of growth were agreed on. The second area of dispute related to achievable export levels to world markets. Once more, expectations were generally on the high side, and it required considerable discussion, and contributions by sector specialists, to bring them down. The model was run on the assumption that no plant could export more than 30 percent of production, with the exception of two plants that were specifically dependent on exports to markets outside the Andean region, the existing plant in Venezuela, at Tablazo, and the project in Bolivia at Palmasola. These two plants could export up to 70 percent of production. It is on this basis that the results described below were achieved.

Under the auspices of the secretariat, many versions of the model were run. In the process, insight was gained into the nature of the planning problems. Moreover, errors in data specification were detected. Although we shall confine ourselves here to the description of a small number of scenarios—as the secretariat did for its own internal purposes—it should be borne in mind that much more analysis was actually carried out.

Models of the type discussed here yield a wide variety of results. In table 9-1, as an example, we list the reports that were mechanically generated by the computer in our collaborative work with the Andean secretariat. For any specific application of the model, a problem-relevant set of such reports can be produced using either standard report generators or custom-written ones. To report on all of these in detail is normally unnecessary, because one can usually determine during the conduct of the study what type of results are important to a specific audience. Such reporting is also undesirable for two reasons. First, a voluminous report on largely irrelevant details diverts attention from essential aspects, thus reducing the effectiveness of negotiations. Second, extensive attention to minor result categories—such as low-volume interplant shipments—creates the false impression of extreme reliability, thus attaching unwarranted significance to small numerical magnitudes. Emphasis should be on the broad pattern of supply revealed by the model, as the logical implication of a set of assumptions and projections, rather than the minute aspects generated as by-products by a nondiscriminating instrument such as the computer.

Table 9-1. *Result Categories Generated for the Andean Model*

---

1. Discounted total cost by period and by country.
2. Cost categories by period and by country, undiscounted.
3. Timing of project package installation by project package and period.
4. Capacity utilization by country and by period.
5. Capacity utilization by plant and by period.
6. Capacity utilization by productive unit and by period.
7. Intraregional trade flows by countries and by period, valued at c.i.f. prices.
8. Extraregional trade flows by country and by period, imports valued at c.i.f. prices, exports valued at f.o.b. prices.
9. Trade flows by volume, by country, by product, and by period.
10. Effective capacity by productive unit and by period for existing plants.
11. Slack capacity by productive unit and by period for existing plants.
12. Imports of final product in volume terms by product and by marketing region per period.
13. Imports of intermediates and raw materials in volume terms by product and by plant site per period.
14. Capacity expansion by plant and by productive unit per period.

Against this background, the following sections dealing with the results achieved with the Andean model focus primarily on costs and trade. When relevant, capacity expansion and utilization will be discussed as well.[1]

Scenario 1: The Implications of Current Plans

Under this scenario, the countries are assumed to implement in the short run, and simultaneously, all the project packages contemplated. This means that productive capacity will be available starting from the second planning period, 1984–86. Although regional trade is allowed if competitive with imports from outside the Andean region, it is clearly limited to meet deficits in each country.[2] Moreover, as much as 30 per-

---

1. It should be noted that for the purpose of this book, all versions of the model were re-run in Washington, D.C., using the latest available information. Sometimes in important respects the results reported here differ from those achieved several years earlier in Lima, Peru.

2. It should be remembered that all our runs incorporate the common external tariff on raw materials and intermediates of 15 percent, and on final products of 10 percent.

cent of the production of each plant may be exported to world markets, except in the case of El Tablazo and Palmasola, where 70 percent may be exported.

Costs

The costs associated with the immediate implementation of all plans, discounted to the present, amount to $3,150 million. This total is the sum of investment charges during the planning period, operating costs of old and new plants, purchases of domestic materials, import costs, tariffs on imports from world markets, and intraregional transport costs, minus export revenues. The various cost elements and export revenue are given in table 9-2 in undiscounted terms. We shall discuss each of these cost elements and export revenues separately, for each time period in the model and in undiscounted terms.

Capital costs are charged from the second period, 1984–86, onward; note that investments in old plants are treated as sunk cost that do not result in annual charges. As all new investments are made in the second period, charges in all subsequent periods are identical.

Table 9-2. *Average Annual Costs under Scenario 1 (All Projects Implemented 1984–86), by Period*
(millions of U.S. dollars)

	Period				Undis-counted costs
Cost category	1 (1981–83)	2 (1984–86)	3 (1987–89)	4 (1990–92)	
Capital charges	—	187.7	187.7	187.7	1,689.3
Operating costs	50.5	178.5	185.1	193.4	1,822.5
Regional raw material purchases	44.5	132.2	132.5	136.4	1,337.1
Import costs	116.9	45.6	54.3	109.7	979.2
(Tariff revenue)	(12.8)	(5.4)	(6.6)	(13.4)	(114.6)
Regional transport costs	45.5	73.4	85.4	99.0	909.6
Total costs	257.4	618.4	644.9	726.0	6,740.1
Export revenue	45.8	192.9	165.7	145.6	1,653.3
Net costs	211.6	424.6	479.2	580.3	5,086.8

Note: Objective function (present value): $3,150.0 million.

It should be remembered that these annual charges are incurred to finance a capacity expansion program that involves ten project packages, of which two are in Bolivia, two in Colombia, one in Ecuador, three in Peru, and two in Venezuela. The project components are reproduced in table 9-3.

Annual operating costs increase sharply after the first period. This increase is, of course, associated with the operation of the new projects; subsequent increases are due to increased levels of capacity utilization. The same explanation is valid for *regional raw material purchases.*

Import costs and tariff revenues are closely related and do not require separate discussion. Obviously, once the new project packages have been implemented in the second period, imports from world markets, and consequently tariff revenues, drop considerably. Given that the region remains in deficit for potash and phosphate, import costs rapidly grow to earlier levels. Colombia and, to a much lesser extent, Venezuela and Peru remain major importers of fertilizer material if no new projects are implemented in subsequent periods.

Transport costs in the region grow markedly. This trend reflects the rapid increase in intraregional trade, once the new project packages are implemented.

Exports to world markets, particularly from Venezuela, expand initially as a result of excess capacity, particularly in nitrogenous fertilizer material. However, increasing regional demand permits growing sales within the common market, and even though all countries are competi-

Table 9-3. *Capacity Expansion under Scenario 1, by Project,
1984–86*

(thousands of tons per year)

Product	Bayovar	Caripito	La Dorada	Palmasola	Potosi	Puerto Bolivar	Punta Caiman
Ammonia (natural gas)	214.830	495.000	330.000	52.800	—	143.550	—
Diammonium phosphate (DAP)	209.880	—	—	—	—	—	185.130
NPK[a]	—	—	—	—	—	—	749.760
Phosphoric acid	440.220	—	214.500	—	41.250	—	273.900
Potassium chloride	99.990	—	—	—	—	—	—
Sulfuric acid	660.000	—	323.400	—	—	—	410.850
Triple superphosphate (TSP)	355.080	—	290.400	—	56.100	—	79.860
Urea	287.100	339.900	528.000	82.500	—	247.500	—

a. NPK denotes compounded fertilizers of various compositions.

tive in world markets, it appears more profitable to sell regionally as exports outside the region decline during the last period for all countries.

A major concern regarding the wisdom of implementing all national plans at the earliest possible moment, in combination with relatively realistic projections of the scope for exports to world markets, is the effect this rapid implementation may have on rates of capacity utilization. The results obtained contain a wealth of information on capacity utilization, by country, by plant location, by productive unit, and by time-period. Only some of the more outstanding features will be discussed here.

The introduction of all project packages in the period 1984–86 results in countrywide rates of capacity utilization that are well below 100 percent, but in most countries the rates are not as low as might have been expected and not for long. Moreover, the countrywide averages are strongly influenced by low rates of utilization of a limited number of productive units. In Bolivia, the ammonia and urea complex at Palmasola is fully utilized from the start; however, the phosphate plant at Potosi uses only 40 percent of capacity throughout the planning period. The countrywide average for Colombia during the second and third periods is the lowest in the region. Closer inspection of the detailed results reveals that this is primarily because the phosphate plant at La Dorada, although forced into the investment program under the assumptions of this scenario, is in fact not utilized at all, implying that it cannot compete with alternative sources of supply, even at marginal costs, except during the last period. Moreover, the introduction of urea production at La Dorada forces production cutbacks at Barrancabermeja during the second period.

The plant at Cuzco, Peru, ceases production as it cannot compete with alternative sources of supply of nitrogenous fertilizer. The Bayovar complex appears very efficient: with the exception of the urea plant during the second period, all units produce at full capacity throughout the planning period.

In Venezuela, the new plant at Caripito and the existing plant at El Tablazo produce at full capacity throughout the planning period. However, several individual units at Moron, notably the nitric acid, urea, and NPK plants, produce well below capacity. The new NPK unit at Punta Caiman is also heavily underutilized.

On balance, the analysis of rates of capacity utilization suggests that the new project packages are more efficient than many of the older plants; however, it should be noted that forcing the new packages into the solution of the model means that all supply alternatives are valued at marginal costs and that investments in both old and new plants are treated as sunk cost.

Trade

The results obtained for trade flows distinguish between intraregional trade and international trade. We shall first discuss each country separately, and then provide information on the results for the region as a whole.

BOLIVIA. The relevant trade data for Bolivia are given in table 9-4. Before the implementation of current plans, Bolivia is a net importer of fertilizers. The solution of our model implies that most of Bolivia's fertilizer requirements should be imported from the Andean region, with the remainder coming from world markets. The construction of the plants at Palmasola and Potosi changes the picture drastically. Both regionally and internationally, Bolivia becomes an exporter, although with regard to the former only during the second period. From then onward, regional imports resume. However, exports of urea and some ammonia from Palmasola to Argentina and Uruguay continue at a high level, clearly because of transport cost advantages that these export markets have over other Andean partner countries.

COLOMBIA. Colombia remains a major importer of fertilizer material during the planning period, mainly for potash and phosphate, product groups for which at present insufficiently large expansion plans have been drawn up. Expansion plans in other Andean countries, particularly Peru and Venezuela, permit a switch from imports from outside the re-

Table 9-4. *Annual Trade Flows for Bolivia under Scenario 1,*
by Period
(millions of U.S. dollars)

Type of flow	1981–83	1984–86	1987–89	1990–92
Intraregional imports[a]	−1.822	−0.120	−3.524	−7.865
Intraregional exports[a]	—	0.705	—	—
Balance	−1.822	0.585	−3.524	−7.865
Extraregional imports	−0.942	−0.036	−0.062	−0.062
Extraregional exports[b]	—	6.724	7.228	7.041
Balance	−0.942	6.688	7.166	6.979
Overall trade balance	−2.764	7.273	3.642	−0.886

a. Valued at c.i.f. prices.
b. For valuation, see text.

gion to sources within the region, although growth in demand in partner countries reverses this trend toward the end of the planning period.

The product composition of Colombia's current expansion plans, involving nitrogenous fertilizers for which the region as a whole would develop a surplus and a phosphate plant that is so high cost that its capacity is not used until the last period, limit Colombia's scope for intraregional exports. Nonetheless, Colombia is in a good position to export urea to world markets. Its overall trade balance, however, remains rather substantially negative, as shown in table 9-5.

ECUADOR. Although Ecuador plans to construct a nitrogenous fertilizer plant, it remains a regional and international importer of phosphate and potash fertilizers. During the second period when its new plant commences operation, a small amount of regional exports (of urea to the Selva in Peru) is possible. Extraregional exports of urea could continue at a fairly high level, leading to a sharp drop in the overall trade deficit during the second period, but with a resumption of growth from then onward, as shown in table 9-6.

PERU. The implementation of Peru's three projects at Bayovar transforms the country drastically from a major net importer, both regionally and internationally, to a net exporter (see table 9-7). Both intraregional and international imports remain necessary throughout the planning period, however, mainly on account of urea requirements.

Table 9-5. *Annual Trade Flows for Colombia under Scenario 1, by Period*
(millions of U.S. dollars)

Type of flow	1981–83	1984–86	1987–89	1990–92
Intraregional imports[a]	−17.697	−77.687	−103.098	−60.696
Intraregional exports[a]	3.856	3.508	2.812	2.025
Balance	−13.841	−74.179	−100.286	−58.671
Extraregional imports	−69.840	−23.937	− 29.470	−75.086
Extraregional exports[b]	—	23.349	28.910	18.079
Balance	−69.840	− 0.588	− 0.560	−57.007
Overall trade balance	−83.681	−74.767	−100.846	−115.678

a. Valued at c.i.f. prices.
b. For valuation, see text.

Table 9-6. *Annual Trade Flows for Ecuador under Scenario 1,*
by Period
(millions of U.S. dollars)

Type of flow	1981–83	1984–86	1987–89	1990–92
Intraregional imports[a]	−10.090	−15.115	−19.967	−29.219
Intraregional exports[a]	—	0.522	—	—
Balance	−10.090	−14.593	−19.967	−29.219
Extraregional imports	−14.152	− 4.014	− 6.570	−10.403
Extraregional exports[b]	—	8.694	8.788	8.735
Balance	−14.152	4.680	2.218	− 1.668
Overall trade balance	−24.242	− 9.913	−17.749	−30.887

a. Valued at c.i.f. prices.
b. For valuation, see text.

Table 9-7. *Annual Trade Flows for Peru under Scenario 1, by Period*
(millions of U.S. dollars)

Type of flow	1981–83	1984–86	1987–89	1990–92
Intraregional imports[a]	−12.949	−24.017	−17.543	−18.520
Intraregional exports[a]	0.124	58.658	78.799	69.045
Balance	−12.825	34.641	61.256	50.525
Extraregional imports	−19.725	− 2.123	− 1.246	− 3.081
Extraregional exports[b]	—	34.660	18.223	16.612
Balance	−19.725	32.537	16.977	13.531
Overall trade balance	−32.550	67.178	78.233	64.056

a. Valued at c.i.f. prices.
b. For valuation, see text.

VENEZUELA. Not surprisingly, given the size and product mix of its expansion plans, Venezuela becomes the major fertilizer exporter of the Andean Group, mainly of ammonia and urea, but initially of diammonium phosphate (DAP) as well. Both regionally and internationally, its trade balance is positive throughout the planning period, as shown in table 9-8.

ANDEAN COMMON MARKET. The trade flows for the Andean Common Market as a whole are given in table 9-9. The value of intraregional trade nearly triples during the second period because of the increases in capacity in the member countries. As a result, extraregional imports are

Table 9-8. *Annual Trade Flows for Venezuela under Scenario 1,*
by Period
(millions of U.S. dollars)

Type of flow	1981–83	1984–86	1987–89	1990–92
Intraregional imports[a]	− 2.701	− 2.370	—	− 2.573
Intraregional exports[a]	41.279	55.916	62.521	47.804
Balance	38.578	53.546	62.521	45.231
Extraregional imports	−12.222	−15.561	−16.887	−20.958
Extraregional exports[b]	45.763	119.506	102.600	95.202
Balance	33.541	103.945	85.713	74.244
Overall trade balance	72.119	157.491	148.234	119.475

a. Valued at c.i.f. prices.
b. For valuation, see text.

Table 9-9. *Annual Trade Flows for the Andean Common Market*
under Scenario 1, by Period
(millions of U.S. dollars)

Type of flow	1981–83	1984–86	1987–89	1990–92
Intraregional trade[a]	45.259	119.309	144.132	118.873
Extraregional imports	−116.881	−45.671	−54.235	−109.590
Extraregional exports[b]	45.763	192.933	165.749	145.669
Extraregional trade balance	−71.118	147.262	111.514	36.079

a. Valued at c.i.f. prices.
b. For valuation, see text.

considerably reduced, whereas the exports to world markets quadruple.

After the second period, demand increases while capacities remain constant. This results in another—but much smaller—increase in intraregional trade in the third period. In the fourth period the value of intraregional trade decreases as preference is given to meeting domestic demand. Imports from world markets grow somewhat during the third period and substantially in the fourth period to attain about the same level as in the first period. Exports to world markets decrease regularly during the third as well as the fourth period, but their level is still much higher than during the first period.

The extraregional trade balance improves considerably during the second period: a change from $70 million to $150 million. After the second period the regional trade balance deteriorates again because of the increase in regional demand and the constant production capacities in the member countries. The latter are clearly not realistic: there is no reason why the countries cannot continue to develop export markets.

Scenario 2: No Capacity Expansion

As table 9-2 made clear, the implementation of all current plans in the second period results in a drastic increase in the cost of meeting fertilizer requirements, much more than the growth in the market would suggest. Clearly, this supply pattern has very high costs. How would it compare with doing nothing at all? The implications of this policy, which relies entirely on regional production in existing plants and imports, can also be examined using the model.

Costs

The total discounted cost of this supply pattern—$2.762 million—is considerably less than that of scenario 1, for a savings of more than 12 percent. As can be expected, most of the total costs are accounted for by imports of fertilizer material. Exports, particularly in the later periods, are marginal, and most productive capacity is used to meet regional demand. Consequently, the trade balance with the rest of the world deteriorates rapidly, from an average annual deficit of $71 million in the first period to $386 million in the last one, in undiscounted terms.

A comparison between tables 9-2 and 9-10 shows that, while scenario 2 expectedly implies lower costs, on account of lower capital charges, operating costs, regional raw material charges, and regional transport cost, and has much lower export revenues, import costs are substantially higher. However, in undiscounted terms, the costs of meeting all fertilizer requirements throughout the planning period without further capacity expansion is almost $600 million less than would have to be incurred by implementing all national plans immediately. Moreover, higher costs are recorded for each period after 1983: 38 percent more in the second period, 14 percent in the third, and 4 percent in the fourth.

Trade

Even if no capacity expansion takes place, very considerable intraregional trade remains possible, as shown in table 9-11. It should be noted,

Table 9-10. *Average Annual Costs under Scenario 2 (No Capacity Expansion), by Period*
(millions of U.S. dollars)

| Cost category | Period | | | | Undis-counted costs |
	1 *(1981–83)*	*2* *(1984–86)*	*3* *(1987–89)*	*4* *(1990–92)*	
Capital charges	—	—	—	—	—
Operating costs	50.5	51.9	52.6	53.7	625.8
Regional raw material purchases	44.6	44.8	43.6	44.8	533.4
Import costs	116.9	179.8	259.3	388.3	2,832.9
(Tariff revenue)	(13.1)	(19.5)	(27.7)	(40.7)	(303.0)
Regional transport costs	45.5	58.2	69.2	75.0	743.7
Total costs	257.4	334.6	424.6	561.8	4,735.2
Export revenue	45.8	27.1	2.9	2.7	235.5
Net costs	211.6	307.5	421.7	559.1	4,499.7

Note: Objective function (present value): $2,761.6 million.

Table 9-11. *Annual Trade Flows for the Andean Common Market under Scenario 2, by Period*
(millions of·U.S. dollars)

Type of flow	1981–83	1984–86	1987–89	1990–92
Intraregional trade	45.259	80.147	108.810	95.381
Extraregional imports	−116.881	−179.828	−259.243	−388.343
Extraregional exports	45.763	27.145	2.918	2.694
Overall trade balance	−71.118	−152.683	−256.325	−385.649

however, that most of the intraregional trade consists of export of urea from Venezuela to other Andean countries.

The trade balance with the rest of the world deteriorates rapidly, as noted before. Exports to the rest of the world decline to marginal levels, while annual imports soar to almost $400 million a year by the end of the planning period.

Scenario 3: The Andean Least-Cost Strategy

To determine the least-cost strategy that may be attainable, the Andean Common Market Secretariat took as its starting point all currently firmly planned projects in the region. The model was subsequently used to select from among the set of possible projects those that would, jointly with the existing plants, lead to a supply pattern that minimizes total net costs of meeting all fertilizer requirements in the region during 1981-92. Thus, whenever imports from outside the region are cheaper than regional suppliers, considering regional production costs, import cost, and differences in regional transport costs to marketing areas, imports are selected as the least-cost strategy by the model.

Costs

Of the seven proposed projects, three were selected under scenario 3. The model recommends the implementation of two projects in the second period (1984-86): a TSP and DAP project at Bayovar, Peru, and an ammonia and urea project at La Dorada, Colombia. A third project—to manufacture TSP, NPK, and DAP at Punta Caiman, Venezuela—is recommended in the fourth period (1990-92).

If these project packages were implemented according to the recommended schedule, and all other project packages were indefinitely postponed, the total cost of meeting fertilizer requirements in the Andean Common Market during the period 1981-92 would amount to $2,666.7 million. This amount is 15 percent less than the costs of implementing all packages at once (scenario 1) and 3.5 percent less than not implementing any packages (scenario 2). Table 9-12 gives details by cost category.

This strategy results in rapidly improving rates of capacity utilization overall, for existing plants as well as new ones. The major exceptions remain Cuzco, which is not used at all, and the Indus plant at Callao, Peru, which is used at only 60 percent of capacity. In all other cases, plants are operated at 85 percent of capacity.

Trade

As table 9-13 shows, intraregional trade increases sharply in periods 2 and 3, to decline slightly in period 4 when domestic demand in the countries absorbs a greater share of domestic production and Venezuela begins production at Punta Caiman. Venezuela no longer dominates regional exports; instead Colombia and, particularly, Peru play an important role in regional fertilizer supply. Overall, the region remains in substantial deficit. Extraregional imports grow steadily, while exports decline sharply in the third and fourth period, after increasing in the second.

Table 9-12. *Average Annual Costs under Scenario 3 (Least-Cost Strategy), by Period*
(millions of U.S. dollars)

| | Period | | | | Undis-counted costs |
Cost category	1 (1981–83)	2 (1984–86)	3 (1987–89)	4 (1990–92)	
Capital charges	—	50.9	50.9	73.6	525.8
Operating costs	50.5	98.0	99.0	117.1	1,093.5
Regional raw material purchases	44.6	84.0	82.9	111.7	969.1
Import costs	116.9	71.4	133.4	167.1	1,466.4
(Tariff revenue)	(12.7)	(8.8)	(15.1)	(19.6)	(168.6)
Regional transport costs	45.5	66.5	77.3	89.8	837.2
Total costs	257.4	370.7	443.4	559.2	4,892.0
Export revenue	45.8	72.1	43.1	30.3	573.7
Net costs	211.6	298.6	400.3	528.9	4,318.3

Note: Objective function (present value): $2,666.7 million.

Table 9-13. *Annual Trade Flows for the Andean Common Market under Scenario 3, by Period*
(millions of U.S. dollars)

Type of flow	1981–83	1984–86	1987–89	1990–92
Intraregional trade	45.3	120.7	137.5	132.2
Extraregional imports	116.9	71.4	133.4	167.1
Extraregional exports	45.8	72.1	43.1	30.3
Overall trade balance	71.1	−0.7	90.3	136.8

Scenario 4: A More Equitable Investment Strategy

The Andean Common Market Secretariat was very concerned that an uneven distribution of project packages in the region would be unacceptable to the partner countries, particularly Bolivia, Ecuador, and Venezuela. It was therefore decided to introduce a new constraint on the investment pattern by requiring that each country would host at least one project. This constraint is the key feature of scenario 4.

Costs

The total costs of this strategy, discounted to the present, amount to $2,676.8 million, or almost the same as the least-cost strategy and 15 percent less than the cost of implementing all current plans at once. A summary of results is given in table 9-14.

The costs projected under scenario 4 are identical to the least-cost strategy for the first three periods. Only the fourth period has different costs for all components. The reason for this similarity of results is to be found in the investment pattern recommended by the model, which closely follows the least-cost strategy. In the second period, the projects at Bayovar, Peru, and La Dorada, Colombia, are to be implemented, as they were under scenario 2. In the fourth period, the project at Punta Caiman, Venezuela, is also recommended, as in scenario 2, as well as two other projects—an ammonia and urea project at Puerto Bolivar, Ecuador, and a TSP project at Potosi, Bolivia.

In other words, when forced to locate a project package in each country, the model selects exactly the same investment program for Peru, Colombia, and Venezuela, with identical timing, as it did for the least-cost strategy, and then adds the smallest possible project in Bolivia and the only possible one in Ecuador, but postpones their implementation as long as possible. During the first three periods, therefore, the supply pattern in the region is identical to the least-cost strategy.

With the exception of Bolivia, capacity utilization rates increase very rapidly to high levels; even the new plant in Ecuador reaches nearly full

Table 9-14. *Average Annual Costs under Scenario 4 (Equitable Investment Strategy), by Period*
(millions of U.S. dollars)

| | Period | | | | Undis-counted costs |
Cost category	1 (1981–83)	2 (1984–86)	3 (1987–89)	4 (1990–92)	
Capital charges	—	50.9	50.9	99.5	603.6
Operating costs	50.5	98.0	99.0	131.0	1,135.3
Regional raw material purchases	44.6	84.0	82.9	116.8	984.6
Import costs	116.9	71.4	133.4	158.7	1,441.1
(Tariff revenue)	(12.7)	(8.8)	(15.1)	(18.8)	(166.2)
Regional transport costs	45.5	66.5	77.3	86.1	826.0
Total costs	237.4	370.7	443.4	592.1	4,990.6
Export revenue	45.8	72.1	43.1	55.2	648.5
Net costs	211.6	298.6	400.3	536.9	4,342.1

Note: Objective function (present value): $2,676.8 million.

capacity utilization in the fourth period. The new plant in Bolivia is used at only 40 percent of its capacity.

Trade

During the first three periods, the same trade pattern is observed as in the case of the least-cost strategy. In the fourth, intraregional trade is lower because of greater self-sufficiency in Bolivia and Ecuador, while extraregional imports decline and extraregional exports increase. Consistently, the overall trade balance improves. Details are provided in table 9-15.

Sensitivity Analysis

As is usual in planning exercises of this kind, it is prudent to conduct a certain amount of sensitivity analysis to determine the impact of projection errors in some of the major variables. The Andean secretariat identified three such variables: (a) demand, (b) capital costs, and (c) natural gas prices. All sensitivity analyses were carried out on scenario 4, the relatively equitable investment strategy.

Lower Demand

Because the projection of demand for fertilizer in the Andean region was a contentious issue, it was felt that sensitivity analysis for lower demand was needed. The reduction in the growth of demand decided upon by the Andean Common Market Secretariat varied by period and by nutrient and reflected disagreements expressed by participants at the work-

Table 9-15. *Annual Trade Flows for the Andean Common Market under Scenario 4, by Period*
(millions of U.S. dollars)

Type of flow	1981–83	1984–86	1987–89	1990–92
Intraregional trade	45.3	120.7	137.5	107.8
Extraregional imports	116.9	71.4	133.4	158.7
Extraregional exports	45.8	72.1	43.1	55.2
Overall trade balance	71.1	−0.7	90.3	103.4

shop of 1979 with regard to the feasibility of national forecasts. The percentage reductions used for sensitivity analysis are given in table 9-16.

If demand grows more slowly, the cost of meeting total requirements is obviously much less than in the earlier scenarios: $2,067.8 million with lower demand projections, compared with $2,676.8 million in scenario 4. The investment program, which would continue to insist that each country have at least one project package, would not be affected by lower demand in its timing or composition. The La Dorada (urea) project in Colombia and Bayovar (TSP and DAP) in Peru would still be implemented in the second period, and Venezuela, Ecuador, and Bolivia would get a project in the fourth period.

Rates of capacity utilization, too, would not be much affected by lower demand, except in Ecuador during the first two periods when lower demand for phosphates would affect the production level of the SSP plant at Guayaquil. As more capacity would be available for export and import requirements would be lower, the trade balance with the rest of the world would improve. During the second period, the Andean Group would be a net exporter of fertilizer material.

Capital Cost

If capital cost for new investments were 15 percent higher than assumed so far, total net discounted cost would increase by 1.8 percent as compared with scenario 4 and would amount to $2,726.1 million. Neither the composition nor the timing of the investment program would be affected by this increase in cost, and a trade pattern emerges that is nearly identical to that of scenario 4. In capital cost, therefore, the least-cost investment program is fairly robust, given the limits on flexibility of investment imposed by the model.

Table 9-16. *Reduction in Forecast Demand Levels, by Period and Nutrient*
(percent)

Nutrient	1981–83	1984–86	1987–89	1990–92
Nitrogen	−14.3	−12.6	−11.2	−9.3
Phosphate	−22.6	−25.1	−22.7	−18.5
Potash	−25.0	−26.0	−27.1	−27.5

Natural Gas Prices

If there were an increase of 50 percent in the price of natural gas, total costs would rise to $2,791.0 million, an increase of 4.3 percent from scenario 4. The composition of the investment program would not be affected, nor would the pattern of intraregional and extraregional trade.

Recapitulation

The scenarios considered by the Andean secretariat all took as given the project packages formulated by the countries at the beginning of the planning period. The model was used to determine the implications of alternative combinations of such project packages, without modifying their size and product mix.

Under these circumstances, the least-cost strategy would be to construct no new capacity in Bolivia and Ecuador, but to concentrate on Peru, Colombia, and Venezuela. In Peru, the TSP and DAP plant at Bayovar would be built in the second period. In Colombia, the urea plant at La Dorada would be constructed in the same period. The TSP, NPK, and DAP plant at Punta Caiman in Venezuela would be added in the last period.

If this strategy were not politically acceptable, as the secretariat expected, it would be possible at relatively low cost to add a project in Ecuador and one in Bolivia, as in scenario 4. In Ecuador the only possible project considered was a medium-sized urea plant at Puerto Bolivar, while in Bolivia a small phosphate plant at Potosi was chosen rather than the export-oriented urea plant at Palmasola. Both projects would be added during the last period.

Scenario 4 was selected by the secretariat as a basis for a coordinated investment program that could be presented to the countries. A certain amount of sensitivity analysis was carried out, which demonstrated that the plan was fairly robust. However, because the basic design of the projects was taken as fixed, it should not be surprising that the plan was not strongly affected by the changes in assumptions that were stipulated in the sensitivity analysis. In the next chapter, dealing with further work on the model at the World Bank, we shall describe the results obtained under more relaxed constraints.

10

Further Analysis
of the Andean Model

The ANDEAN COMMON MARKET SECRETARIAT decided from the start on two important issues in the search for an attractive set of recommendations for the regional development of the fertilizer industry: (a) it would not attempt to redesign projects formulated by the member countries, and (b) it would only focus on alternative combinations of these fixed projects and the timing of their implementation to attain a degree of equity in the proposed programs.

In many respects, these were sensible decisions. Modification of project packages that had already been the subject of intense national discussions would have introduced an additional element of negotiation into the process. Moreover, using the model as a project *design* tool rather than a project *selection* tool would probably have exceeded the available capability for efficient computer use at the time. The latter argument also applies to the introduction of other considerations of equity besides project distribution.

In this chapter, we shall carry the analysis one step further and use the model as a project design tool to determine what additional efficiency gains can be derived from a flexible view with regard to project size, as well as timing. This model variant is run on two alternative conditions: (a) to find the "true" least-cost supply pattern, and (b) to locate at the lowest cost possible at least one project in each country. Having described the results of these two variants, we shall describe some possible additional experiments that could be conducted to approach the question of equity on other aspects, such as trade.

Scenario 5: The "True" Least-Cost Supply Pattern

We shall discuss the results achieved with the model under this heading in comparison to the results achieved in scenario 3, referred to in chapter 9 as the Andean least-cost supply pattern. The only difference between the two supply patterns lies in whether or not the project packages are considered to be of fixed size. Once the issue of project size is left open, to be resolved by the model on the basis of least-cost considerations, a number of important changes occur in the investment and trade pattern, as well as in costs. These patterns will be described as scenario 5.

Total discounted costs fall to their lowest level under scenario 5: $2,583 million, or 3.1 percent less than the cost associated with the least-cost investment plan with fixed project packages (scenario 3, as described in table 9-12). Detailed cost information, by category and period, is given in table 10-1. The greater efficiency of this investment plan, compared with scenario 3, is primarily due to changes in the external trade pattern. In undiscounted terms, total extraregional imports fall from $1.5 billion to $0.9 billion, or by 35 percent, while extraregional exports increase from $0.6 billion to $1.4 billion. How is this achieved?

Table 10-1. *Average Annual Costs under Scenario 5 (Least-Cost Strategy with Variable Project Size), by Period*
(millions of U.S. dollars)

Cost category	Period				Undis-counted costs
	1 (1981–83)	*2 (1984–86)*	*3 (1987–89)*	*4 (1990–92)*	
Capital charges	—	71.2	91.4	124.3	860.8
Operating costs	50.5	128.4	145.5	178.8	1,509.5
Regional raw material purchases	44.6	106.8	135.3	145.7	1,297.1
Import costs	116.9	55.2	68.8	75.2	948.3
(Tariff revenue)	(12.7)	(6.4)	(8.2)	(8.5)	(107.4)
Regional transport costs	45.5	72.8	88.1	98.2	913.4
Total costs	257.4	434.4	529.1	622.2	5,529.1
Export revenues	45.8	141.3	142.9	130.1	1,380.0
Net costs	211.6	293.1	386.2	492.1	4,149.1

Note: Objective function (present value): $2,583.4 million.

The true least-cost investment pattern involves the construction of projects in Peru, Colombia, and Venezuela, as was the case in the least-cost program with fixed project packages. However, project size and timing of implementation are different, and in Peru not only triple superphosphate (TSP) and diammonium phosphate (DAP), but also ammonia and urea are produced efficiently. The inclusion of the ammonia and urea project in scenario 5 suggests that project design, not product choice, is responsible for the absence of the project in all earlier scenarios.

In table 10-2, we present the details of the investment program in this solution to the model, and, to facilitate comparison, the investment program of scenario 3 in chapter 9. In Colombia, a larger version of the ammonia and urea project at La Dorada could be implemented, but not

Table 10-2. *Least-Cost Investment Programs under Scenarios 3 and 5*

Country and product	Fixed projects (scenario 3)		Variable projects (scenario 5)	
	Period implemented	Annual capacity (tons)	Period implemented	Annual capacity (tons)
Colombia				
Ammonia, La Dorada	1984–86	330,000	1990–92	395,200
Urea, La Dorada	1984–86	528,000	1990–92	670,500
Peru				
TSP, Bayovar	1984–86	355,000	1984–86	270,800
Phosphoric acid, Bayovar	1984–86	440,000	1984–86	712,500
Sulfuric acid, Bayovar	1984–86	660,000	1984–86	1,068,800
DAP, Bayovar	1984–86	210,000	1984–86	600,000
Ammonia, Bayovar	—	—	1984–86	625,800[a]
Urea, Bayovar	—	—	1984–86	835,500[a]
Venezuela				
TSP, Punta Caiman	1990–92	80,000	—	—
Phosphoric acid, Punta Caiman	1990–92	274,000	1987–89	375,500
Sulfuric acid, Punta Caiman	1990–92	411,000	1987–89	563,200
NPK, Punta Caiman	1990–92	750,000	—	—
DAP, Punta Caiman	1990–92	185,000	1987–89	393,400

Note: TSP signifies triple superphosphate; DAP signifies diammonium phosphate; and NPK signifies compounded fertilizers of various compositions.

a. The fixed project package was much smaller, with ammonia capacity of 214,800 tons, and urea of 287,100 tons of capacity.

before 1990. It would immediately be fully utilized, making Colombia self-sufficient in urea and permitting extraregional exports of over 200,000 tons a year. No intraregional exports of urea from Colombia take place.

In Peru, a large number of changes take place. With project size variable, less TSP and three times as much DAP would be produced at Bayovar, and, as stated earlier, ammonia and urea production would be efficient as long as it is at a larger scale than originally designed. As in the case of Colombia, the new projects in Bayovar would be fully utilized from the start. Very substantial intraregional and extraregional exports of urea, TSP, and DAP would be possible throughout the period.

In Venezuela, the Punta Caiman complex would be installed in the period 1987–89, which is earlier than in scenario 3, and would concentrate on DAP, deleting the production of TSP and NPK. The DAP plant could be twice as large as originally planned and would be fully utilized. The third period is the only one with substantial intraregional exports of DAP, mainly to Colombia.

Overall trade results are presented in table 10-3. As indicated before, the possibility of redesigning the project packages has a very substantial impact on trade patterns. First, much more intraregional trade takes place; in each year after 1984, intraregional trade is at least 40 percent larger than would be the case under scenario 3. Second, the Andean region is, from 1984 onward, consistently a net exporter of fertilizer to the rest of the world, even though the export constraint of 30 percent of production for most plants remains in force. The principal exporting countries in the second and third periods are Peru and Venezuela (urea and DAP), to be joined by Colombia in the fourth period (urea). During the first two periods, Venezuela exports ammonia as well.

Table 10-3. *Annual Trade Flows for the Andean Common Market under Scenario 5, by Period*
(millions of U.S. dollars)

Type of flow	1981–83	1984–86	1987–89	1990–92
Intraregional trade	45.3	171.0	202.1	192.2
Extraregional imports	116.9	55.2	68.8	75.2
Extraregional exports	45.8	141.3	142.9	130.1
Overall trade balance	71.1	−86.1	−74.1	−54.8

Scenario 6: A Flexible and Equitable Investment Program

In chapter 9, scenario 4 was called an equitable investment program because it was achieved under the constraint that each country should have at least one project. With project design taken as given, this constraint could be satisfied only at higher total cost to the region, $10 million in discounted terms.

We shall now relax the constraint on project design and solve the model leaving the issue of size and composition of projects open. However, we retain the constraint that each country have at least one project. The solution of the model under these conditions is scenario 6. The comparison will be made to scenario 4, and, occasionally, scenario 5.

Considerable cost savings can be achieved, even forcing a project in each country, by letting the model decide on project size. Compared with scenario 4, with fixed project packages, scenario 6 can save almost $60 million in discounted terms; the objective function value falls from $2,676.8 million to $2,617.1 million. Equity among the countries, however, is achieved at greater overall cost with flexible project sizes than with fixed project packages. In the latter case (scenario 4), total costs are only $10 million larger than the fixed size, least-cost program in discounted terms. With flexible project size, total costs increase from $2,583.4 million for the least-cost program to $2,617.1 million for the more equitable one, a rise of $34 million. Nevertheless, this increase represents only 1.3 percent, a relatively small price to pay if the alternatives are the immediate implementation of all national plans, which is $533 million more costly, or a do-nothing approach, which costs $145 million more. All amounts are discounted totals for the entire planning period.

A summary of the annual costs in each period is given in table 10-4. Higher investment and operating cost are incurred in the program with flexible project sizes than in the one with fixed sizes, because larger plants are generally recommended. Much lower imports from world markets are needed, and export revenues could be double the size of those achieved in scenario 4. As can be seen from table 10-5, the overall trade balance with the rest of the world is in surplus from 1984 onward, at approximately the same level as in scenario 5. Intraregional trade is even larger, over $200 million in each year after 1984.

The composition of products in the investment program in scenario 6 is similar to that obtained in scenario 4. Project sizes, however, vary considerably. Details are given in table 10-6.

Table 10-4. *Average Annual Costs under Scenario 6 (Equitable Investment Strategy with Variable Project Size), by Period*
(millions of U.S. dollars)

| Cost category | Period | | | | Undis-counted costs |
	1 (1981–83)	*2 (1984–86)*	*3 (1987–89)*	*4 (1990–92)*	
Capital charges	—	71.7	91.5	127.6	872.4
Operating costs	50.5	128.9	146.0	178.9	1,512.9
Regional raw material purchases	44.6	106.6	134.2	146.0	1,294.1
Import costs	116.9	55.2	68.3	75.2	946.6
Transport costs	45.5	78.8	93.5	103.4	963.4
Total costs	257.4	441.2	533.4	631.1	5,589.4
Exports	45.8	141.4	142.8	130.3	1,380.9
Net costs	211.6	299.8	390.7	500.8	4,208.5

Note: Objective function (present value): $2,617.1 million.

Table 10-5. *Annual Trade Flows for the Andean Common Market under Scenario 6, by Period*
(millions of U.S. dollars)

Type of flow	1981–83	1984–86	1987–89	1990–92
Intraregional trade	45.3	206.6	232.2	221.9
Extraregional imports	116.9	55.2	68.3	75.2
Extraregional exports	45.8	141.4	142.8	130.3
Overall trade balance	71.1	−86.2	−74.5	−55.1

The least-cost strategy that would locate a project in Bolivia would be to construct a small TSP plant in Potosi, less than half the size currently planned, in the last period. It produces only for the domestic market, at 100 percent of effective capacity.

The ammonia and urea project in Colombia, to be located at La Dorada, should be somewhat larger than currently planned. However, compared with scenario 4, its implementation should be postponed until the end of the planning period. This result and the disappearance of the ammonia and urea project in Peru (as compared with the least-cost strategy) are both explained by the establishment of a very much larger ammonia and urea complex in Ecuador. If Ecuador is to have a project, it would be advisable to construct a sizable ammonia and urea plant at

Table 10-6. *Equitable Investment Programs under Scenarios 4 and 6*

Country and product	Fixed projects (scenario 4)		Variable projects (scenario 6)	
	Period implemented	*Annual capacity (tons)*	*Period implemented*	*Annual capacity (tons)*
Bolivia				
TSP, Potosi	1990–92	56,100	1990–92	23,100
Phosphoric acid, Potosi	1990–92	41,250	1990–92	17,100
Colombia				
Ammonia, La Dorada	1984–86	330,000	1990–92	381,000
Urea, La Dorada	1984–86	528,000	1990–92	647,000
Ecuador				
Ammonia, Puerto Bolivar	1990–92	143,550	1984–86	641,200
Urea, Puerto Bolivar	1990–92	247,500	1984–86	861,600
Peru				
TSP, Bayovar	1984–86	355,000	1984–86	261,500
Phosphoric acid, Bayovar	1984–86	440,000	1984–86	705,700
Sulfuric acid, Bayovar	1984–86	660,000	1984–86	1,058,500
DAP, Bayovar	1984–86	210,000	1984–86	600,000
Venezuela				
TSP, Punta Caiman	1990–92	80,000	—	—
Phosphoric acid, Punta Caiman	1990–92	274,000	1987–89	364,000
Sulfuric acid, Punta Caiman	1990–92	411,000	1987–89	546,000
NPK, Punta Caiman	1990–92	750,000	—	—
DAP, Punta Caiman	1990–92	185,000	1987–89	380,000

Puerto Bolivar, implemented in the period 1984–86. In addition to meeting domestic urea requirements, this plant would enable Ecuador to become a major supplier of urea within the Andean region, exporting to all Andean countries except Venezuela and to world markets from 1984 onward.

As indicated earlier, the imposition of projects in all countries affects the relative efficiency of ammonia and urea production at Bayovar, Peru. Nonetheless, a project complex for TSP and DAP should be erected there, as in scenario 4, but it should produce less TSP and more DAP. Ammonia for DAP production is imported from Ecuador, which explains the imbalance of the ammonia and urea complex at Puerto Bolivar.

Finally, in Venezuela, the Punta Caiman project should concentrate on DAP production, dropping plans for TSP and NPK production. The DAP plant should be twice the size that was originally planned. The complex should be implemented in 1987–89, earlier than in scenario 4.

This completes the description of the use of the model as a project design tool. Clearly, many more scenarios could be developed. Additional constraints could be introduced with regard to the pattern of project implementation: for example, prescribing that all projects should be implemented within one period, for the model to select, or within two periods. Moreover, the definition of the planning problem itself could be altered: for example, by specifying more potential producing locations or more products. Although such further analysis may be called for in a given application of the model, here it would add little to the demonstration of the uses of the model. Instead, we shall discuss the relative merits of the six scenarios.

A Comparison of Costs by Country

Before describing the results obtained on costs by country for the various scenarios that have been evaluated, we need to explain how costs are treated in the model. The standard cost-minimizing optimization framework generates results that ascribe all production costs to the plant where production occurs, and, therefore, to the country in which the plant is located. No transfer prices need to be stipulated in order to find the least-cost supply pattern. For this exercise, however, the standard results are not satisfactory, as no country is credited for intraregional exports or charged for intraregional imports. A simple procedure was used to correct this anomaly, namely, all intraregional trade flows were valued at c.i.f. prices relevant for each period, and the cost thus computed was added to the total cost of the importing country, and deducted as revenue from the cost of the exporting country. This procedure implies that the gains associated with each least-cost supply pattern are entirely allocated to the producing country. Clearly, an infinite range of alternative supply patterns can be designed to introduce greater equity in the distribution of gains. For example, if one scenario is 10 percent less costly than another, transfer prices for intraregional trade could be placed at 90 percent of c.i.f. values. However, this was not done for the analysis described below and summarized in table 10-7.

Table 10-7. *Undiscounted Costs under Scenarios 1-6, by Period and Country*
(millions of U.S. dollars)

Scenario and country	1981–83	1984–86	1987–89	1990–92
Scenario 1 (all in second period)				
Bolivia	3.7	23.8	28.5	34.3
Colombia	123.8	207.9	244.2	265.1
Ecuador	28.6	53.0	62.4	76.7
Peru	50.5	79.6	72.8	90.3
Venezuela	5.0	60.2	71.4	113.9
Scenario 2 (no expansion)				
Bolivia	3.7	8.5	14.6	20.7
Colombia	123.8	178.6	223.2	251.9
Ecuador	28.6	41.9	57.8	74.9
Peru	50.5	72.6	91.3	110.7
Venezuela	5.0	5.9	34.6	111.0
Scenario 3 (least-cost, fixed projects)				
Bolivia	3.7	8.6	14.7	20.8
Colombia	123.8	173.0	203.3	236.8
Ecuador	28.6	43.4	58.8	74.8
Peru	50.5	52.9	69.4	91.0
Venezuela	5.0	20.7	54.1	105.5
Scenario 4 (equitable, fixed projects)				
Bolivia	3.7	8.6	14.7	24.6
Colombia	123.8	173.0	203.3	236.3
Ecuador	28.6	43.4	58.8	71.6
Peru	50.5	52.9	69.4	90.6
Venezuela	5.0	20.7	54.1	113.6
Scenario 5 (least-cost, variable projects)				
Bolivia	3.7	8.9	15.0	21.1
Colombia	123.8	193.1	235.7	244.8
Ecuador	28.6	44.1	62.4	78.8
Peru	50.5	15.1	21.2	27.3
Venezuela	5.0	32.0	52.0	120.1
Scenario 6 (equitable, variable projects)				
Bolivia	3.7	8.9	15.0	23.4
Colombia	123.8	194.6	235.2	247.2
Ecuador	28.6	12.6	18.6	37.0
Peru	50.5	51.6	65.8	72.8
Venezuela	5.0	32.1	56.1	120.4

From Bolivia's point of view, the country-specific total cost figures confirm what was already apparent from the earlier discussion: Bolivia is not an efficient producer of fertilizer material, and it would be better off not to do anything at all. Implementing all its projects is by far the most expensive option, leading to very high cost especially in the earlier periods. In 1984–86, the annual costs are almost three times those resulting if no capacity expansion occurs. Insisting upon at least one project as part of an Andean investment strategy increases the cost of meeting fertilizer requirements in Bolivia in the last period only, by about $4 million a year in the case of fixed projects; for variable projects, the costs are higher in every year after 1983, to attain a difference of $2.7 million a year in the last period, compared with a strategy of no capacity expansion.

For Colombia, too, scenario 1 is the most expensive for all time periods. However, in contrast to Bolivia, the differences in annual costs are not as large, particularly in the later years. Although no expansion at all leads to a lower cost supply pattern than the immediate implementation of all projects, very considerable cost savings are possible by implementing only the ammonia and urea complex at La Dorada and by dropping the phosphate project. As this strategy is what emerges in both scenarios 3 and 4, the costs for both are virtually identical.

The relaxation of the constraint on project size results in higher costs to Colombia, both for the least-cost strategy and for the one that requires a project in each country. This outcome is due to changes in the pattern of trade, which in turn stem from changes in the timing and, in the case of flexible project sizes, changes in the design of projects. Let us focus on a comparison between scenarios 4 and 6. During the period 1987–89, the annual costs of meeting Colombia's fertilizer requirements with flexible projects is almost $35 million larger than with fixed projects, net of export proceeds. Closer inspection of the detailed results provides the following explanation for this cost increase. First, with flexible project size and the need to establish a project in each country, it is efficient from the whole Andean region's point of view to postpone the installation of Colombia's ammonia-urea project at La Dorada from the second until the fourth period. Until that time, Colombia is therefore much more dependent on imports, which it purchases from Ecuador in the form of urea and from Peru in the form of DAP. In contrast, with fixed project size, Colombia is self-sufficient in its nitrogen requirements from 1984 onward, when it installs the La Dorada project. It obtains its phosphate requirements from the Peruvian TSP plant at Bayovar. In other words, the introduction of flexible project packages changes the timing of capacity construction in Colombia, changes its supply pattern from domestic to imported urea, and changes its product composition from TSP to DAP. Although these changes are beneficial for the Andean region, they are not so for Colombia, which will host a project much later but will face a more costly supply pattern than it would if project packages were fixed. Clearly, therefore, a more attractive transfer price for intraregional trade would need to be established for Colombia for that country to be willing to join an agreement. A 22 percent reduction in the c.i.f. price for intraregional trade would make Colombia break even; however, that adjustment would not provide compensation for a delay in plant construction.

In Ecuador, the first five scenarios imply total annual costs that are very similar, particularly after the second period. Nevertheless, implementation of all current plans is again the most expensive strategy, and a do-nothing approach is superior for Ecuador, as is either strategy with fixed projects, except during the final period. Ecuador is the principal beneficiary of the implementation of scenario 6, an equitable investment strategy with variable project size. As described in the previous section, in that case Ecuador would host a large ammonia and urea complex that would permit very substantial exports of urea, principally to Colombia. Credited against the cost of meeting its domestic fertilizer requirements, the revenues from intraregional exports reduce total net annual costs to less than one-third of what they are in any of the other scenarios. The redesign of the Ecuadorean urea plant is responsible for the delay in the construction of the urea plant in Colombia, and, consequently, the increase in total costs in that country. Compared with the fixed-projects strategies (scenarios 3 and 4), Ecuador's gain under a flexible investment program is almost exactly equal to Colombia's loss.

Peru presents another interesting case. For the first time, the no-capacity-expansion case is not in every period superior to the implementation of all current plans, annual costs in the third and fourth period being considerably lower for the latter scenario. This result is simply another demonstration of the relative efficiency of some of Peru's projects, particularly those for phosphatic fertilizer. However, as the results for the second period in scenarios 3 and 4 show, not all projects at Bayovar are efficient, and deletion of the potash and nitrogen projects permits a considerable reduction in total costs compared with scenario 1, which includes them. By far the cheapest scenario for Peru is scenario 5, the least-cost investment strategy with variable project size. It will be remembered that in that case Peru produces TSP, DAP, and urea, the last two products at scales far beyond those originally planned, and the country becomes a major Andean exporter. The imposition of an equity constraint on the investment program (scenario 6) shifts the ammonia and urea capacity to Ecuador (as it leads to postponement of the Colombian plant) and reduces export revenues.

Venezuela would clearly be better off with a do-nothing approach, at least during the second and third periods. The reason is that the country has by far the largest installed production capacity in the sector and would be able to export substantial quantities of fertilizer material to neighboring countries. In contrast, the implementation of all current plans would be very expensive to Venezuela, both because it inhibits Andean exports and because some of its own projects are not very efficient. Comparing the scenarios that take current expansion plans as fixed with those assuming the possibility of project redesign, it appears that Venezuela would, on the whole, benefit from inefficient project design in the partner countries. The main impact of the relation of the constraint on project design for Venezuela is that neither the TSP nor the NPK plant would be constructed, and that a much larger DAP plant would be constructed earlier. Although Venezuela, as a result, achieves a greater degree of self-sufficiency, it also has a much reduced scope for intraregional exports. As a consequence, the net cost of meeting fertilizer requirements increases over the level possible with fixed projects.

Recapitulation

The foregoing discussion of the costs by country of the various scenarios has shown that a joint investment program entails difficult questions relating to the distribution of costs and benefits among the partner countries. While our definition of equity has focused on the distribution of projects over the Andean region, it should be realized that each investment pattern implies costs by country that may be seen to be unequal. Our analysis has been limited to one very simple pricing scheme for intraregional trade, that is, world market prices. This approach implies that all gains associated with regional production over imports are allocated to the producing country. As we have seen, this may not be the most promising pricing system to achieve agreement among partner countries.

One alternative among many would be opportunity cost pricing. Assume that the alternative to a regional investment strategy is a no-capacity-expansion policy. In this case, it can be determined at what cost each marketing center would be able to obtain its needed supplies at lowest cost. Assume further that the regional investment strategy would make possible a 10 percent reduction in total supply costs. In that case, a straightforward pricing policy would be based on opportunity costs reduced by the regional cost advantage. However, in reality such a simple rule is unlikely to be feasible, as it requires one very critical agreement among the countries: that the only relevant alternative to the regional investment program is no capacity expansion at all. This will rarely be the case, and some countries are likely to implement more or less efficient national investment projects. Under such circumstances, the analyst has no alternative but to determine the optimal investment strategy for each country individually, to derive resulting supply prices, and to design a regional investment strategy that represents an improvement over the most efficient national strategy. This may once more be done by reflecting the overall regional cost advantage in the supply prices at each marketing center.

Although an infinite number of alternative pricing schemes is feasible, and negotiations will normally have to be conducted to reach agreement, it should be realized that the range within which agreement needs to be sought is limited to the overall benefits of the particular scenario. In the long run, no cooperation agreement is likely to survive if it implies supply costs to one or more countries that are higher than readily available alternative supply patterns.

11

Conclusions

MULTICOUNTRY INVESTMENT ANALYSIS has been approached here in both general and specific terms. Generally, this book extends the methodology of investment analysis in the presence of economies of scale for national economies to planning situations that require the explicit consideration of equity among geographic units. Specifically, it applies that approach to a case study, the fertilizer sector in the Andean Common Market countries.

There is much evidence that regional cooperation among developing countries remains of considerable interest. The world recession of the late seventies and early eighties, and the resulting slowdown in the growth of international trade, has provided developing countries with the impetus to explore the scope for South-South trade. Surely, increased trade among developing countries can and will take place without regional cooperation agreements. However, many such schemes exist, and the main objective of this volume is to contribute to the formulation of efficient investment projects based upon such agreements. No single factor contributes more decisively to the long-term viability of multicountry investment agreements than the efficiency of the projects subject to such agreements.

As we have demonstrated in the case study, equity considerations among the countries involved need to be considered as thoroughly as efficiency considerations. Typically, there will be tradeoffs. However, it will usually be possible to introduce an element of equity into the investment program without eliminating the gains from regional cooperation, as compared with the implementation of inefficient national plans or a do-nothing approach. If it is not possible to achieve an adequate degree of equity by a modification of the regional investment program, at reasonable cost, other forms of equity may be sought, such as lump-sum transfers or relatively favorable transfer prices. However, these alternatives have proved to be rather unstable in practice.

As our experience with the Andean region has shown, our approach to multicountry investment analysis should not be judged by its success in contributing to a regional investment plan. In such terms, our case study could easily be seen to have been a failure, as the Andean Common Market could not agree on a joint strategy. A political malaise within the region, and widespread disenchantment with the lack of success of earlier industrial agreements, led to lukewarm reception of the proposals formulated in Lima. Nonetheless, the secretariat was praised for the quality of the analysis that was carried out and was encouraged to make efforts to keep the data base up to date and to achieve improvements in areas where the data were known to be weak, such as transport and distribution costs. Periodic use of the model to analyze the implications of changes in circumstances, such as the introduction of specific projects, the identification of new project possibilities, and variations in world market conditions, would in fact be a very effective approach, as long as the results of such further analysis lead to greater coordination of actions in the Andean region. Ideally, the secretariat ought to establish and maintain a data base on the most important industrial subsectors in the Andean region, using the model as a data organizational framework, as well as for analytic purposes to report to the countries on trends in each subsector from a regional point of view. Whether such analysis leads to regional investment projects or, less ambitiously, to national investment decisions that have benefited from better information on the regional context is not important: either result is likely to have benefits that far exceed the costs of the analysis and data maintenance. It is in this flexible spirit that the approach in this volume should be used.

APPENDIX

A Computer-Readable Statement of the Model

```
    4   SET  W     COUNTRIES IN ANDEAN COMMON MARKET  / BOLIVIA, COLOMBIA, ECUADOR, PERU, VENEZUELA /
    5
    6        WR    COUNTRIES AND REGION
    7
    8        I     PLANT LOCATIONS    /
    9
   10              PALMASOLA     PTA-PEQUENA
   11              PTO-SUAREZ    PTA-GRANDE
   12              POTOSI        ENAF
   13              BARANQUILL    MONOMEROS
   14              CARTAGENA     ABOCOL
   15
   16              BARRANCABR    FERTICOL
   17              LA-DORADA     LA-DORADA
   18              GUAYAQUIL     FERTIZA
   19              PT-BOLIVAR    CEPE
   20              CALLAO-F      FERTIZA
   21
   22              CUZCO         CACHIMAYO
   23              TALARA        PETROPERU
   24              CALLAO-I      INDUS
   25              BAYOVAR       BAYOVAR
   26              MORON         IVP
   27
   28              PTA-CAIMAN    PEDEVESA
   29              CARIPITO      IVP
   30              TABLAZO       NITROVEN   /
   31
   32
   33   WI(W,I)    COUNTRY-PLANT LOCATION MAPPING     /
   34
   35              BOLIVIA.(PALMASOLA,PTO-SUAREZ,POTOSI)
   36              COLOMBIA.(BARANQUILL,CARTAGENA,BARRANCABR,LA-DORADA )
   37              ECUADOR.(GUAYAQUIL,PT-BOLIVAR)
   38              PERU.(CALLAO-F,CUZCO,TALARA,CALLAO-I,BAYOVAR)
   39              VENEZUELA.(MORON,PTA-CAIMAN,CARIPITO,TABLAZO)   /
   40
   41        J     DEMAND REGIONS    /
   42
   43              COCHABAMBA    VALLES
   44              SANTA-CRUZ    LLANOS-ORIENTALES
   45              POTOSI        ALTIPLANO
   46              BOGOTA        CENTRAL
   47              BUCARAMANG    NOR-ORIENTAL
   48
   49              ARMENIA       CAFETERA
   50              CALI          SUR
   51              QUITO         NOR-OCCIDENTAL
   52              BABAHOYO      CENTRO-OCCIDENTAL
   53              MACHALA       SUR-OCCIDENTAL
   54              CHICLAYO      NORTE
```

184

```
 55          ICA          CENTRO
 56          AREQUIPA     SUR
 57          TINGO-MAR    SELVA
 58          MATURIN      ORIENTAL
 59
 60          MARACAIBO    OCCIDENTAL
 61          CALABOZO     CENTRO-ORIENTE
 62          ACARIGUA     CENTRO-OCCIDENTE  /
 63
 64
 65  WJ(W,J)  COUNTRY DEMAND REGION MAPPING  /  BOLIVIA.(COCHABAMBA,SANTA-CRUZ,POTOSI)
 66                                              COLOMBIA.(BOGOTA,BUCARAMANG,ARMENIA,CALI)
 67                                              ECUADOR.(QUITO,BABAHOYO,MACHALA)
 68                                              PERU.(CHICLAYO,ICA,AREQUIPA,TINGO-MAR)
 69                                              VENEZUELA.(MATURIN,MARACAIBO,CALABOZO,ACARIGUA)  /
 70
 71
 72  P        PROCESSES  /
 73
 74          AMM-ELEC     AMMONIA: ELECTROLYSIS
 75          AMM-N-GAS    AMMONIA: NATURAL GAS
 76          AMM-F-OIL    AMMONIA: FUEL OIL
 77          NITR-ACID    NITRIC ACID
 78          AMM-NITR     AMMONIUM NITRATE
 79
 80          UREA         UREA
 81          SSP          SINGLE SUPERPHOSPHATE
 82          TSP          TRIPLE SUPERPHOSPHATE
 83          S-SP         SINGLE SUPERPHOSPHATE ON SS-TSP UNIT
 84          T-SP         TRIPLE SUPERPHOSPHATE ON SS-TSP UNIT
 85
 86          PHOS-ACID    PHOSPHORIC ACID
 87          SULF-ACID    SULFURIC ACID
 88          DAP          DIAMMONIUM PHOSPHATE
 89          DAP-G        DIAMMONIUM PHOSPHATE ON GRANULATOR UNIT
 90          COMP-G       COMPOUND FERTILIZER ON GRANULATOR UNIT
 91
 92          C-20-18-10   COMPOUND FERTILIZER
 93          C-13-13-20   COMPOUND FERTILIZER
 94          C-15-21-10   COMPOUND FERTILIZER
 95          C-16-12-12   COMPOUND FERTILIZER
 96          C-08-24-12   COMPOUND FERTILIZER
 97
 98          C-12-12-12   COMPOUND FERTILIZER
 99          POT-CHLOR    POTASSIUM CHLORIDE
100          AMM-SULF     AMMONIUM SULFATE  /
101
102
103  G        PLANT TYPE  / OLD, NEW /
104
105  M        PRODUCTIVE UNITS  /
106
```

185

A N D E A N   FERTILIZER MODEL
SET DEFINITIONS

```
107              AMM-ELEC     AMMONIA: ELECTROLYSIS
108              AMM-N-GAS    AMMONIA: NATURAL GAS
109              AMM-F-OIL    AMMONIA: FUEL OIL
110              NITR-ACID    NITRIC ACID
111              AMM-NITR     AMMONIUM NITRATE
112
113
114              UREA         SINGLE SUPERPHOSPHATE
115              SSP          TRIPLE SUPERPHOSPHATE
116              TSP          COMBINED SSP TSP PLANT
117              SS-TSP       PHOSPHORIC ACID
118              PHOS-ACID    SULFURIC ACID
119              SULF-ACID
120
121              DAP          DIAMMONIUM PHOSPHATE
122              GRANULATOR   UNIT FOR DAP NPK AND TSP GRANULATION
123              NPK          COMPOUND FERTILIZER
124              AMM-SULF     AMMONIUM SULFATE
125              POT-CHLOR    POTASSIUM CHLORIDE                    /
126
127
128      CQ      NUTRIENTS                  /
129
130              N            NITROGEN
131              P205         PHOSPHORUS
132              K20          POTASH                /
133
134
135      C       ALL COMMODITIES            /
136
137              UREA
138              AMM-NITR     AMMONIUM NITRATE
139              SSP          SINGLE SUPERPHOSPHATE
140              TSP          TRIPLE SUPERPHOSPHATE
141              DAP          DIAMMONIUM PHOSPHATE
142
143              C-20-18-10
144              C-13-13-20
145              C-15-21-10
146              C-16-12-12
147              C-08-24-12   COMPOUND FERTILIZER
148              C-12-12-12
149              AMM-SULF     AMMONIUM SULFATE
150              POT-CHLOR    POTASSIUM CHLORIDE
151              AMMONIA
152              NITR-ACID    NITRIC ACID
153
154              CARB-DIOX    CARBON DIOXIDE
155              ELECTR       ELECTRICITY          (1000 KWH    )
156              NAT-GAS      NATURAL GAS          (1000 STD.CUB.F)
157              FUEL-OIL
158
```

```
159
160          PHOS-ACID    PHOSPHORIC ACID
161
162          PHOS-ROCK    PHOSPHATE ROCK      ( .75 PCT BPL  )
163          SULF-ACID    SULFURIC ACID
164          EL-SULFUR    ELEMENTAL SULFUR
165          BRINE                                 /
166
167    CF(C) FINAL PRODUCTS      /
168
169          UREA, AMM-NITR, AMM-SULF, SSP, TSP, POT-CHLOR, DAP
170          C-20-18-10, C-13-13-20, C-15-21-10, C-16-12-12, C-08-24-12, C-12-12-12 /
171
172
173    CO(C) COMPOUNDS      / C-20-18-10, C-13-13-20, C-15-21-10, C-16-12-12, C-08-24-12, C-12-12-12 /
174
175
176    CR(C) DOMESTIC RAW MATERIALS   / ELECTR, NAT-GAS, FUEL-OIL, PHOS-ROCK, EL-SULFUR, SULF-ACID, BRINE /
177
178
179    CIS(C) PRODUCTS FOR INTERPLANT SHIPMENT   /
180
181          UREA, AMM-NITR, AMM-SULF, SSP, TSP, POT-CHLOR, DAP, PHOS-ACID, AMMONIA /
182
183
184    CE(C) PRODUCTS FOR EXPORT   / UREA, AMM-NITR, AMM-SULF, SSP, TSP, POT-CHLOR, DAP, PHOS-ACID, AMMONIA  /
185
186
187    CV(C) PRODUCTS FOR IMPORT      /
188
189          UREA, AMM-NITR, AMM-SULF, TSP, POT-CHLOR, DAP, PHOS-ACID, AMMONIA, PHOS-ROCK, EL-SULFUR /
190
191
192    WNPK(W,C) COUNTRY COMPOUND MAPPING   / VENEZUELA.(C-20-18-10,C-13-13-20)
193                                           COLOMBIA.(C-16-12-12,C-15-21-10)
194                                           ECUADOR.(C-08-24-12)
195                                           PERU.(C-12-12-12)              /
196
197
198    T     TIME PERIODS   / 1981-83, 1984-86, 1987-89, 1990-92 /
199
200
201    TE(T) EXPANSION PERIODS   / 1984-86, 1987-89, 1990-92 /
202
203    CORES(CO,I,J) COMPOUND SHIPMENT POSSIBILITIES ;
204
205
206    ALIAS(I,IP),(J,JP),(T,TP),(TE,TEP),(W,WP);
207
208    WR(W)       = YES; WR("ANDEAN")=YES;
209    CORES(CO,I,J) = SUM(W$(WI(W,I)*WJ(W,J)), WNPK(W,CO));
210    DISPLAY WR,CORES;
```

187

TABLE DEM82(J,CQ) NUTRIENT DEMAND PROJECTIONS FOR 1982 (1000 TPY)

	N	P205	K20
COCHABAMBA	1.2	2.3	
SANTA-CRUZ	1.2	.6	
POTOSI	.3	2.4	
BOGOTA	74.2	57.1	34.2
BUCARAMANG	29.4	7.1	5.4
ARMENIA	54.3	44.3	29.3
CALI	30.8	25.3	15.4
QUITO	12.6	10.3	6.1
BABAHOYO	16.2	13.2	7.9
MACHALA	7.2	5.8	3.4
CHICLAYO	58.0	15.8	9.4
ICA	43.2	11.8	7.1
AREQUIPA	17.2	4.7	2.8
TINGO-MAR	4.9	1.3	.8
MATURIN	24.8	18.3	11.7
MARACAIBO	16.5	12.2	7.8
CALABOZO	42.7	31.5	20.2
ACARIGUA	53.7	39.6	25.4

TABLE DEM85(J,CQ) NUTRIENT DEMAND PROJECTIONS FOR 1985 (1000 TPY)

	N	P205	K20
COCHABAMBA	3.7	3.2	
SANTA-CRUZ	4.6	1.1	
POTOSI	0.9	3.0	
BOGOTA	90.7	65.9	37.2
BUCARAMANG	34.9	8.4	6.1
ARMENIA	76.8	63.5	43.7
CALI	38.9	31.8	16.9
QUITO	14.4	11.6	7.0
BABAHOYO	23.1	18.5	11.3
MACHALA	10.6	8.5	5.1
CHICLAYO	70.8	21.5	12.8
ICA	45.8	13.9	8.3
AREQUIPA	23.6	7.2	4.3
TINGO-MAR	7.4	2.2	1.4
MATURIN	30.6	23.6	14.1
MARACAIBO	20.4	15.7	9.4
CALABOZO	52.6	40.7	24.2
ACARIGUA	66.2	51.1	30.5

DEMAND DATA

260	TABLE DEM88(J,CQ)	NUTRIENT DEMAND PROJECTIONS FOR 1988 (1000 TPY)		
261		N	P205	K20
262				
263				
264	COCHABAMBA	5.7	4.7	
265	SANTA-CRUZ	7.4	1.7	
266	POTOSI	3.3	4.3	
267	BOGOTA	99.9	71.1	42.0
268	BUCARAMANG	38.3	9.9	7.6
269	ARMENIA	100.8	82.6	49.8
270	CALI	46.6	38.4	18.8
271	QUITO	16.0	12.8	7.7
272	BABAHOYO	32.0	25.8	15.5
273	MACHALA	16.0	12.8	7.7
274	CHICLAYO	81.5	29.2	17.4
275	ICA	48.2	17.3	10.3
276	AREQUIPA	28.3	10.2	6.0
277	TINGO-MAR	8.3	3.0	1.8
278	MATURIN	39.2	32.9	17.2
279	MARACAIBO	26.2	21.9	11.5
280	CALABOZO	67.5	56.7	29.7
281	ACARIGUA	84.9	71.3	37.4
282				
283				
284	TABLE DEM91(J,CQ)	NUTRIENT DEMAND PROJECTIONS FOR 1991 (1000 TPY)		
285		N	P205	K20
286				
287				
288	COCHABAMBA	8.0	6.9	
289	SANTA-CRUZ	10.4	3.0	
290	POTOSI	4.6	5.4	
291	BOGOTA	104.2	74.2	43.2
292	BUCARAMANG	44.4	12.3	9.0
293	ARMENIA	121.1	100.8	59.1
294	CALI	54.3	44.3	20.5
295	QUITO	16.7	13.3	8.1
296	BABAHOYO	43.1	34.8	20.9
297	MACHALA	23.3	18.7	11.3
298	CHICLAYO	90.6	38.8	23.2
299	ICA	51.6	21.4	12.7
300	AREQUIPA	33.3	14.3	8.5
301	TINGO-MAR	11.1	4.8	2.8
302	MATURIN	51.0	47.3	21.2
303	MARACAIBO	34.0	31.5	14.2
304	CALABOZO	87.9	81.6	36.6
305	ACARIGUA	110.5	102.6	46.1
306				

DEMAND DATA

TABLE DB(J,*) MINIMUM AMMONIUM SULFATE REQUIREMENT (1000 TPY)

	1981-83	1984-86	1987-89	1990-92
COCHABAMBA	.5	.5	.5	.5
SANTA-CRUZ	.5	.5	.5	.5
POTOSI	.3	.3	.5	.5
BOGOTA	9.8	12.4	13.4	15.5
BUCARAMANG	4.7	4.7	6.9	8.0
ARMENIA	9.4	12.0	13.4	15.5
CALI	4.7	4.7	6.4	7.5
QUITO	1.8	2.3	2.8	3.1
BABAHOYO	1.8	2.3	2.4	2.6
MACHALA	1.4	1.5	1.9	2.2
CHICLAYO	3.8	4.5	5.3	6.5
ICA	3.8	4.5	5.3	6.5
AREQUIPA	3.2	3.9	4.6	5.7
TINGO-MAR	1.3	1.9	2.7	3.3
MATURIN	15.4	16.9	20.5	21.5
MARACAIBO	11.5	11.8	11.9	12.5
CALABOZO	23.3	24.5	27.0	28.4
ACARIGUA	28.8	32.9	34.0	35.7

TABLE ALPHA(C,CQ) NUTRIENT CONTENT

	N	P205	K20
AMMONIA	.80		
NITR-ACID	.22		
PHOS-ACID		.54	
PHOS-ROCK		.30	
BRINE			.0004
UREA	.46		
AMM-NITR	.33		
AMM-SULF	.205		
SSP		.20	
TSP		.46	
POT-CHLOR			.60
DAP	.18	.46	
C-20-18-10	.20	.18	.10
C-13-13-20	.13	.13	.20
C-15-21-10	.15	.21	.10
C-16-12-12	.16	.12	.12
C-08-24-12	.08	.24	.12
C-12-12-12	.12	.12	.12

PARAMETERS D(J,CQ,T) DEMAND FOR NUTRIENTS   (1000 TPY);

D(J,CQ,"1981-83") = DEM82(J,CQ);
D(J,CQ,"1984-86") = DEM85(J,CQ);

```
360        D(J,CQ,"1987-89") = DEM88(J,CQ);
361        D(J,CQ,"1990-92") = DEM91(J,CQ);
362
363        DISPLAY D;
```

TABLE TRSP TRANSPORT COST (US$ PER TON)

	PALMASOLA	PTO-SUAREZ	POTOSI	BARANQUILL	CARTAGENA	BARRANCABR	LA-DORADA	GUAYAQUIL	PT-BOLIVAR
POTOSI	31.25	55.97	18.17	70.68	70.68	93.97	97.58	70.32	70.32
COCHABAMBA	21.50	46.22	28.25	74.34	74.34	97.63	101.24	71.10	71.10
SANTA-CRUZ	3.00	27.72	28.25	86.84	86.84	110.13	113.74	83.60	83.60
BOGOTA	122.72	1000.00	103.56	32.88	35.61	16.44	12.00	64.04	64.04
BUCARAMANG	113.13	1000.00	93.97	23.28	26.03	8.22	21.28	54.45	54.45
ARMENIA	101.63	1000.00	82.66	31.15	31.15	21.91	11.47	42.33	42.33
CALI	106.15	1000.00	87.18	25.67	20.67	32.98	16.95	36.75	36.75
QUITO	91.13	1000.00	87.92	48.76	48.67	72.05	47.40	20.80	26.00
BABAHOYO	88.52	1000.00	75.92	36.76	36.76	60.05	63.66	5.60	13.20
MACHALA	88.52	1000.00	73.32	34.16	34.16	57.45	61.06	9.60	3.00
CHICLAYO	84.36	1000.00	66.25	36.14	36.14	59.43	63.04	32.90	32.90
ICA	65.35	1000.00	47.40	51.05	51.05	74.34	77.95	47.81	47.81
AREQUIPA	124.99	1000.00	106.44	41.99	41.99	65.28	68.89	38.25	38.75
TINGO-MAR	95.81	1000.00	74.49	72.61	72.61	95.90	99.51	69.37	69.37
MATURIN	105.12	1000.00	74.49	39.61	39.61	55.46	66.51	39.11	39.11
MARACAIBO	103.95	1000.00	83.80	22.61	31.61	38.17	49.51	39.11	39.11
CALABOZO		1000.00	83.80	44.22	49.14	45.65	60.21	48.42	48.42
ACARIGUA		1000.00	82.63	37.33	49.33	38.64	53.70	47.25	47.25
PTS-PLANT	60.00	1000.00	40.00	-.009	-.009	23.30	25.00	-.009	-.009

+	CALLAO-F	CUZCO	TALARA	CALLAO-I	BAYOVAR	MORON	PTA-CAIMAN	CARIPITO	TABLAZO	PTS-MARKET
POTOSI	75.40	55.45	77.02	75.40	77.02	75.12	67.48	67.48	67.48	33.00
COCHABAMBA	68.40	47.85	70.02	68.40	70.02	80.94	73.30	73.30	73.30	50.50
SANTA-CRUZ	80.90	64.70	82.52	80.90	82.52	93.44	85.80	85.80	85.80	71.50
BOGOTA	66.02	1000.00	66.02	66.02	66.02	73.34	65.48	65.48	65.48	32.90
BUCARAMANG	56.43	1000.00	56.43	56.43	56.43	63.75	55.89	55.89	55.89	23.30
ARMENIA	44.93	1000.00	44.93	44.93	44.93	53.33	44.43	44.43	44.43	12.30
CALI	39.43	1000.00	39.45	39.45	39.45	47.85	38.95	38.95	38.95	6.90
QUITO	46.42	1000.00	46.42	46.42	46.42	58.60	49.70	49.70	49.70	17.60
BABAHOYO	34.42	1000.00	34.42	34.42	34.42	46.60	37.70	37.70	37.70	5.60
MACHALA	31.82	1000.00	31.82	31.82	31.82	44.00	35.10	35.10	35.10	3.00
CHICLAYO	21.82	1000.00	21.82	21.82	21.82	44.00	35.10	35.10	35.10	3.10
ICA	17.91	49.00	17.91	17.91	36.73	58.91	50.01	50.01	50.01	18.00
AREQUIPA	27.20	24.70	27.67	27.20	27.67	49.85	40.95	40.95	40.95	8.90
TINGO-MAR	39.47	1000.00	58.29	39.47	58.29	80.47	71.57	71.57	71.57	39.50
MATURIN	39.11	106.02	39.11	39.11	39.11	20.86	21.03	7.01	28.74	7.00
MARACAIBO	39.11	1000.00	39.11	39.11	39.11	15.88	17.52	32.01	7.01	7.00
CALABOZO	48.42	1000.00	48.42	48.42	48.42	11.68	13.08	15.65	23.26	11.70
ACARIGUA	47.25	1000.00	47.25	47.25	47.25	10.51	12.27	24.65	11.21	10.50
PTS-PLANT	-.009	29.80	-.009	-.009	-.009	-.009	-.009	-.009	-.009	

```
413  TABLE TRAN TRANSPORT COST FOR INTERPLANT SHIPMENT (US$ PER TON)
414
415              PALMASOLA PTO-SUAREZ POTOSI BARANQUILL CARTAGENA BARRANCABR LA-DORADA GUAYAQUIL PT-BOLIVAR
416
417  PTO-SUAREZ     87.22
418  POTOSI         31.25    55.97
419  BARANQUILL     89.80   114.56    70.68     5.00
420  CARTAGENA      89.80   114.56    70.68    23.28     26.00
421  BARRANCABR    115.80   137.85    93.97    35.90     35.90
422  LA-DORADA      90.16   141.46    97.58    31.20     31.20     13.06
423  GUAYAQUIL      88.52   111.32    70.32    31.14     31.20     54.20     56.10     9.60
424  PT-BOLIVAR     91.52   111.32    70.32    33.10     33.10     54.45     56.43    28.80     28.82
425  CALLAO-F       85.52   108.62    75.40    69.69     69.69     89.98     56.43    63.45     63.45
426  CUZCO          90.25    92.42    72.10    77.02     77.02     56.43     93.59    28.80     28.82
427  TALARA         88.52   110.24    77.02    75.40     75.40     56.43     56.43    29.90     28.82
428  CALLAO-I       85.52   108.62    75.40    77.02     77.02     56.43     60.00    29.90     28.82
429  BAYOVAR        75.12   110.24    77.02    40.50     40.50     43.30     56.43    29.90     28.82
430  MORON          67.48   121.16    75.10    32.60     32.60     45.00     57.90    39.70     39.70
431  PTA-CAIMAN     67.48   113.52    67.50    32.60     32.60     55.48     60.22    39.11     32.10
432  CARIPITO       67.48   113.52    67.48    31.60     31.60     38.17     66.51    39.11     32.10
433  TABLAZO        67.48   113.52    67.48                        49.51     39.11    32.10
434
435  +          CALLAO-F  CUZCO  TALARA  CALLAO-I  BAYOVAR  MORON  PTA-CAIMAN  CARIPITO
436
437  CUZCO        51.90   52.37
438  TALARA       18.82   51.90   52.37
439  CALLAO-I     51.90   52.37   18.80
440  BAYOVAR      21.82   52.37          18.80
441  MORON        39.70   77.00   39.70    39.70     39.70
442  PTA-CAIMAN   32.10   61.80   32.10    32.10     32.10    7.20
443  CARIPITO     39.11   77.00   39.11    39.11     39.11   20.90      21.03
444  TABLAZO      39.11   77.00   39.11    39.11     39.11   23.40      17.52     28.74
445
446
447  PARAMETERS
448  MUR          TRANSPORT COST: IMPORTED RAW MATERIAL.     (US$ PER TON)
449  MUE          TRANSPORT COST: EXPORT                     (US$ PER TON)
450  MUF          TRANSPORT COST: FINAL PRODUCTS             (US$ PER TON)
451  MUI          TRANSPORT COST: INTERPLANT SHIPMENT        (US$ PER TON)
452  MUX          TRANSPORT COST: FACTOR FOR ACIDS
453  MUFV         TRANSPORT COST: IMPORTED FINAL PRODUCTS     (US$ PER TON) ;
454
455  MUR(I)       = TRSP("PTS-PLANT",I) ;
456  MUFV(J)      = TRSP(J,"PTS-MARKET") ;
457  MUF(I,J)     = TRSP(J,I) ;
458  MUE(I)       = TRSP("PTS-PLANT",I) ;
459  *HANDLE SPECIAL MARKET ARRANGEMENTS FOR PALMASOLA TO ARGENTINA.
460  MUE("PALMASOLA") = 0.01;
461  MUX(C)       = 1; MUX("PHOS-ACID") =2; MUX("AMMONIA") =2;
462  MUI(I,IP)    = (TRAN(I,IP) + TRAN(IP,I));
463
464  DISPLAY MUR,MUE,MUF,MUI,MUFV,MUX;
```

193

TABLE A(C,P) INPUT-OUTPUT MATRIX

Line		AMM-ELEC	AMM-N-GAS	AMM-F-OIL	NITR-ACID	AMM-NITR	UREA	PHOS-ACID	SULF-ACID	SSP
469	NITR-ACID				1.0	-.760				
470	AMM-NITR					1.0				
471	UREA						1.0			
472	PHOS-ACID							1.0		
473	SULF-ACID							-1.5	1.0	-.380
474	SSP									1.0
476	AMMONIA	1.0	1.0	1.0	-.270	-.2	-.580			
477	CARB-DIOX		1.0	1.0			-.580			
478	ELECTR	-87.0								
479	NAT-GAS		-27.0							
480	FUEL-OIL			-.840						
481	PHOS-ROCK							-1.8		-.7
482	EL-SULFUR								-.330	

+

Line		TSP	S-SP	T-SP	DAP	DAP-G	COMP-G	C-20-18-10	C-13-13-20	C-15-21-10
486	NITR-ACID									
487	UREA						-.283	-.150	-.283	-.150
488	PHOS-ACID	-.740		-.740	-.840	-.840	-.293	-.1	-.293	-.2
489	SULF-ACID		-.380							
490	SSP		1.0							
491	TSP	1.0		1.0						
492	DAP				1.0	1.0		-.170		-.170
493	C-20-18-10							1.0		
494	C-13-13-20								1.0	
495	C-15-21-10									1.0
496	POT-CHLOR						-.334	-.170	-.334	-.170
497	AMM-SULF							-.150		-.150
498	AMMONIA				-.230	-.230		-.190		-.080
499	PHOS-ROCK	-.450	-.7	-.450						-.2

+

Line		C-16-12-12	C-08-24-12	C-12-12-12	POT-CHLOR	AMM-SULF
503	NITR-ACID	-.170				
504	UREA	-.260				
505	PHOS-ACID	-.040	-.320			
506	SULF-ACID		-.340			-.760
507	SSP			-.210		
508	DAP			-.170		
509	C-16-12-12	1.0				
510	C-08-24-12		1.0			
511	C-12-12-12			1.0		
512	POT-CHLOR	-.2	-.2	-.2	1.0	
513	AMMONIA		-.053			-.265
514	AMM-SULF					1.0
515	PHOS-ROCK	-.330	-.107	-.420		
516	BRINE				-150.0	

TABLE B(M,P) PRODUCTIVE UNIT-PROCESS MAP

	AMM-ELEC	AMM-N-GAS	AMM-F-OIL	NITR-ACID	AMM-NITR	UREA	PHOS-ACID	SULF-ACID	SSP
AMM-ELEC	1.0								
AMM-N-GAS		1.0							
AMM-F-OIL			1.0						
NITR-ACID				1.0					
AMM-NITR					1.0				
UREA						1.0			
PHOS-ACID							1.0		
SULF-ACID								1.0	
SSP									1.0

+	TSP	S-SP	T-SP	DAP	DAP-G	COMP-G	C-20-18-10	C-13-13-20	C-15-21-10
TSP	1.0								
DAP				1.0					
SS-TSP		1.0	1.0						
GRANULATOR					1.045				
NPK						1.0	1.0	1.0	1.0

+	C-16-12-12	C-08-24-12	C-12-12-12	POT-CHLOR	AMM-SULF
POT-CHLOR				1.0	
AMM-SULF					1.0
NPK	1.0	1.0	1.0		

SET MISC MISCELLANIOUS INPUTS / ELECTR, WATER-PR, WATER-C, NAT-GAS, STEAM, MISC, BAGS /

PARAMETER MISCOST(MISC) COST OF MISCELLANEOUS INPUTS /
ELECTR = 2.0, WATER-PR = .3, WATER-C = .05, NAT-GAS = 1.1, STEAM = 3.0, MISC = 1.0, BAGS = .28 /

TABLE AM(I,P,MISC) MISCELLANIOUS INPUTS BY PLANT AND PROCESS

	ELECTR	WATER-PR	WATER-C	NAT-GAS	STEAM	MISC	BAGS
BARANQUILL.NITR-ACID	.7	1.2	180.0		.6	.4	
BARANQUILL.AMM-SULF	.18				.05	.3	22.0
BARANQUILL.SULF-ACID	.05		15.2		.1	.4	
BARANQUILL.C-15-21-10	.80		17.0	0.5	2.1	.7	22.0
BARANQUILL.C-16-12-12	.80		17.0	0.5	2.1	.7	22.0
CARTAGENA.AMM-N-GAS	9.9	1.0	150.0		6.0	.6	
CARTAGENA.NITR-ACID	1.6	1.1	160.0			.4	
CARTAGENA.UREA	.56	2.5	190.0	2.0	1.1	.9	22.0
CARTAGENA.C-15-21-10	.75		20.0				22.0

TECHNOLOGY DATA

Line								
570	CARTAGENA.C-16-12-12	.75		20.0			.9	22-0
571								
572	BARRANCABR.AMM-N-GAS	10.4	4.2	500.0		4.1	1.6	
573	BARRANCABR.NITR-ACID	1.74	1.0	170.0			.5	
574	BARRANCABR.UREA	2.7	3.2	180.0		1.8	2.6	22-0
575	BARRANCABR.AMM-NITR	0.74		34.0	0.6	0.5	2.2	22-0
576								
577	GUAYAQUIL.PHOS-ACID	4.0	4.0	100.0		2.0	3.0	
578	GUAYAQUIL.SSP	.2		15.2			1.6	22-0
579	GUAYAQUIL.SULF-ACID	.05		.2		.1	.4	
580	GUAYAQUIL.C-08-24-12	.3			0.6	.2	1.8	22-0
581								
582	CALLAO-F.AMM-F-OIL	17.0	4.2	70.0		4.1	1.1	
583	CALLAO-F.NITR-ACID	.2	1.1	160.0			.4	
584	CALLAO-F.AMM-NITR	.75		35.0		0.5	2.3	22-0
585	CALLAO-F.AMM-SULF	.13				0.1	1.0	22-0
586								
587	CUZCO.AMM-ELEC	15.0		58.0		6.0	2.2	
588	CUZCO.NITR-ACID	3.1	.4	150.0			0.9	
589	CUZCO.AMM-NITR	.8	1.5	30.0		.4	2.8	22-0
590								
591	TALARA.AMM-N-GAS	7.9	2.9	105.0		1.3	.6	
592	TALARA.UREA	.94	1.0	50.0		1.0	1.1	22-0
593								
594	CALLAO-I.SSP	.1		1.6			3.6	22-0
595	CALLAO-I.C-12-12-12	.33		.3	1.5	.03	1.8	22-0
596								
597	MORON.AMM-N-GAS	.25	1.9	254.0			.4	
598	MORON.UREA	1.63	1.5	56.0		1.1	1.0	22-0
599	MORON.AMM-SULF	.18				.05	1.8	22-0
600	MORON.S-SP	.10					1.6	22-0
601	MORON.T-SP	.20		.1			1.6	22-0
602	MORON.SULF-ACID	.05		15.2		.1	.4	
603	MORON.PHOS-ACID	.95	3.8	123.0		1.5	.6	
604	MORON.NITR-ACID	1.24	1.2	168.0		.23	.5	
605	MORON.DAP-G	.30				.1	1.6	22-0
606	MORON.COMP-G	.25			1.4	0.1	1.2	22-0
607	MORON.C-13-13-20	.25			.3	0.1	1.2	22-0
608	MORON.C-20-18-10	.25			.3	0.1	1.2	22-0
609								
610	TABLAZO.AMM-N-GAS	.22	1.9	254.0			.4	
611	TABLAZO.UREA	1.63	1.5	56.0		1.1	1.0	22-0
612								
613								

614 *NOTE:
615 * THE INPUTS FOR NITR-ACID AT MORON ARE WEIGHTED AVERAGES OF THE OTHER
616 * NITR-ACID PLANTS. THE NORMS FOR THE GRANNULATOR AT MORON ARE ASSUMED TO
617 * BE THE SAME AS THE COMPOUND PLANT.
618
619

```
621
622   TABLE OPCOST(M,*) OPERATING COST FOR NEW PLANTS (US$ PER TON PER YEAR)
623
624                        CAPACITY    PROCESS
625
626   AMM-ELEC             34.5        12.3
627   AMM-N-GAS            34.5        12.3
628   AMM-F-OIL            34.5        12.3
629   NITR-ACID           10.6         2.2
630   AMM-NITR             8.4        10.4
631   AMM-SULF             8.0         0.2
632   UREA                17.8         8.0
633   SSP                  9.3         1.7
634   TSP                  9.3         1.7
635   SS-TSP               9.3         1.7
636   PHOS-ACID           16.8         9.0
637   SULF-ACID            0.3         2.5
638   NPK                  6.5         2.9
639   DAP                  7.7         5.5
640   GRANULATOR           9.3         1.7
641   POT-CHLOR           13.0        22.0
642
643   PARAMETERS ONEW(P)    VARIABLE OPERATING COST FOR NEW PLANTS (US$ PER UNIT LEVEL)
644            OOLD(P,I)    VARIABLE OPERATING COST OF OLD PLANTS (US$ PER UNIT LEVEL)
645            OZ(G,P,I)    VARIABLE OPERATING COST (US$ PER UNIT LEVEL)
646            OCAP(M)      FIXED OPERATING COST;
647
648
649   OOLD(P,I)     = SUM(MISC,MISCOST(MISC)*AM(I,P,MISC));
650   ONEW(P)       = SUM(M, B(M,P)*OPCOST(M,"PROCESS")) ;
651
652   OZ("OLD",P,I) = OOLD(P,I) ;
653   OZ("NEW",P,I) = ONEW(P) ;
654   OCAP(M)       = OPCOST(M,"CAPACITY");
655
656   DISPLAY OZ,ONEW,OOLD;
```

```
658   TABLE DCAP(I,M) INSTALLED CAPACITY IN OPERATION IN 1980 (TONS PER DAY)
659
660           AMM-ELEC AMM-N-GAS AMM-F-OIL NITR-ACID NITR-ACID AMM-NITR AMM-SULF UREA SSP SS-TSP PHOS-ACID SULF-ACID NPK GRANULATOR
661
662   BARANQUILL                          230                    212                                              162    850
663   CARTAGENA           340             68                     500                                                    425
664   BARRANCABR           65             85             150      65                                               80    180
665   GUAYAQUIL                                                  120                                       17
666   CALLAO-F                      70    107       140
667   CUZCO            50                  90        118
668   TALARA                                                      50
669   CALLAO-I           300                                     510                                                     240
670   MORON             600             88                       100   200   300   650              1200       460
671   TABLAZO          1800                                            750                                                920
672                                                                    2400
673
674   PARAMETERS  K(M,I,T)         EFFECTIVE CAPACITY OF OLD PLANTS   (1000 TPY)
675              CAPUT(M,I,T)      CAPACITY UTILIZATION FOR OLD PLANTS
676              DCAPW(*,M)        NAMEPLATE CAPACITY BY COUNTRY       (1000 TPY)
677              KW(M,*,T)         EFFECTIVE CAPACITY BY COUNTRY       (1000 TPY)
678              UMIN(T)           UTILIZATION: LOWER LIMIT;
679
680   UMIN(T)         = .7 ; UMIN("1981-83") = .6 ; UMIN("1984-86") = .65;
681
682   CAPUT(M,I,T) = .9 ; CAPUT(M,I,T)$(WI("PERU",I)+WI("VENEZUELA",I)) = .75 ;
683
684   K(M,I,T)                     = .33*CAPUT(M,I,T)*DCAP(I,M) ;
685   K("AMM-SULF","MORON","1987-89") = .75*.33*390 ;
686   K("AMM-SULF","MORON","1990-92") = .75*.33*390 .
687
688   DCAPW(W,M)         = SUM(ISWI(W,I), DCAP(I,M));
689   KW(W,M,T)          = SUM(ISWI(W,I), K(M,I,T));
690   DCAPW("REGION",M)  = SUM(W, DCAPW(W,M));
691   KW(M,"REGION",T)   = SUM(W, KW(M,W,T));
692
693   DISPLAY CAPUT,K,DCAPW,KW;
694   * COMMENTS ON INSTALLED CAPACITY:
695   * THE INSTALLED CAPACITY FOR UREA AT CARTAGENA IS ASSUMED TO BE 500 MT/DAY.
696   * THE CONSTRUCCION OF THE PLANT HOWEVER IS NOT YET COMPLETED.
697   * THE SS-TSP UNIT AT MORON CAN PRODUCE EITHER TSP OR SSP AT 300 MT/DAY.
698   * THE GRANULATOR AT MORON IS DESIGNED TO PRODUCE DAP AT 880 MT/DAY OR
699   * NPK AT 920 MT/DAY. THIS PARTICULAR UNIT CAN ALSO BE USED TO GRANULATE
700   * POWDERED TSP FROM OTHER UNITS AT 1400 MT/DAY.
701   * THE AMMONIUM SULFATE PRODUTION CAPACITY AT MORON VENZUELA IS ASSUMED
702   * TO BE 390 MT/DAY FOR THE PERIODS 1987-89 AND 1990-92.
703
```

198

705
706
707 TABLE PV(C,T) IMPORT PRICES CIF (US$ PER TON)
708

	1981-83	1984-86	1987-89	1990-92
EL-SULFUR	73.3	78.3	80.0	80.0
PHOS-ROCK	57.4	60.3	61.3	61.3
PHOS-ACID	169.2	193.0	200.0	200.0
AMMONIA	119.4	160.1	179.0	179.0
UREA	163.7	186.8	198.0	198.0
AMM-NITR	145.4	165.0	174.0	174.0
AMM-SULF	112.2	120.3	123.0	123.0
SSP	92.2	101.2	104.2	104.2
TSP	166.1	187.0	194.2	194.2
POT-CHLOR	98.8	103.6	105.2	105.2
DAP	211.4	242.9	254.2	254.2
C-20-18-18	172.01	191.01	199.01	199.01
C-13-13-20	149.01	160.01	165.01	165.01
C-15-15-10	165.01	183.01	190.01	190.01
C-16-12-12	140.01	154.01	160.01	160.01
C-08-24-12	154.01	170.01	176.01	176.01
C-12-12-12	125.01	138.01	143.01	143.01

709-725 (table rows above)

726
727
728 PARAMETER PE(C,T)   EXPORT PRICE (US$ PER TON) ;
729 PE(CE,T) = .8*PV(CE,T)-20*MUX(CE);
730 DISPLAY PV,PE;
731
732 * NOTE:
733 * NOT ALL TRUE ANYMORE
734 *   THE WORLDMARKET PRICES FOR THE COMPOUNDS ARE ESTIMATES SINCE THEY
735 *   ARE NOT TRADED ON THE MARKET ON A REGULAR BASIS .
736 *   PRICES ARE ESTIMATED ON THEIR NUTRIENT CONTENT USING TSP, UREA AND
737 *   POT-CHLOR WITH A $20.00 SURCHARGE FOR BLENDING . THIS METHOD WAS
738 *   CALIBRATED WITH THE KNOWN PRICE FOR C-15-15-15 OF $150.00 AND GAVE
739 *   A REASONABLE FIT.
740
741
742
743 TABLE PD(I,C) DOMESTIC RAW MATERIAL PRICES (US$ PER UNIT)
744

	SULF-ACID	ELECTR	NAT-GAS	FUEL-OIL	PHOS-ROCK	EL-SULFUR	BRINE
PALMASOLA			1.02				
PTO-SUAREZ			1.02				
POTOSI	10.00				45.00		
CARTAGENA			1.02				
BARRANCABR			1.02				
LA-DORADA			1.02			50.00	
PT-BOLIVAR			1.02				
CALLAO-F	40.00			39.00			
CUZCO		2.00					
TALARA			1.02				
CALLAO-I	40.00						

745-756 (table rows above)

199

```
757    BAYOVAR                     1.02              30.00      40.00    .20
758    MORON                       1.02              49.70      45.00
759    PTA-CAIMAN                                    42.00      45.00
760    CARIPITO                    1.02
761    TABLAZO                     1.02
762
763  * NOTE THAT IF THE PARAMETER PDLIM BELOW IS ZERO IT IS THEN IMPLIED THAT THERE IS NO DOMESTIC SUPPLY LIMIT.
764    PARAMETER PDLIM(I,C)  DOMESTIC MATERIAL LIMITS (1000 TPY) / POTOSI.PHOS-ROCK = 35 / ;
765
766    SCALAR  TARIFFVI   TARIFF ON IMPORTED INTERMEDIATE GOODS    / .15 /
767            TARIFFVF   TARIFF ON IMPORTED FINAL GOODS           / .1 /
768
769    DISPLAY PD,PDLIM;
770
```

TABLE INVDAT(M,*)   INVESTMENT DATA

	FIXED (MILL US$)	PROP (US$/TPY)	LIMIT (1000 TPY)
AMM-N-GAS	84.7	185	550
NITR-ACID	5.0	43	200
AMM-NITR	5.4	36	200
AMM-SULF	4.7	48	300
UREA	29.4	93	550
SSP	10.2	35	200
TSP	9.5	47	200
DAP	8.6	63	400
NPK	8.6	63	300
POT-CHLOR	10.2	153	800
PHOS-ACID	17.4	100	150
SULF-ACID	14.8	58	500
			700

SETS   N   PACKAGES / BOL-1, BOL-2, COL-1, COL-2, ECU-1, PER-1, PER-2, PER-3, VEN-1, VEN-2 /

PARAMETER   NDEF(N,I,M)   PACKAGE DEFINITIONS (TONS PER DAY)   /

BOL-1.PALMASOLA.AMM-N-GAS   160
BOL-1.PALMASOLA.UREA   250

BOL-2.POTOSI.TSP   170
BOL-2.POTOSI.PHOS-ACID   125

COL-1.LA-DORADA.AMM-N-GAS   1000
COL-1.LA-DORADA.UREA   1600

COL-2.LA-DORADA.TSP   880
COL-2.LA-DORADA.PHOS-ACID   650
COL-2.LA-DORADA.SULF-ACID   980

ECU-1.PT-BOLIVAR.AMM-N-GAS   435
ECU-1.PT-BOLIVAR.UREA   750

PER-1.BAYOVAR.AMM-N-GAS   651
PER-1.BAYOVAR.UREA   870

PER-2.BAYOVAR.SULF-ACID   2000
PER-2.BAYOVAR.PHOS-ACID   1334
PER-2.BAYOVAR.TSP   1076
PER-2.BAYOVAR.DAP   636

PER-3.BAYOVAR.POT-CHLOR   303

VEN-1.PTA-CAIMAN.PHOS-ACID   830
VEN-1.PTA-CAIMAN.SULF-ACID   1245
VEN-1.PTA-CAIMAN.NFK   2272

```
824        VEN-1.PTA-CAIMAN.TSP           242
825        VEN-1.PTA-CAIMAN.DAP           561
826
827        VEN-2.CARIPITO.AMM-N-GAS       1500
828        VEN-2.CARIPITO.UREA            1030   /
829
830     PARAMETERS  NUP(N)       PACKAGE COST                      (1000 US$)
831                 NUPF(N)      FIXED PACKAGE COST                (1000 US$)
832                 POP(N)       FIXED OPERATING COST              (1000 US$)
833                 HP(N,I,M)    EFFECTIVE PACKAGE SIZE            (1000 TPY)
834                 UNEW         NEW PLANT UTILIZATION
835                 HB(M)        MAXIMUM PLANT SIZE                (1000 TPY)
836                 NU(M)        PROPORTIONAL INVESTMENT          (US$ PER TPY)
837                             ;
838
839     NUP(N)      = SUM((I,M)$NDEF(N,I,M), 1000*INVDAT(M,"FIXED") + .33*INVDAT(M,"PROP")*NDEF(N,I,M));
840     NUPF(N)     = SUM((I,M)$NDEF(N,I,M), 1000*INVDAT(M,"FIXED"));
841     UNEW        = .85 ;
842     POP(N)      = SUM((I,M)$NDEF(N,I,M), 0.33*OPCOST(M,"CAPACITY")*NDEF(N,I,M));
843     HP(N,I,M)   = .33*NDEF(N,I,M);
844     HB(M)       = INVDAT(M,"LIMIT");
845     NU(M)       = INVDAT(M,"PROP");
846
847     DISPLAY NUP,POP,UNEW,HP,HB,NUPF,NU;
848
849     PARAMETERS  DELTA(T)     DISCOUNT FACTOR
850                 RHO          DISCOUNT RATE
851                 LIFE         LIFE OF PRODUCTIVE UNIT (YEARS)
852                 MIDYEAR(T)   MIDYEAR FOR EACH PERIOD
853                 SIGMA        CAPITAL RECOVERY FACTOR
854                 TS           TIME SUMMATION MATRIX ;
855
856     LIFE = 15; RHO = .1; SIGMA  = RHO*(1+RHO)**LIFE/((1+RHO)**LIFE-1); TS(T,TP)$(ORD(T) GE ORD(TP)) = 1;
857     MIDYEAR(T) = 1979 + 3*ORD(T);
858     DELTA(T)   = (1+RHO)**(1981-MIDYEAR(T)) + (1+RHO)**(1982-MIDYEAR(T)) + (1+RHO)**(1983-MIDYEAR(T));
859
860     DISPLAY DELTA,RHO,LIFE,MIDYEAR,SIGMA,TS;
```

```
862    SET  NMAP          MAP OF PACKAGES TO LOCATIONS
863         WN            MAP OF COUNTRIES TO PACKAGES
864         CFV(CF)       IMPORTED FINAL PRODUCTS THAT ARE NOT COMPOUNDS
865         OLD(G)        OLD VINTAGE PLANTS                        / OLD /
866         NEW(G)        NEW VINTAGE PLANTS                        / NEW /
867         MC(C,I,J)     MARKETING POSSIBILITIES;
868
869    PARAMETER NNUM      PACKAGE UNITY
870              NPACK     MINIMUM NUMBER OF PACKAGES IN EACH COUNTRY
871              DPACK     DIFFERENCE IN PACKAGE NUMBERS BETWEEN COUNTRIES
872              PLE       MATRIX FOR COUNTRY PACKAGE COMPARISONS IN THE INEQUALITY CONSTRAINT
873              GAMMA     PACKAGE SIZE MULTIPLIER FOR EXPERIMENTS WITH FLEXIBLE PACKAGE SIZES
874              LAM       MAXIMUM EXPORT CAPABILITY OF PLANT AS FUNCTION OF PRODUCTION LEVEL;
875
876    NNUM  = 1;
877    NPACK = 0;
878    DPACK = NA;
879    PLE(W,WP)$(ORD(W) NE ORD(WP)) = 1;
880    GAMMA         = 1;
881    LAM(I)  = 0.3;  LAM("TABLAZO") = 0.7;  LAM("PALMASOLA") = 0.7;
882
883    NMAP(N,I)     = SUM(M, NDEF(N,I,M));
884    WN(W,N)       = SUM((M,I)$WI(W,I), NDEF(N,I,M));
885    CFV(CF)       = CV(CF) - CO(CF);
886    MC(CF,I,J)    = YES;  MC(CO,I,J)$(NOT CORES(CO,I,J) = NO;
887
888    *
889    *  MODEL REDUCTION
890    *
891    SET  MPOS(G,M,I)=YES;  PPOS(G,P,I)=YES;  CPOSM(C,I)=YES;  CPOSP(C,I)=YES;  HPOS(M,I)=YES;  NFIX(M,I)=YES;
892         PPOS(G,*,I)        PROCESS POSSIBILITIES
893         CPOSM(C,I)         CONSUMPTION POSSIBILITIES
894         CPOSP(C,I)         PRODUCTION POSSIBILITIES
895         HPOS(M,I)          UNIT EXPANSION POSSIBILITIES
896         NFIX(M,I)          FIXED PACKAGE EXPANSIONS;
897
898    MPOS(G,M,I)=YES;  PPOS(G,P,I)=YES;  CPOSM(C,I)=YES;  CPOSP(C,I)=YES;  HPOS(M,I)=YES;  NFIX(M,I)=YES;
899
900    MPOS("OLD",M,I)   = SUM(T, K(M,I,T));
901    MPOS("NEW",M,I)   = SUM(N, NDEF(N,I,M));
902    PPOS(G,P,I)       = SUM(M$( NOT MPOS(G,M,I)), B(M,P) NE 0) EQ 0;
903    PPOS(G,CO)$SUM($SVI(W,I) NOT WNPK(W,CO)) = NO;
904    CPOSM(C,I)        = SUM((G,P)$PPOS(G,P,I), A(C,P) LT 0);
905    CPOSP(C,I)        = SUM((G,P)$PPOS(G,P,I), A(C,P) GT 0);
906    HPOS(M,I)         = MPOS("NEW",M,I);
907    NFIX(M,I)         = HPOS(M,I);
```

```
909  *NUTRIENT PRODUCTION/CAPACITY ANALYSIS
910   SETS    PPOSK(*,I)   I POSSIBILITIES
911           CPOSXP(C,I)  COMMODITY OUTPUT POSSIBILITY;
912
913   PARAMETERS AX(C,P,I)  REDUCED I-O MATRIX FOR NUTRIENT POTENTIAL
914              KX(M,I)    EFFECTIVE CAPACITY
915              WEIGHT(CQ) NUTRIENT WEIGHTS / N = 100, P205 = 10, K20 = 1 /
916              NUTXX(C)   NUTRIENT WEIGHT FOR PRODUCTS
917              XREP       MAXIMUM NUTRIENT SHIPMENTS (1000 TPY);
918
919   AX(C,P,I) = AX(C,P) ; AX(C,P,I)$((AX(C,P) LT 0) AND (1$CV(C) OR PD(I,C))) = 0 ;
920   NUTXX(CF)  = SUM(CQ, WEIGHT(CQ)*ALPHA(CF,CQ)); DISPLAY NUTXX;
921   KX(M,I)    = 1; FPOSK(P,I) = YES; CPOSXP(C,I) = YES;
922
923   VARIABLES  ZX(P,I)    PROCESS LEVEL                 (1000 TPY)
924              XX(C,I)    OUTPUT OF FINAL PRODUCTS      (1000 TPY)
925              NUT        TOTAL NUTRIENT VALUE          (1000 TPY)
926              POSITIVE VARIABLES ZX, XX;
927
928   EQUATIONS  MBX(C,I)   MATERIAL BALANCE              (1000 TPY)
929              CCX(M,I)   CAPACITY CONSTRAINT           (1000 TPY)
930              DNUT       NUTRIENT DEFINITION ;
931
932   MBX(C,I).. SUM(P$PPOSK(P,I), AX(C,P,I)*ZX(P,I)) =G= XX(C,I)$(CPOSXP(C,I)*CF(C));
933
934   CCX(M,I).. SUM(P$PPOSK(P,I), B(M,P)*ZX(P,I)) =L= KX(M,I);
935
936   DNUT..     NUT  =E= SUM((C,I)$(CPOSXP(C,I)*CF(C)), NUTXX(C)*XX(C,I)) -.1*SUM((P,I)$PPOSK(P,I), ZX(P,I));
937
938   MODEL CAPCHECK /MBX, CCX, DNUT / ;
939
940   * KX(M,I) = K(M,I,"1990-92"); USED FOR COMPUTING MAXIMUM NUTRIENT OUTPUT, NO EXPANSION.
941   * KX(M,I) = K(M,I,"1990-92") + SUM(N, HP(N,I,M)); USED FOT COMPUTING MAXIMUM NUTRIENT OUTPUT, WITH EXPANSION.
942     KX(M,I)  = K(M,I,"1981-83");
943     PPOSK(P,I)   = SUM(M$(NOT KX(M,I)), B(M,P)) NE 0) EQ 0 ;
944     PPOSK(CO,I)$SUM(W$WI(W,I), NOT WNPK(W,CO)) = NO ;
945     CPOSXP(C,I)  = SUM(P$PPOSK(P,I), AX(C,P,I) GT 0);
946
947   DISPLAY "MAXIMUM NUTRIENT OUTPUT FOR N, P AND K"
948           "YEAR 1981-83";
949
950   SOLVE CAPCHECK MAXIMIZING NUT USING LP;
951   XREP(W,CO)   = SUM((CF,I)$WI(W,I), ALPHA(CF,CQ)*XX.L(CF,I));
952   XREP("REGION",CO) = SUM(W, XREP(W,CQ));
953   DISPLAY XX.L, XREP;
954
955   *TRADE AND TRANSPORT ANALYSIS
956   PARAMETER  EVIIP(I,IP,CIS,T)  INTERNATIONAL TRADE ADVANTAGE (US$ PER TON)
957              EVIJ(I,J,CF,T)     INTERNATIONAL TRADE ADVANTAGE (US$ PER TON);
958
959   EVIIP(I,IP,CIS,T)$(CV(CIS)*CE(CIS)) = MAX(0,MUX(CIS)*(MUI(I,IP)-MUR(IP)-MUE(I)) - (TARIFFVI+1)*PV(CIS,T) + PE(CIS,T));
960
```

```
961     EVIJ(I,J,CF,T)$(CV(CF)*CE(CF))    = MAX(0,MUX(CF)*(MUF(I,J)-MUFV(J)-MUE(I)) - (TARIFFVF+1)*PV(CF,T) + PE(CF,T));
962
963     DISPLAY EVIIP,EVIJ;
964
965
966     *NUTRIENT DEMAND GROWTH RATES: COMPUTED ON 1976 NUTRIENT CONSUMPTION BY COUNTRY.
967
968     TABLE CON76(*,CQ)  NUTRIENT CONSUMPTION IN 1976 (1000 TPY)
969
970                     N     P205    K20
971
972     BOLIVIA         1     2
973     COLOMBIA      108    69      42
974     ECUADOR        20    17      10
975     PERU          101    17      13
976     VENEZUELA     133    95      71
977
978     PARAMETER DR(CQ,T,*)    DEMAND FOR NUTRIENTS           (1000 TPY)
979               DBR(*,T),     DEMAND FOR AMMONIUM SULFATE    (1000 TPY)
980               DGR(*,CQ,*)   DEMAND GROWTH RATES;
981
982     DR(CQ,T,W)     = SUM(J$WJ(W,J), D(J,CQ,T));
983     DR(CQ,T,"ANDEAN")  = SUM(W, DR(CQ,T,W));
984     DBR(W,T)       = SUM(J$WJ(W,J), DB(J,T));
985     DBR("ANDEAN",T) = SUM(W, DBR(W,T));
986
987     CON76("ANDEAN",CQ)  = SUM(W, CON76(W,CQ));
988     DGR("76/82",CQ,WR) = (DR(CQ,"1981-83",WR)/CON76(WR,CQ))**(1/6)  - 1 ;
989     DGR("76/91",CQ,WR) = (DR(CQ,"1990-92",WR)/CON76(WR,CQ))**(1/16) - 1 ;
990     DGR("82/85",CQ,WR) = (DR(CQ,"1984-86",WR)/DR(CQ,"1981-83",WR))**(1/3) - 1 ;
991     DGR("85/88",CQ,WR) = (DR(CQ,"1987-89",WR)/DR(CQ,"1984-86",WR))**(1/3) - 1 ;
992
993     DGR("88/91",CQ,WR) = (DR(CQ,"1990-92",WR)/DR(CQ,"1987-89",WR))**(1/3) - 1 ;
994     DGR("82/91",CQ,WR) = (DR(CQ,"1990-92",WR)/DR(CQ,"1981-83",WR))**(1/9) - 1 ;
995
996     DISPLAY DB,DGR,CON76;
```

MODEL DEFINITION

998	VARIABLES	Z(G,P,I,T)	PROCESS LEVEL	(1000 UNITS PER YEAR)
999		XF(C,I,J,T)	DOMESTIC SHIPMENT ACTIVITY: FINAL	(1000 TPY)
1000		XI(C,I,IP,T)	DOMESTIC SHIPMENT ACTIVITY: INTERPLANT	(1000 TPY)
1001		VF(CF,J,T)	IMPORTS: FINAL PRODUCTS	(1000 TPY)
1002		TVF(W,T)	VALUE OF IMPORTS: FINAL PRODUCTS	(MILL US$ PER YEAR)
1003		VI(C,I,T)	IMPORTS: INTERMEDIATES AND RAW MATERIALS	(1000 TPY)
1004		TVI(W,T)	VALUE OF IMPORTS: INTERMEDIATES	(MILL US$ PER YEAR)
1005		E(C,I,T)	EXPORTS	(1000 TPY)
1006		U(C,I,T)	DOMESTIC MATERIAL PURCHASES	(1000 TPY)
1007		H(M,I,TE)	CAPACITY EXPANSION	(1000 TPY)
1008		YP(N,TE)	PACKAGE DECISION VARIABLE	(BINARY)
1009		YW(W,TE)	PACKAGE DECISION VARIABLE BY COUNTRY	
1010		PHIK(W,T)	CAPITAL COST	(MILL US$ PER YEAR)
1011		PHIP(W,T)	OPERATING COST	(MILL US$ PER YEAR)
1012		PHIG(W,T)	DOMESTIC MATERIAL COST	(MILL US$ PER YEAR)
1013		PHIW(W,T)	WORKING CAPITAL COST	(MILL US$ PER YEAR)
1014		PHIM(W,T)	IMPORT COST	(MILL US$ PER YEAR)
1015		PHIT(W,T)	TARIFFS	(MILL US$ PER YEAR)
1016		PHIL(W,T)	TRANSPORT COST	(MILL US$ PER YEAR)
1017		PHIE(W,T)	EXPORT REVENUE	(MILL US$ PER YEAR)
1018		PHI(W,T)	COST PER YEAR	(MILL US$ PER YEAR)
1019		PHITOT	DISCOUNTED TOTAL COST	(MILL US$ DISCOUNTED)
1020	POSITIVE VARIABLES	Z, XF, VI, E, U, H, XI;		
1021	BINARY VARIABLE	YP;		
1022	EQUATIONS			
1023		MBD(CQ,J,T)	MATERIAL BALANCE ON DEMAND	(1000 TPY)
1024		MBA(J,T)	AMMONIUM SULFATE REQUIREMENTS	(1000 TPY)
1025		MB(C,I,T)	MATERIAL BALANCE AT PLANTS	(1000 TPY)
1026		UBND(C,I,T)	BOUNDS ON LOCAL MATERIALS	(1000 TPY)
1027		ATVF(W,T)	DEFINITION OF IMPORT VALUE: FINALS	(MILL US$ PER YEAR)
1028		ATVI(W,T)	DEFINITION OF IMPORT VALUE: INTERMEDIATES	(MILL US$ PER YEAR)
1029		ELIM(C,I,T)	EXPORT LIMITS	(1000 TPY)
1030		CC(G,M,I,T)	CAPACITY CONSTRAINTS	
1031		CCMIN(C,I,T)	MINIMUM NPK UTILIZATION	
1032		BINV(M,I,TE)	BINARY CONSTRAINT: VARIABLE PLANT SIZE	(1000 TPY)
1033		BINF(M,I,TE)	BINARY CONSTRAINT: FIXED PLANT SIZE	(1000 TPY)
1034		MINPACK(W)	MINIMUM NUMBER OF PACKAGES PER COUNTRY	
1035		BW(W,TE)	AGGREGATION OF PACKAGES IN COUNTRY	
1036		CPIR(W,WP,TE)	INTER-COUNTRY CONSTRAINT ON PACKAGE - INEQUALITY	
1037		EX(N)	PACKAGE MUTUAL EXCLUSIVITY	(UNITS)
1038		ACC(W,T)	ACCOUNTING: CAPITAL COST	(MILL US$ PER YEAR)
1039		ACP(W,T)	ACCOUNTING: OPERATING COST	(MILL US$ PER YEAR)
1040		ACG(W,T)	ACCOUNTING: DOMESTIC MATERIALS	(MILL US$ PER YEAR)
1041		ACW(W,T)	ACCOUNTING: WORKING CAPITAL	(MILL US$ PER YEAR)
1042		ACM(W,T)	ACCOUNTING: IMPORT COST	(MILL US$ PER YEAR)
1043		ACT(W,T)	ACCOUNTING: TARIFFS	(MILL US$ PER YEAR)
1044		ACL(W,T)	ACCOUNTING: TRANPORT COST	(MILL US$ PER YEAR)
1045		ACE(W,T)	ACCOUNTING: EXPORT REVENUE	(MILL US$ PER YEAR)
1046		AC(W,T)	ACCOUNTING: TOTAL COST	(MILL US$ PER YEAR)
1047		OBJ	TOTAL DISCOUNTED COST;	(MILL US$ PER YEAR)

1050   MBD(CQ,J,T).. SUM(CF, ALPHA(CF,CQ)*(SUM(I$(MC(CF,I,J)*CPOSP(CF,I)), XF(CF,I,J,T)) + VF(CF,J,T)$CFV(CF))) =G= D(J,CQ,T);

1051

1052   MBA(J,T).. SUM(I$CPOSP("AMM-SULF",I), XF("AMM-SULF",I,J,T)) + VF("AMM-SULF",J,T) =G= DB(J,T) ;

1053

1054   MB(C,I,T)..

1055   SUM((G,P)$PPOS(G,P,I), A(C,P)*Z(G,P,I,T)) + (VI(C,I,T)$CV(C) + U(C,I,T)$PD(I,C)

1056 + SUM(IP$CPOSP(C,IP), XI(C,IP,I,T))$CIS(C))$CPOSM(C,I) =G= (SUM(IP$CPOSM(C,IP), XI(C,I,IP,T))$CIS(C) + E(C,I,T)$CE(C)

1057 + SUM(J$MC(C,I,J), XF(C,I,J,T)))$CPOSP(C,I) ;

1058

1059   UBND(CR,I,T)$(CPOSM(CR,I)$PDLIM(I,CR)).. U(CR,I,T) =L= PDLIM(I,CR);

1060

1061   ELIM(CE,I,T)$CPOSP(CE,I).. E(CE,I,T) =L= LAM(I)*SUM((G,P)$((A(CE,P) GT 0)$PPOS(G,P,I)), A(CE,P)*Z(G,P,I,T));

1062

1063   CC(G,M,I,T)$MPOS(G,M,I)..

1064   SUM(P$PPOS(G,P,I), B(M,P)*Z(G,P,I,T)) =L= K(M,I,T)$OLD(G) + SUM(TE$TS(T,TE), UNEW*H(M,I,TE))$NEW(G) ;

1065

1066   CCMIN(I,T)$K("NPK",I,T).. SUM(P$PPOS("OLD",P,I), B("NPK",P)*Z("OLD",P,I,T)) =G= UMIN(T)*K("NPK",I,T);

1067

1068   BINV(M,I,TE)$HPOS(M,I).. H(M,I,TE) =L= GAMMA*SUM(N$NDEF(N,I,M), HB(M)*YP(N,TE)) ;

1069

1070   BINF(M,I,TE)$NFIX(M,I).. H(M,I,TE) =E= SUM(N$NDEF(N,I,M), HP(N,I,M)*YP(N,TE)) ;

1071

1072   MINPACK(W).. SUM((N,TE)$WN(W,N), YP(N,TE)) =G= NPACK;

1073

1074   BW(W,TE).. YW(W,TE) =E= SUM(N$WN(W,N), YP(N,TE));

1075

1076   GPLE(W,WP,TE)$PLE(W,WP)..   YW(W,TE) - YW(WP,TE) =L= DPACK;

1077

1078   EX(N)..   SUM(TE, YP(N,TE)) =L= NNUM ;

1079

1080   ACC(W,T) ..   PHIK(W,T) =E= SIGMA*SUM(TE$TS(T,TE), SUM((M,I)$(WI(W,I)*MPOS("NEW",M,I)), NU(M)*H(M,I,TE))

1081   + SUM(N$WN(W,N), NUPF(N)*YP(N,TE)))/1000;

1082

1083   ACP(W,T)...   PHIP(W,T) =E= SUM(I$WI(W,I), SUM((G,P)$PPOS(G,P,I), OZ(G,P,I)*Z(G,P,I,T))

1084   + SUM((M,TE)$(TS(T,TE)$HPOS(M,I)),OCAP(M)*H(M,I,TE))/1000;

1085

1086   ACG(W,T)..   PHIG(W,T) =E= SUM((CR,I)$(WI(W,I)*CPOSM(CR,I)$PD(I,CR)), PD(I,CR)*U(CR,I,T))/1000;

1087

1088   ACW(W,T)..

1089   PHIW(W,T) =E= .025*(PHIP(W,T)+PHIG(W,T)+SUM((CV,I)$(WI(W,I)*CPOSM(CV,I)), (PV(CV,T)+MUX(CV)*MUR(I))*VI(CV,I,T)))/1000;

1090

1091   ACM(W,T)..   PHIM(W,T) =E= TVI(W,T) + TVF(W,T);

1092

1093   ACT(W,T)..   PHIT(W,T) =E= TARIFFVI*TVI(W,T) + TARIFFVF*TVF(W,T) ;

1094

1095   ATVF(W,T)..   TVF(W,T) =E= SUM((CFV,J)$WJ(W,J), PV(CFV,T)*VF(CFV,J,T))/1000;

1096

1097   ATVI(W,T)..   TVI(W,T) =E= SUM((CV,I)$(WI(W,I)$CPOSM(CV,I)), PV(CV,T)*VI(CV,I,T))/1000;

1098

1099   ACL(W,T)..

1100   PHIL(W,T) =E= (SUM((CF,J)$WJ(W,J), SUM(I$(MC(CF,I,J)*CPOSF(CF,I)), MUF(I,J)*XF(CF,I,J,T)) + MUFV(J)*VF(CF,J,T)$CFV(CF))

1101   + SUM(I$WI(W,I), SUM(CE$CPOSF(CE,I), MUX(CE)*MUE(CE,I,T)) + SUM(CV$CPOSM(CV,I), MUX(CV)*MUR(I)*VI(CV,I,T))

```
1102            + SUM((CIS,IP)$(CPOSM(CIS,IP)*CPOSP(CIS,I)), MUX(CIS)*MUI(I,IP)*XI(CIS,I,IP,T)))/1000;

1103

1104  ACE(W,T)..  PHIE(W,T) =E= SUM((CE,I)$(WI(W,I)*CPOSP(CE,I)), PE(CE,T)*E(CE,I,T))/1000;

1105

1106  AC(W,T)..  PHI(W,T) =E= PHIK(W,T) + PHIP(W,T) + PHIG(W,T) + PHIW(W,T) + PHIM(W,T) + PHIL(W,T) - PHIE(W,T) ;

1107

1108  OBJ..  PHITOT =E= SUM((W,T), DELTA(T)*PHI(W,T));
```

```
1111   * CONTINOUS OPTIMUM FOR FLEXIBLE PACKAGE SIZES - BASE CASE
1112     GAMMA = 2;
1113     NPACK = 0;
1114     DPACK = 1000;
1115     NFIX(M,I) = NO;
1116     DISPLAY NFIX,NPOS;
1117
1118   MODEL AOPT1 /MBD,MBA,MB,ELIM,UBND,CC,CCMIN,BINV,BINF,MINPACK,BW,GPLE,EX,ACC,ACP,
1119                ACG,ACW,ACM,ACT,ATVF,ATVI,ACL,ACE,AC,OBJ /
1120
1121     SOLVE AOPT1 MINIMIZING PHITOT USING MIP;
```

210

```
1123   PARAMETERS  FLOWF             FINAL PRODUCT FLOW
1124               FLOWI             INTERMEDIATE AND RAW MATERIAL FLOW
1125               CIFCIF            VALUE FLOWS
1126               TRADECOST         TRADE FLOW ADVANTAGE AT FOB COST
1127               AREP              CAPACITY REPORT BY PLANT UNIT AND TIME
1128               BREP              CAPACITY REPORT BY COUNTRY UNIT AND TIME
1129               AUT               CAPACITY UTILIZATION BY PLANT AND UNIT
1130               BUT               CAPACITY UTILIZATION BY UNIT
1131               CUT               CAPACITY UTILIZATION BY PLANT
1132               DUT               CAPACITY UTILIZATION BY COUNTRY;
1133
1134   SET IE / EXTRA-IMP, INTRA-IMP, TOTAL-IMP, EXTRA-EXP, INTRA-EXP, TOTAL-EXP, BALANCE /
1135
1136       WIM / BOLIVIA, COLOMBIA, ECUADOR, PERU, VENEZUELA, EXTRA /
1137       WEX / BOLIVIA, COLOMBIA, ECUADOR, PERU, VENEZUELA, EXTRA /
1138       CAP / ECAP, SLACK, UTILIZE /;
1139
1140
1141   FLOWF(W,WP,CF,T)             = SUM((I,J)$(WI(W,I)*WJ(WP,J)), XF*L(CF,I,J,T));
1142   FLOWF("EXTRA",WP,CF,T)      = SUM(J$WJ(WP,J), VF*L(CF,J,T));
1143   FLOWF(W,"EXTRA",CF,T)       = SUM(I$WI(W,I), E*L(CF,I,T));
1144
1145   FLOWF(WIM,WEX,"FINAL",T)    = SUM(CF, FLOWF(WIM,WEX,CF,T));
1146   FLOWI(W,WP,CIS,T)           = SUM((I,IP)$(WI(W,I)*WI(WP,IP)), X1*L(CIS,I,IP,T));
1147   FLOWI("EXTRA",WP,CV,T)      = SUM(IP$WI(WP,IP), VI*L(CV,IP,T));
1148
1149   FLOWI(W,"EXTRA",CE,T)$(NOT CF(CE)) = SUM(I$WI(W,I), E*L(CE,I,T));
1150   FLOWI(WIM,WEX,"INTERM",T)   = SUM(C, FLOWI(WIM,WEX,C,T));
1151
1152
1153   CIFCIF(WIM,WEX,T)           = SUM(C, PV(C,T)*(FLOWF(WIM,WEX,C,T)+FLOWI(WIM,WEX,C,T)))/1000;
1154   CIFCIF("INTRA",W,T)         = SUM(WPS(ORD(W) NE ORD(HP)), CIFCIF(WP,W,T));
1155   CIFCIF(W,"INTRA",T)         = SUM(WPS(ORD(W) NE ORD(HP)), CIFCIF(W,WP,T));
1156   CIFCIF(W,"TOTAL",T)         = CIFCIF(W,"INTRA",T) + CIFCIF(W,"EXTRA",T);
1157   CIFCIF("TOTAL",W,T)         = CIFCIF("EXTRA",W,T) + CIFCIF("INTRA",W,T);
1158   CIFCIF(W,"BALANCE",T)       = CIFCIF("TOTAL",W,T) - CIFCIF("TOTAL",W,T);
1159
1160
1161   TRADECOST(WEX,"EXTRA-IMP",T)   = CIFCIF("EXTRA",WEX,T);
1162   TRADECOST(WEX,"INTRA-IMP",T)   = CIFCIF("INTRA",WEX,T);
1163   TRADECOST(WEX,"TOTAL-IMP",T)   = TRADECOST(WEX,"EXTRA-IMP",T) + TRADECOST(WEX,"INTRA-IMP",T);
1164   TRADECOST(WEX,"EXTRA-EXP",T)   = SUM(C, PE(C,T)*(FLOWF(WEX,"EXTRA",C,T)+FLOWI(WEX,"EXTRA",C,T))/1000;
1165   TRADECOST(WEX,"INTRA-EXP",T)   = CIFCIF(WEX,"INTRA",T);
1166   TRADECOST(WEX,"TOTAL-EXP",T)   = TRADECOST(WEX,"EXTRA-EXP",T)+TRADECOST(WEX,"INTRA-EXP",T);
1167   TRADECOST(WEX,"BALANCE",T)     = TRADECOST(WEX,"TOTAL-EXP",T) - TRADECOST(WEX,"TOTAL-IMP",T) ;
1168
1169
1170   AREP(I,M,T,"ECAP")         = K(M,I,T) + SUM(TE$TS(T,TE), UNEW*H-L(M,I,TE));
1171   AREP(I,M,T,"SLACK")        = SUM(G, CC-UP(G,M,I,T) - CC-L(G,M,I,T));
1172
1173   AREP(I,M,T,"UTILIZE")$(AREP(I,M,T,"ECAP") NE 0) = (AREP(I,M,T,"ECAP")-AREP(I,M,T,"SLACK"))/AREP(I,M,T,"ECAP");
1174
```

REPORT ANDEAN MODEL

```
1175   AREP("TOTAL",T,CAP)   = SUM(M, AREP(I,M,T,CAP));
1176   AREP("TOTAL",M,T,CAP) = SUM(I, AREP(I,M,T,CAP));
1177
1178   AREP(I,"TOTAL",T,"UTILIZE")$(AREP(I,"TOTAL",T,"ECAP") NE 0) = (AREP(I,"TOTAL",T,"ECAP")-AREP(I,"TOTAL",T,"SLACK"))/
1179                                                                  AREP(I,"TOTAL",T,"ECAP");
1180
1181   AREP("TOTAL",M,T,"UTILIZE")$(AREP("TOTAL",M,T,"ECAP") NE 0) = (AREP("TOTAL",M,T,"ECAP")-AREP("TOTAL",M,T,"SLACK"))/
1182                                                                  AREP("TOTAL",M,T,"ECAP");
1183
1184
1185   BREP(W,M,T,CAP)       = SUM(ISWI(W,I), AREP(I,M,T,CAP));
1186
1187   BREP(W,M,T,"UTILIZE")$(BREP(W,M,T,"ECAP") NE 0) = (BREP(W,M,T,"ECAP")-BREP(W,M,T,"SLACK"))/BREP(W,M,T,"ECAP");
1188         ' ,
1189   BREP("TOTAL",M,T,CAP) = AREP("TOTAL",M,T,CAP);
1190   BREP(W,"TOTAL",T,CAP) = SUM(M, BREP(W,M,T,CAP));
1191
1192   BREP(W,"TOTAL",T,"UTILIZE")$(BREP(W,"TOTAL",T,"ECAP") NE 0) = (BREP(W,"TOTAL",T,"ECAP")-BREP(W,"TOTAL",T,"SLACK"))/
1193                                                                  BREP(W,"TOTAL",T,"ECAP");
1194
1195
1196   AUT(I,M,T)        = AREP(I,M,T,"UTILIZE");
1197   AUT(I,"TOTAL",T)  = AREP(I,"TOTAL",T,"UTILIZE");
1198   AUT("TOTAL",M,T)  = AREP("TOTAL",M,T,"UTILIZE");
1199
1200   BUT(M,T)  = AUT("TOTAL",M,T);
1201   CUT(I,T)  = AUT(I,"TOTAL",T);
1202   DUT(W,T)  = BREP(W,"TOTAL",T,"UTILIZE");
1203
1204   DISPLAY YP.L;
1205   DISPLAY PHIK.L;
1206   DISPLAY PHITOT.L,PHIP.L,PHIG.L,PHIW.L,PHIM.L,PHIT.L,PHIL.L,PHIE.L,PHI.L;
1207   DISPLAY DUT,CUT,BUT,CIFCIF,TRADECOST,FLOWZ,FLOWI,AREP.BREP,AUT;
1208   DISPLAY VF.L,VI.L,U.L,E.L,TVF.L,TVI.L,YP.L,H.L;
```

VARIABLES	TYPE	REFERENCES									
A	PARAM	REF	904	905	2*919	1055	2*1061	DEFINED	466	DCL	466
AC	EQU	REF	1119		DEFINED	1106		DCL	1046		
ACC	EQU	REF	1118		DEFINED	1080		DCL	1038		
ACE	EQU	REF	1119		DEFINED	1104		DCL	1045		
ACG	EQU	REF	1119		DEFINED	1086		DCL	1040		
ACL	EQU	REF	1119		DEFINED	1099		DCL	1044		
ACM	EQU	REF	1119		DEFINED	1091		DCL	1042		
ACP	EQU	REF	1118		DEFINED	1083		DCL	1039		
ACT	EQU	REF	1119		DEFINED	1098		DCL	1043		
ACW	EQU	REF	1119		DEFINED	1088		DCL	1041		
ALPHA	PARAM	REF	920	950	1050	332	DEFINED	332	DCL	332	
AM	PARAM	REF	649	555	555	332					
AOPTI	MODEL	REF	1121		DEFINED	1119		DCL	1118		
AREP	PARAM	REF	4*1173	1175	1176	1179	3*1181	1182	1185	1189	
			1196	1197	1207	1170	1171	1173	1175	1176	
			1178	1181	DCL						
			3*1178						1198		
ATVF	EQU	REF	1119		DEFINED	1095		DCL	1027		
ATVI	EQU	REF	1119		DEFINED	1097		DCL	1028		
AUT	PARAM	REF	1200	1201	1207	1196	DEFINED	1197	DCL	1198	1129
AX	PARAM	REF	932	945	DEFINED	934	913	DCL	519		
B	PARAM	REF	650	902	943	1064	1066	DEFINED	DCL		
BINF	EQU	REF	1118		DEFINED	1070		DCL	1033		
BINV	EQU	REF	1118		DEFINED	1068		DCL	1032		
BREP	PARAM	REF	4*1187	1190	3*1192	1193	1202	DEFINED	1207	1185	1187
				1192	1128						
BUT	PARAM	REF	1189	1207	1200	1074	1130	1035	DCL		
BW	EQU	REF	167	173	176	179	184	187	192	466	
			728	742	765	867	893	894	904	911	
C	SET	REF	705	4*919	924	928	4*932	4*936	945	999	1000
			913	1006	1025	1026	5*1055	9*1056	3*1057	1150	
			1003	1005	135	1029	461	28898	1164	905	2*919
			3*1164	932	1135	CONTROL	1150	1153	DCL	135	
			921	936	945	1190	1138		CONTROL	1175	
CAP	SET	REF	1176	1189	1185	1185	DEFINED	192	332		
			1185	1176	1190	1189	DEFINED	1138			
CAPCHECK	MODEL	REF	949		DEFINED	938		DCL	938		
CAPUT	PARAM	REF	685	694	DEFINED	2*683		DCL	676		
CC	EQU	REF	1118	2*1171	1066	1063	DCL	1031	1030		
CCMIN	EQU	REF	1118		DEFINED	1066		DCL	1031		
CCX	EQU	REF	938		DEFINED	934		DCL	929		
CE	SET	REF	2*729	959	961	1056	4*1061	3*1104	2*1149	DEFINED	
			184	729	961	1101	1104	DCL	184	5*961	167
CF	SET	REF	6*1050	2*885	1142	920	936	2*950	957	5*961	1001
			864	1141	1143	1145	1149	1100	1141	167	CONTROL
			885	920	950	961	1050	DEFINED	1142	1142	1143
CFV	SET	REF	1145	DCL	DEFINED	885	CONTROL	1095	DCL	864	
			1050	1155	1157	1158	1161	1162	1165		
CIFCIF	PARAM	REF	1153	1154	2*1156	1157	1158	1156	1125	1207	
			DEFINED								

REFERENCE MAP OF VARIABLES

VARIABLES	TYPE	REFERENCES
CIS	SET	REF 956 5*959 2*1056 4*1102 1146 DEFINED 179 CONTROL 959 · 1102 179
CO	SET	REF 1146 203 209 · 179 885 209 · 944 903 · 988 903 · 903 886 944 968 · 987 987 DEFINED 173 CONTROL DCL 968
CON76	PARAM	REF 886 987 209 944 903 988 996 DEFINED 203 209 DCL 987 968
CORES	SET	REF 987 988 886 1059 210 DEFINED 203 1101 987 DCL 898
CPOSM	SET	REF 210 2*1056 1086 1059 209 1089 DEFINED 1097 DCL 1101 1102 1104
CPOSP	SET	REF 904 DCL 893 1052 1056 1057 894 1061 1100 1101 1102 1104
CPOSP	SET	DEFINED 1050 905 1056 DCL 898
CPOSXP	SET	REF 932 936 DEFINED 921 945 332 356 358 911 359 360
Cq	SET	REF 212 2*920 236 260 284 951 968 978 980 358 982 983
Cq	SET	915 2*988 2*989 2*990 2*991 2*993 2*994 2*1050
		CONTROL 987 988 989 990 991 993 994 950 951 DEFINED 982
		128 987 989 990 991 920 994 1023 DCL
CR	SET	REF 4*1059 4*1086 DEFINED 176 CONTROL 1131 1059 1086 176
CUT	PARAM	REF 1207 885 1201 961 1055 DCL 1147 3*1097 3*1101 1147
CV	SET	REF 187 919 959 1089 1097 1101 DCL 187
		DEFINED 363 982 1050 DEFINED 358 360 361 DCL
D	PARAM	REF 356 CONTROL 982 1089 1097 358 359 360 361
DB	PARAM	REF 984 996 1052 DEFINED 308 308
DBR	PARAM	REF 985 DEFINED 984 985 DCL 979
DCAP	PARAM	REF 685 689 658 689 658
DCAPW	PARAM	REF 691 694 DEFINED 689 691 DCL 677
DELTA	PARAM	REF 860 1108 DEFINED 858 849
DEM82	PARAM	REF 358 DEFINED 212 DCL 236
DEM85	PARAM	REF 359 DEFINED 236 DCL 260
DEM88	PARAM	REF 360 DEFINED 260 DCL 284
DEM91	PARAM	REF 361 DEFINED 284 989 990
DGR	PARAM	REF 996 988 DCL 930 991 994 DCL
		980
DNUT	EQU	REF 938 936 DEFINED 871 993
DPACK	PARAM	REF 1076 878 DEFINED 983 982 2*993 2*994 DEFINED 982
DR	PARAM	REF 983 988 978 DCL 2*991 2*990
DUT	PARAM	REF 1207 1202 DEFINED 1132 1143 1149 1208 DCL
E	VAR	REF 1020 1061 1056 1104 1101
		1005
ELIM	EQU	REF 1118 1061 DEFINED 1029 DCL
EVIIP	PARAM	REF 963 959 DEFINED 956 DCL
EVIJ	PARAM	REF 963 961 DEFINED 957 DCL
EX	EQU	REF 1118 1078 DEFINED 1037 DCL
FLOWF	PARAM	REF 1145 1164 1153 1207 1141 1142 1143 1145
		1123 DCL
FLOWI	PARAM	REF 1150 1153 1164 DEFINED 1146 1147 1149 1150
		1124 DCL
G	SET	REF 645 865 866 891 892 902 904 905 998

214

REFERENCE MAP OF VARIABLES

```
VARIABLES  TYPE    REFERENCES

GAMMA              1030     2*1055   2*1061   1063     4*1064   3*1083   2*1171   DEFINED  103      CONTROL
                   2*898    902      903      904      905      1055     1061     1063     1083     1171
GPLE       PARAM   DCL      103
H          EQU     REF      1068     DEFINED  DEFINED  1112     DCL      873
           VAR     REF      1118     DEFINED  1076     DCL      1036     1061
                   1007     1020     1064     1068     1070     1080     1080     1170     1208     DCL
HB         PARAM   REF      847      1068     DEFINED  844      835      835      906      DCL      895
HP         PARAM   REF      847      1070     DEFINED  843      833      833      458      2*462    555
                   644      907      203      1084     1116     898      898      2*683    2*685    2*689
HPOS       SET     REF      33       206      209      209      455      457      895      896      667
I          SET     644      645      649      652      658      675      676      910      911      900
                   2*690    742      765      793      833      839      840      3*934    4*936    913
                   883      2*884    886      891      892      893      894      998      998      942
                   901      902      903      904      905      906      907      1029     1030     999
                   914      919      923      924      928      957      2*959    4*1059   5*1061   1031
                   943      904      2*945    2*950    956      1025     2*959    5*1086   4*1089   1063
                   1000     1003     1005     1006     1007     1025     1026     2*1149   2*1170   3*1097
                   1032     1033     2*1052   4*1070   3*1080   4*1083   3*1057   1197     1201     2*1171
                   4*1064   4*1066   3*1068   3*1104   2*1141   2*1143   2*1084   649      652      DEFINED
                   4*1100   7*1101   3*1102   3*1178   2*1141   2*1185   2*1146   843      881      653
                   4*1173   1175     1176     209      457      458      1196     904      905      883
                   8        685      689      455      839      840      462      943      944      906
                   2*683    2*886    6*898    900      901      902      842      1061     1063     945
                   884      2*919    3*921    932      934      2*936    903      1100     1101     1066
                   907      959      961      1050     1052     1054     942      1173     1175     1104
                   950      1070      1080     1083     1086     1089     1059                       1176
                   1068     1143     1146      1197     1201     1170     1097
                   1115     1185      1196                       DCL     1171
                   1178                                                  8
IE         SET     DEFINED  1134     DCL      844      845      4*1056   772      DCL      772
INVDAT             1134     DCL                        1000     1147     3*1102   2*1146
IP         PARAM   REF      2*462    956      2*959    1146     212      DCL      206      2*1147
                   2*462    959      2*1056   1102     209      456      236      260
J          SET     462      65       203      206      361      1023     457      867
                   356      358      359      360      999      1001     1024     4*1050
                   2*961    2*982    2*984    2*1142   2*1142           982      209
                   2*1095   6*1100   2*1141   457      1142     40       CONTROL  984
                   360      361      456      1141                       961     982
                   1057     1095     1100                               DEFINED  40
JP         SET     DCL      206                                         1142
K          PARAM   206      690      694      900      942      1064     2*1066   1170      DEFINED  685
                   REF      690      694      675      690                        678
KW         PARAM   686      687      DCL      DEFINED  690      692      DCL      914
KX         PARAM   687      692      943      675      921      942      DCL
LAM        PARAM   934      934      DEFINED  3*881    DCL      874      851
LIFE       PARAM   1061     1061     860      646      856      DCL      658      675      676      677
                   2*856    2*856    DEFINED  2*650    654      654      772      793      833      835
M          SET     519      519      621      691      691      692      845      883      884      891
                   2*685    2*685    689      690      690      692
                   836      4*839    2*840    3*842    843      844
```

REFERENCE MAP OF VARIABLES

VARIABLES	TYPE	REFERENCES									
MAX	FUNCT	895	896	900	901	2*902	906	907	914	929	2*934
		942	2*943	1007	1030	1032	1033	1063	3*1064	4*1068	4*1070
		3*1080	3*1084	1190	2*1171	4*1173	1175	1176	1176	1182	1185
		4*1187	2*683	1189	1196	1198	1200	691	106	CONTROL	650
		654	685	845	689	690	884	692	839	840	842
		843	844	921	883	942	928	900	901	902	906
		907	921	934	1200	943	1063	1068	1070	1080	1084
		1115	1170	961	1175	1176	1181	1185	1187	1189	
		1190	1196	1198		106					
MB	EQU	REF									
MBA	EQU	REF									
MBD	EQU	REF									
MBX	EQU	REF					DEFINED				
MC	SET	REF				2*886	DCL	852	867		
MIDYEAR	PARAM	REF	3*858	860	1100	DEFINED	1034				
MINPACK	EQU	REF	1118	DEFINED	857	DCL	548	548	DCL	548	
MISCOST	SET	REF	550	555	2*649	DEFINED	550	CONTROL			
MPOS	SET	REF	902	906	1063	1080	898	649	900	901	DCL
		991				DEFINED					
MUE	PARAM	REF	464	959	961	DEFINED	458	460		DCL	
MUF	PARAM	REF	464	961	1100	DEFINED	457	DCL	449	DCL	
MUFV	PARAM	REF	464	961	1100	DEFINED	456	DCL	452		
MUI	PARAM	REF	464	959	1102	DEFINED	462	DCL	450		
MUR	PARAM	REF	464	959	1089	961	1089	455	DCL	448	
MUX	PARAM	REF	451	729	959	1101	2*1101	1102	447	DEFINED	3*461
		DCL									
N	SET	REF	793	830	831	832	833	840	2*842	843	
		883	884	1008	2*842	2*1068	2*1068	2*1072	2*1074	1078	
		3*1081	1068	901	1072	839	840	842	883	884	
NDEF	PARAM	901	DEFINED	790	2*842	1074	1078	1081	DCL	790	1070
		REF	793	840	793	843	883	884	901	1068	
NEW	SET	DEFINED	1064	1116	866	DCL	866	1115	DCL	896	
NFIX	SET	REF	1070	DCL	898	898	907				
NMAP	SET	DEFINED	883	DCL	862	DCL	DCL				
NNUM	PARAM	DEFINED	1078	DEFINED	876	DCL	869	870			
NPACK	PARAM	REF	1072	1080	877	1113	DCL	DCL	836		
NU	PARAM	REF	847	DEFINED	839	845	830	831			
NUP	PARAM	REF	847	1081	DEFINED	840	DCL	840			
NUPF	PARAM	REF	847	949	DEFINED	DCL	925	831			
NUT	VAR	REF	936	936	936	920	920	916			
NUTXX	PARAM	REF	920	DEFINED	DEFINED	DCL	1047	916	DCL		
OBJ	EQU	REF	1119	1108	654	646	646				
OCAP	PARAM	REF	1084	DEFINED	654	865	865	DCL			
OLD	SET	REF	1064	DEFINED	865	DCL	DCL	DCL			
ONEW	PARAM	REF	653	656	650	DCL	643	DCL			
OOLD	PARAM	REF	652	656	649	649	644	DCL			
OPCOST	PARAM	REF	650	654	842	DEFINED	621	621		1070	

GAMS 1.0   A N D E A N   FERTILIZER MODEL   10/20/82   21.16.15.   PAGE 34

REFERENCE MAP OF VARIABLES

```
VARIABLES  TYPE    REFERENCES

OZ         PARAM   REF       656     1083  DEFINED   652     653   DCL       645     650     652
P          SET     REF       466      519     555     643     644     649     649     650     652
                             902   2*904   2*905     913   2*919     923   3*932   3*934   2*936
                             943   2*945     998  3*1055  4*1061  3*1064  3*1066  3*1083            72
                   CONTROL   649     650     652     653     898     902     904     905   2*919
                             921     932     934     936     943     945     955    1061    1064    1066
                            1083     DCL      72

PD         PARAM   REF       770      919    1055  2*1086  DEFINED   742     742   DCL       742
PDLIM      PARAM   REF       770   2*1059  DEFINED   765     765   DCL
PE         PARAM   REF       730      959     961    1104    1164  DEFINED   729   DCL       728
PHI        VAR     REF      1106     1108    1206   DCL     1018    1012
PHIE       VAR     REF      1104     1106    1206    1017   DCL
PHIG       VAR     REF      1086     1089    1106    1206   DCL     1010
PHIL       VAR     REF      1080     1106    1205   DCL     1016
PHIM       VAR     REF      1100     1106    1206   DCL     1014
PHIP       VAR     REF      1091     1106    1206    1206    1011
PHIT       VAR     REF      1083     1089   DCL     1015   DCL
PHITOT     VAR     REF      1093     1206    1206    1019   DCL
PHIW       VAR     REF      1108     1121    1206    1013   DCL
PLE        PARAM   REF      1089     1106    1206     872   DCL
POP        PARAM   REF      1076  DEFINED    879     842     832    1066  DEFINED            898
PPOS       SET     REF       847  DEFINED    905     842    1055    1061    1083   DCL
PPOSX      SET     REF       904      905   DCL       945     921     943     944
                   910       932      934     936     945     961    1089  DEFINED   1097    1095
PV         PARAM   REF       729      730     860  DEFINED   856    1095    1097    1153  DEFINED
RHO        REF     705       DCL    3*856    3*858  1080   DEFINED   856   DCL     850   DEFINED
SIGMA      PARAM   REF       860      206     356     675     678     679     685     690
T          SET     REF       201      728     729     849     852     856     857     858     900
                             705      957   2*959    1001    1002    1003    1004    1005    1006     985
                             692      999    1000    1014    1015    1016    1017    1018    1023     984
                             956     1012    1013    1028    1029    1030    1031    1038    1039    1010
                            1011     1026    1027    1044    1045    1046  3*1050  3*1052  3*1055    1024
                            1025     1042    1043  3*1064  4*1066  2*1080  2*1083  2*1086  3*1056    1040
                            1041     1059   2*1061  3*1097  3*1100  2*1101    1084  8*1106  2*1086  3*1056
                          3*1091   3*1093  3*1095  2*1145    1146    1147    1102  3*1104  3*1153  5*1089
                            1141     1142    1143  2*1158    1161    1162    1149    1150    1165  2*1108
                          2*1155   2*1156  2*1157  4*1173    1175    1176  3*1163  3*1164  3*1181  2*1166
                          2*1167   2*1170  2*1171    1190  3*1192    1193  3*1178    1197    1198    1182
                          4*1187     1189     198     900     681   2*683     685     690   3*1181  1200
                            1201     1202  DEFINED   858  CONTROL   959     961     982     983     692
                             729      856      857    1052    1061    1063    1066    1080    1083     984
                             985     1050     1054    1059    1061    1099    1104    1106    1080    1083
                            1086     1088     1091    1093    1095    1149    1150    1153    1106    1108
                            1141     1142     1143    1145    1146    1147    1163    1164    1165    1154
                            1155     1156     1157    1158    1161    1162    1178    1181    1185    1166
                            1167     1170     1171    1173    1175    1176                            1187
```

REFERENCE MAP OF VARIABLES

VARIABLES	TYPE	1189	1190	1192	1196	1197	1198	1200	1201	1202	DCL
		198									
TARIFFVF	PARAM	REF	961	1093	DEFINED	768	DCL	768	1035	1036	2*1064
TARIFFVI	PARAM	REF	959	1093	DEFINED	767	DCL	767	1081	2*1084	2*1170
TE	SET	REF	206	1007	1008	1009	1032	1033	1074	1076	1078
		2*1068	201	1072	2*1074	1068	1078	2*1080			
		DEFINED	1084		DCL	201	1070				
		1080									
TEP	SET	DCL	206	CONTROL	856	DCL	206				
TP	SET	REF	856	2*1166	2*1167	1207	DEFINED	365	DCL	365	1164
TRADECOST	PARAM	1165	1166	1167	DCL	1126	DEFINED	DEFINED	856	DCL	
TRAN	PARAM	REF	2*462	DEFINED	413	DCL	413	365	DCL	365	854
TRSP	PARAM	REF	455	456	457	458	DEFINED				
TS	PARAM	REF	860	1064	1080	1084	1170	DEFINED			
TVF	VAR	REF	1091	1093	1095	1208	DCL	1002	690	984	692
TVI	VAR	REF	1091	1093	1097	1208	DCL	1004	1006		
U	VAR	REF	1020	1055	1059	1086	1208	DCL			
UBND	EQU	REF	1118	1059	1059	DCL	1026	DCL			
UMIN	PARAM	REF	1066	DEFINED	3*681	DCL	679				
UNEW	PARAM	REF	847	DEFINED	1170	DEFINED	841	DCL	834	DCL	1001
VF	VAR	REF	1020	1064	1052	1095	1100	1142	1208	DCL	1003
VI	VAR	REF	1020	1050	1089	1097	1101	1101	1208	DCL	692
W	SET	REF	33	1055	192	206	3*209	689	690	984	985
		879	65	2*903	2*944	950	951	982	983	1014	1015
		987	884	1004	1009	1010	1011	1012	1013	1038	1039
		1016	1002	1018	1027	1028	1034	1035	1036	2*1074	2*1076
		1040	1017	1042	1044	1043	1045	1046	1072	2*1097	2*1100
		2*1080	1041	2*1083	2*1086	4*1089	3*1091	3*1093	2*1095	2*1154	2*1155
		1101	1081	8*1106	1108	1108	1143	1146	1149	1202	DEFINED
		2*1156	2*1104	2*1158	1185	1141	1146	3*1192	1193	879	884
		4	2*1157	208	209	4*1187	1190	691	692	987	1072
		903	CONTROL	208	689	982	690	691	985	995	1097
		1074	944	1080	1083	1086	983	984	1093	1154	1155
		1099	1076	1106	1108	1141	1088	1091	1149	DCL	4
		1156	1104	1158	1185	1187	1143	1146	1202		
			1157				1190	1192			
WEIGHT	PARAM	REF	920	DEFINED	915	DCL	915	DCL	834	1165	1166
WEX	SET	2*1167	1145	1137	2*1153	1145	1150	2*1163	2*1164	1162	1163
		REF	DEFINED	1166	1167	1161	1162	1153	1161		
WI	SET	REF	1165	1166	CONTROL	1145	1137	903	944	950	1080
		1083	209	2*683	689	690	884	1141	1143	2*1146	1147
		1149	1086	1089	1097	1101	1104				
WIM	SET	REF	1185	DEFINED	33	DCL	33	CONTROL	1145	1150	1153
		REF	1145	1150	2*1153	DCL	1136	1136			
WJ	SET	DCL	1136	982	984	DEFINED	1100	1141	1142	DEFINED	65
		REF	209			1095					
		DCL	65								
WN	SET	REF	1072	1074	1081	DEFINED	884	DCL	863		1080
WNPK	SET	REF	209	903	944	DEFINED	192	DCL	192		1072
WP	SET	REF	879	1036	2*1076	1141	1142	1146	1147	2*1154	2*1155

REFERENCE MAP OF VARIABLES

VARIABLES   TYPE   REFERENCES

VARIABLES	TYPE		879	1076	1141	1142	1146	1147	1154	1155	DCL
WR	SET	CONTROL 206	2*988	2*989	2*990	2*991	2*993	2*994	DEFINED		2*208
XF	VAR	REF	210	988	989	990	991	993	994	DCL	6	
XI	VAR	REF	988	1050	1052	1057	1100	1141	DCL	999	
XREP	PARAM	REF	1020	2*1056	1102	1146	DCL	1000	917		
XX	VAR	REF	951	932	DEFINED	950	951	DCL	924	1204	
YP	VAR	REF	926	1068	1070	1072	952	1078	1081		
YW	VAR	DCL	1021				1074				
Z	VAR	REF	1074	2*1076	1061	1064	1066	1083	DCL	998	1208
ZX	VAR	REF	1020 926	1055 932	934	936	DCL	923	998		

SETS

C	ALL COMMODITIES
CAP	PRODUCTS FOR EXPORT
CE	FINAL PRODUCTS
CFV	IMPORTED FINAL PRODUCTS THAT ARE NOT COMPOUNDS
CIS	PRODUCTS FOR INTERPLANT SHIPMENT
CO	COMPOUNDS
CORES	COMPOUND SHIPMENT POSSIBILITIES
CPOSM	CONSUMPTION POSSIBILITIES
CPOSP	PRODUCTION POSSIBILITIES
CPOSXP	COMMODITY OUTPUT POSSIBILITY
CQ	NUTRIENTS
CR	DOMESTIC RAW MATERIALS
CV	PRODUCTS FOR IMPORT
G	PLANT TYPE
HPOS	UNIT EXPANSION POSSIBILITIES
I	PLANT LOCATIONS
IE	ALIAS FOR I
IP	DEMAND REGIONS
J	ALIAS FOR J
JP	PRODUCTIVE UNITS
M	MARKETING POSSIBILITIES
MC	MISCELLANIOUS INPUTS
MISC	PRODUCTIVE UNIT POSSIBILITIES
MPOS	PACKAGES
N	NEW VINTAGE PLANTS
NEW	FIXED PACKAGE EXPANSIONS
NFIX	MAP OF PACKAGES TO LOCATIONS
NMAP	OLD VINTAGE PLANTS
OLD	PROCESSES
P	PROCESS POSSIBILITIES
PPOS	I POSSIBILITIES
PPOSX	TIME PERIODS
T	

219

SETS

TE   EXPANSION PERIODS
TEP   ALIAS FOR TE
TP   ALIAS FOR T
W   COUNTRIES IN ANDEAN COMMON MARKET
WEX   COUNTRY-PLANT LOCATION MAPPING
WIM
WJ   COUNTRY DEMAND REGION MAPPING
WN   MAP OF COUNTRIES TO PACKAGES
WNPK   COUNTRY COMPOUND MAPPING
WP   ALIAS FOR W
WR   COUNTRIES AND REGION

PARAMETERS

A   INPUT-OUTPUT MATRIX
ALPHA   NUTRIENT CONTENT
AM   MISCELLANEOUS INPUTS BY PLANT AND PROCESS
AREP   CAPACITY REPORT BY PLANT UNIT AND TIME
AUT   CAPACITY UTILIZATION BY PLANT AND UNIT
AX   REDUCED I-O MATRIX FOR NUTRIENT POTENTIAL
B   PRODUCTIVE UNIT-PROCESS MAP
BREP   CAPACITY REPORT BY COUNTRY UNIT AND TIME
BUT   CAPACITY UTILIZATION BY UNIT
CAPUT   CAPACITY UTILIZATION FOR OLD PLANTS
CIFCIF   VALUE FLOWS
CON76   NUTRIENT CONSUMPTION IN 1976 (1000 TPY)
CUT   CAPACITY UTILIZATION BY PLANT
D   DEMAND FOR NUTRIENTS   (1000 TPY)
DB   MINIMUM AMMONIUM SULFATE REQUIREMENT (1000 TPY)
DBR   DEMAND FOR AMMONIUM SULFATE   (1000 TPY)
DCAP   INSTALLED CAPACITY IN OPERATION IN 1980 (TONS PER DAY)
DCAPW   NAMEPLATE CAPACITY BY COUNTRY   (1000 TPY)
DELTA   DISCOUNT FACTOR
DEM82   NUTRIENT DEMAND PROJECTIONS FOR 1982 (1000 TPY)
DEM85   NUTRIENT DEMAND PROJECTIONS FOR 1985 (1000 TPY)
DEM88   NUTRIENT DEMAND PROJECTIONS FOR 1988 (1000 TPY)
DEM91   NUTRIENT DEMAND PROJECTIONS FOR 1991 (1000 TPY)
DGR   DEMAND GROWTH RATES
DPACK   DIFFERENCE IN PACKAGE NUMBERS BETWEEN COUNTRIES
DR   DEMAND FOR NUTRIENTS   (1000 TPY)
DUT   CAPACITY UTILIZATION BY COUNTRY
EVIP   INTERNATIONAL TRADE ADVANTAGE (US$ PER TON)
EVIJ   INTERNATIONAL TRADE ADVANTAGE (US$ PER TON)
FLOWF   FINAL PRODUCT FLOWF
FLOWI   INTERMEDIATE AND RAW MATERIAL FLOWF
GAMMA   PACKAGE SIZE MULTIPLIER FOR EXPERIMENTS WITH FLEXIBLE PACKAGE SIZES
HB   MAXIMUM PLANT SIZE   (1000 TPY)
HP   EFFECTIVE PACKAGE SIZE   (1000 TPY)
INVDAT   INVESTMENT DATA
K   EFFECTIVE CAPACITY OF OLD PLANTS   (1000 TPY)
KW   EFFECTIVE CAPACITY BY COUNTRY   (1000 TPY)
KX   EFFECTIVE CAPACITY
LAM   MAXIMUM EXPORT CAPABILITY OF PLANT AS FUNCTION OF PRODUCTION LEVEL
LIFE   LIFE OF PRODUCTIVE UNIT (YEARS)

PARAMETERS

MIDYEAR	MIDYEAR FOR EACH PERIOD	
MISCOST	COST OF MISCELLANEOUS INPUTS	
MUE	TRANSPORT COST: EXPORT	(US$ PER TON)
MUF	TRANSPORT COST: FINAL PRODUCTS	(US$ PER TON)
MUFV	TRANSPORT COST: IMPORTED FINAL PRODUCTS	(US$ PER TON)
MUI	TRANSPORT COST: INTERPLANT SHIPMENT	(US$ PER TON)
MUR	TRANSPORT COST: IMPORTED RAW MATERIAL	(US$ PER TON)
MUX	TRANSPORT COST: FACTOR FOR ACIDS	
NDEF	PACKAGE DEFINITIONS (TONS PER DAY)	
NNIM	PACKAGE UNITY	
NPACK	MINIMUM NUMBER OF PACKAGES IN EACH COUNTRY	
NU	PROPORTIONAL INVESTMENT (US$ PER TPY)	
NUP	PACKAGE COST (1000 US$)	
NUPF	FIXED PACKAGE COST (1000 US$)	
NUTXX	NUTRIENT WEIGHT FOR PRODUCTS	
OCAP	FIXED OPERATING COST	
ONEW	VARIABLE OPERATING COST FOR NEW PLANTS (US$ PER UNIT LEVEL)	
OOLD	VARIABLE OPERATING COST OF OLD PLANTS (US$ PER UNIT LEVEL)	
OPCOST	OPERATING COST FOR NEW PLANTS (US$ PER TON PER YEAR)	
OZ	VARIABLE OPERATING COST (US$ PER UNIT LEVEL)	
PD	DOMESTIC RAW MATERIAL PRICES (US$ PER UNIT)	
PDLIM	DOMESTIC MATERIAL LIMITS (1000 TPY)	
PE	EXPORT PRICE (US$ PER TON)	
PLE	MATRIX FOR COUNTRY PACKAGE COMPARISONS IN THE INEQUALITY CONSTRAINT	
POP	FIXED OPERATING COST (1000 US$)	
PV	IMPORT PRICES CIF (US$ PER TON)	
RHO	DISCOUNT RATE	
SIGMA	CAPITAL RECOVERY FACTOR	
TARIFFVF	TARIFF ON IMPORTED FINAL GOODS	
TARIFFVI	TARIFF ON IMPORTED INTERMEDIATE GOODS	
TRADECOST	TRADE FLOW ADVANTAGE AT FOB COST	
TRAN	TRANSPORT COST FOR INTERPLANT SHIPMENT (US$ PER TON)	
TRSP	TRANSPORT COST (US$ PER TON)	
TS	TIME SUMMATION MATRIX	
UMIN	UTILIZATION: LOWER LIMIT	
UNEW	NEW PLANT UTILIZATION	
WEIGHT	NUTRIENT WEIGHTS	
XREP	MAXIMUM NUTRIENT SHIPMENTS (1000 TPY)	

VARIABLES

E	EXPORTS	(1000 TPY)
H	CAPACITY EXPANSION	(1000 TPY)
NUT	TOTAL NUTRIENT VALUE (1000 TPY)	
PHI	COST PER YEAR	(MILL US$ PER YEAR)
PHIE	EXPORT REVENUE	(MILL US$ PER YEAR)
PHIG	DOMESTIC MATERIAL COST	(MILL US$ PER YEAR)
PHIK	CAPITAL COST	(MILL US$ PER YEAR)
PHIL	TRANSPORT COST	(MILL US$ PER YEAR)
PHIM	IMPORT COST	(MILL US$ PER YEAR)
PHIP	OPERATING COST	(MILL US$ PER YEAR)
PHIT	TARIFFS	(MILL US$ PER YEAR)

VARIABLES

PHITOT   DISCOUNTED TOTAL COST   (MILL US$ DISCOUNTED)
PHIW   WORKING CAPITAL COST   (MILL US$ PER YEAR)
TVF   VALUE OF IMPORTS: FINAL PRODUCTS   (MILL US$ PER YEAR)
TVI   VALUE OF IMPORTS: INTERMEDIATES   (MILL US$ PER YEAR)
U   DOMESTIC MATERIAL PURCHASES   (1000 TPY)
VF   IMPORTS: FINAL PRODUCTS   (1000 TPY)
VI   IMPORTS: INTERMEDIATES AND RAW MATERIALS   (UNIT TPY)
XF   DOMESTIC SHIPMENT ACTIVITY: FINAL   (1000 TPY)
XI   DOMESTIC SHIPMENT ACTIVITY: INTERPLANT   (1000 TPY)
XX   OUTPUT OF FINAL PRODUCTS   (1000 TPY)
YP   PACKAGE DECISION VARIABLE   (BINARY)
YW   PACKAGE DECISION VARIABLE BY COUNTRY
Z   PROCESS LEVEL   (1000 UNITS PER YEAR)
ZX   PROCESS LEVEL   (1000 TPY)

EQUATIONS

AC   ACCOUNTING: TOTAL COST   (MILL US$ PER YEAR)
ACC   ACCOUNTING: CAPITAL COST   (MILL US$ PER YEAR)
ACE   ACCOUNTING: EXPORT REVENUE   (MILL US$ PER YEAR)
ACG   ACCOUNTING: DOMESTIC MATERIALS   (MILL US$ PER YEAR)
ACL   ACCOUNTING: TRANPORT COST   (MILL US$ PER YEAR)
ACM   ACCOUNTING: IMPORT COST   (MILL US$ PER YEAR)
ACP   ACCOUNTING: OPERATING COST   (MILL US$ PER YEAR)
ACT   ACCOUNTING: TARIFFS   (MILL US$ PER YEAR)
ACW   ACCOUNTING: WORKING CAPITAL   (MILL US$ PER YEAR)
ATVF   DEFINITION OF IMPORT VALUE: FINALS   (MILL US$ PER YEAR)
ATVI   DEFINITION OF IMPORT VALUE: INTERMEDIATES   (MILL US$ PER YEAR)
BINF   BINARY CONSTRAINT: FIXED PLANT SIZE   (1000 TPY)
BINV   BINARY CONSTRAINT: VARIABLE PLANT SIZE   (1000 TPY)
BW   AGGREGATION OF PACKAGES IN COUNTRY
CC   CAPACITY CONSTRAINTS   (1000 TPY)
CCMIN   MINIMUM NPK UTILIZATION
CCX   CAPACITY CONSTRAINT   (1000 TPY)
DNUT   NUTRIENT DEFINITION
ELIM   EXPORT LIMITS   (1000 TPY)
EX   PACKAGE MUTUAL EXCLUSIVITY   (UNITS)
GPLE   INTER-COUNTRY CONSTRAINT ON PACKAGE - INEQUALITY
MB   MATERIAL BALANCE AT PLANTS   (1000 TPY)
MBA   AMMONIUM SULFATE REQUIREMENTS   (1000 TPY)
MBD   MATERIAL BALANCE ON DEMAND   (1000 TPY)
MBX   MATERIAL BALANCE   (1000 TPY)
MINPACK   MINIMUM NUMBER OF PACKAGES PER COUNTRY
OBJ   TOTAL DISCOUNTED COST
UBND   BOUNDS ON LOCAL MATERIALS   (1000 TPY)

MODELS

AOPTI
CAPCHECK

222

Index

Acceptability constraints, 94-96; in dynamic process model, 86, 88; and international trade, 73; and intraregional trade, 72-73; and level of production, 71-72; in static capacity expansion model, 78

Accounting prices, in models, 94

Accounting rate of interest (ARI), 62; country-specific, 98-99; uniform, 99

ACM. See Andean Common Market

Agriculture: agreements to limit production in, 18; cooperation projects in, 18

Ammonia, 53-54, 123, 124, 126

Ammonium nitrate, 54

Ammonium sulfate, 54, 121, 131

Andean Common Market (ACM): fertilizer sector in, 119-28; gross "regional" product of, 117, 118; industry allocation study of, 62-64; membership and population of, 110, 117, 118; trade flows for, 158-60, 161, 163, 165, 171; trade within, 118. See also Andean Common Market case study; Andean fertilizer model

Andean Common Market case study: objectives and approach of, 110-11; phases of, 111-12; proposal for, 113-14. See also Andean Common Market; Andean fertilizer model; Andean fertilizer model results

Andean Common Market Secretariat, 110, 115, 129, 150, 163, 168; investment strategy proposal by, 113

Andean fertilizer model: computer-readable statement of, 183-223; costs in, 143-49, 175-76; existing and proposed plant locations in, 131, 133; objective of, 143-44; planning problems and approach for, 129-31; production relationship in, 136-43. See also Andean fertilizer model results; Andean fertilizer plants

Andean fertilizer model results: costs in, 153-55, 160, 162-65, 169-70, 172-73, 175-79; sensitivity analysis of, 165-67; trade flows in, 156-60, 162-63, 165, 173-74; under Scenario 1 (Implications of Current Plans), 152-60, 176, 177; under Scenario 2 (No Capacity Expansion), 160-61, 176; under Scenario 3 (Andean Least-Cost Strategy), 161-63, 176, 177; under Scenario 4 (Equitable Investment Strategy), 163-65, 174, 176, 177; under Scenario 5 (Least-Cost Supply Pattern), 169-71, 176; under Scenario 6 (Flexible and Equitable Investment Program), 172-78. See also Andean fertilizer model

Andean fertilizer plants: under construction, 142; installed capacity of, 140; investment cost for new, 144; names and

Loet B. M. Mennes is Professor of Development Planning at Erasmus University, Rotterdam, The Netherlands.

Ardy J. Stoutjesdijk is director of the Country Programs Department in the Europe, Middle East, and North Africa Regional Office of the World Bank.

The most recent World Bank publications are described in the annual spring and fall lists. The latest edition is available free of charge from the Publications Sales Unit, Department B, The World Bank, Washington, D.C. 20433, U.S.A.

9649